Press and Politics
in Nigeria, 1880-1937

Ibadan History Series

For further details of the books in this series
please consult the publisher.

Ibadan History Series

General Editor J. F. A. Ajayi, Ph.D.

Press and Politics in Nigeria, 1880-1937

Fred I. A. Omu

Department of History, University of Lagos

Humanities Press
Atlantic Highlands, New Jersey

First published in the United States in 1978
by Humanities Press, Inc.
Atlantic Highlands, New Jersey 07716

First published 1978

Library of Congress Cataloging in Publication Data

Omu, Fred I. A.
    Press and politics in Nigeria, 1880–1937.
    (Ibadan history series)
    Bibliography: p.
    1. Press and politics—Nigeria—History.
    2. Nigeria—Politics and government. I. Title.
    II. Series.
    PN5499.N504   079′.669   77–25099
    ISBN 0–391–00561–8

Printed in Great Britain

Contents

Abbreviations

Civ.	Record of Civil cases
Crim.	Record of Criminal cases
C.M.S.	Church Missionary Society
C.S.O.	List of papers assembled from the Nigerian Secretariat, Lagos (National Archives, Ibadan)
C.O.	Colonial Office (British)
J.A.H.	*Journal of African History*
J.H.S.N.	*Journal of the Historical Society of Nigeria*
L.W.R.	*Lagos Weekly Record*
R.C.	Registrar of Companies
Reg. Crim.	Chief Registrar's Criminal Record Book
U.N.A.C.	United Native African Church

Preface

Looking back in 1964 over journalism in Nigeria since its inception more than a century ago, former President Nnamdi Azikiwe, himself one of the greatest Nigerian journalists, drew attention to the work of 'pioneers of the Nigerian Press' the history of whose activities is 'identical with the intellectual and material developments of this country'. The 'galaxy of immortal journalists produced by Nigeria', Azikiwe believed, had played their part 'in this corner of the earth in the great crusade for human freedom'.[1] This glowing tribute emphasises the fact, widely acknowledged by writers on Nigeria, that the newspaper press has been a significant force in national development. J. S. Coleman in *Nigeria: Background to Nationalism* asserts that 'there can be little doubt that nationalist newspapers and pamphlets have been among the main influences in the awakening of racial and political consciousness'.[2] Kalu Ezera in *Constitutional Developments in Nigeria*, speaks about the influence of the press on constitutional reform during the inter- and post-war years.[3]

The works cited above contain brief references to the names of newspapers and their owners. Such information has been culled from Increase Coker's *70 years of the Nigerian Press*, Lagos, 1952, revised and retitled *Landmarks of the Nigeria Press*, Lagos, 1968. This is a survey of the development of the mass media (newspapers, radio and television broadcasting and Government Information Services) from the beginning to 1965. In the words of the author, 'it is a story told rather imperfectly and in outline'. It is evident that the Nigerian newspaper press has not attracted serious scholarship and it is the aim of this study to satisfy this significant need.

This study, therefore, will attempt to place the rise of the newspaper industry in historical context, to survey the role which the newspapers played in major questions of policy, to examine the influences behind the thoughts and actions of the newspapers, to indicate how the ideas and attitudes of the newspapers developed in relation to changing circumstances and changes in personnel and to attempt, where the evidence permits, an evaluation of the effectiveness of press criticism and agitation. A note of caution is sounded in recognition of the fact that newspaper influence is an intangible phenomenon which defies precise measurement. 'No divining rod can locate it', says Lucy Salmon, 'no plummet sound its depth, no instrument of precision measure it, no astronomer compute its orbit.'[4] A Nigerian newspaper drew attention to the intangibility of press effectiveness when it remarked in 1882:

> How much success has attended our feeble efforts it is not possible for us to know altogether since success in a cause like ours does not always imply the immediate attainment of an object aimed at but also the creation of sentiment and the production of sympathy which may eventually result in co-operation to attain the end desired.[5]

However, the peculiar position of a vigorous opposition press in a situation of Crown Colony rule makes it possible to establish satisfactory conclusions.

When certain non-African philanthropic interests established the first newspapers in Nigeria in the 1850s and 1860s, the aim was primarily to increase the level of literacy; the newspapers advertised the advantages of the acquisition of knowledge through reading short stories and didactic essays on various subjects. The emphasis was on literary content, and politics was secondary, if not incidental. African inheritors of the newspaper idea were also impressed by the needs of philanthropy and their newspapers often carried literary matter, but because Africans were denied effective participation in government and wanted to influence the trend of events and to realise their dreams of greater racial identity and dignity, their anxiety centred on the demands of political and nationalist persuasion and propaganda. This was rendered all the more acute by the fact that many newspapermen were of the commercially frustrated elite forced into journalism by European monopolists who crushed them out of the Niger trade.

It is not surprising, therefore, that the early press was essentially a political press. Of the more than twelve newspapers which appeared in Lagos between 1880 and 1900, for example, only one would not be classed as markedly political in bias. Politics was virtually the only object of excitement and circulations expanded in proportion as interest in it was generated.

What concerned newspapermen and the educated elite in general, therefore, was not merely that people should acquire knowledge but that the knowledge should be such as to form the basis of a strong public opinion which the colonial government could not ignore. Literacy was expanding to the extent that individual newspaper sales of 200 at the beginning of our period would rise to 9 000 by the end of it. If this was related to the commonplace estimate that for every literate person who read an African newspaper, as many as ten to twenty illiterates possibly had its contents read or retailed to them, the readership of a leading newspaper would represent at best a rise from about 4 000 in the 1880s to 180 000 in the 1930s. Inevitably, therefore, the press took on the role of opposition to the government. It encouraged a sense of political and nationalist awareness and involvement by providing the medium of criticism of the authorities, spreading disaffection with aspects of official policies and programmes and co-ordinating movements of agitation. Possessing a high degree of credibility and goodwill among the educated elite as well as the unlettered indigenous masses, and encouraged by the assumption that as British subjects Africans were entitled to enjoy the freedom of the press, and by the sympathy and support of Afrophile groups in Britain, the press waded into one political controversy after another, confident of its power as 'the guardian of the rights and liberties of the people as well as the interpreter of their ideals and aspirations'.

A study of the history of the early Nigerian newspaper press, as of pioneer newspaper presses in general, is bound to be hampered by lack of information on the internal history of the newspapers. For although they are rich sources of historical material, the newspapers are very silent about themselves. Private papers which should have made good the lack do not, as a rule, contain statistics on finance and organisation. Generally, such records were never kept, and even where they were kept and have not been lost, they are too fragmentary to be useful. Nonetheless, the available sources provide sufficient material for the reconstruction of the history of the Nigerian newspaper press.

A pioneer study of the sort attempted here is beset by a number of organisational difficulties arising from the fact that the newspaper press is a complex enterprise. As an industry and a social and political organ, its subject-matter is multiple. However, in a historical study like this, it is impossible to cover every facet of the newspaper concern. For example, it is not intended to go into content analysis, readership survey and similar issues. Throughout the chapters that follow, the establishment of the newspapers will be described within the framework of the social and political circumstances at the time.

There are two main ways in which the subject may be approached. One might see it in terms of a chronological development. But this mode of procedure would hardly permit detailed examination of certain dominant threads which went to make up the history of the industry. The alternative is the thematic approach which has been followed here. The different themes, however, have been studied chronologically. The study is in two Parts. Part I (Chapters 1–3) is concerned with the institutional development of the newspaper press, while Part II (Chapters 4–7) focuses on the role of the press in political questions. The origins of the newspaper press are discussed in Chapter 1, and the following chapter examines ownership and owners. Chapter 3 describes the evolution and organisation of the newspaper industry. Chapters 4 and 5 attempt to show and explain the initial role of the newspapers in public issues. These set the stage for a study of the reaction of the government to newspaper opposition in Chapter 6. In the last chapter, the survey of political developments is concluded. Several matters will be touched on at many points, but confusion will be limited by the use of cross-references.

The date for the termination of the period has not been arbitrarily chosen. In many respects, 1937 marked the end of an epoch and the beginning of another. The revival and revolution in Nigerian journalism began that year and, more important, it was the eve of a new impetus in political development. In 1938, the Nigerian National Democratic Party, which had won the three quinquennial elections between 1923 and 1933, lost to the Nigerian Youth Movement (founded in 1934 as the Lagos Youth Movement) in a fierce battle which ended the Fourteen Years of Peace in Nigeria's political history. This thus reversed the traditions of Legislative Council elections. Furthermore, Nigeria was soon to be involved in the turmoil of the Second World War with its acceleration of nationalist development.

This book is the outcome of my Ph.D. thesis presented to the University of Ibadan. Its completion is owed to the assistance of various individuals. Professor J. F. Ade Ajayi first drew my attention to the possibilities of historical research in an area of mass communication and, as Vice-Chancellor of the University of Lagos, has given me further opportunities of closer association with mass communication studies. Professor John D. Hargreaves, Burnett-Fletcher Professor of History at the University of Aberdeen, should really take much of the credit for the completion of this book. His beneficence resulted in a Leverhulme Visiting Fellowship, tenable at Aberdeen, which enabled me to carry out further research in London. His suggestions for the improvement of organisation and style in revision of the thesis have been invaluable.

My thanks also go to Professor Boniface I. Obichere, Department of History, University of California, Los Angeles (UCLA) whose kindness led to a fruitful offer of a visiting lectureship in the fall of 1973. Professor J. D. Omer-Cooper read the draft at thesis stage and provided much intellectual stimulation. Finally, to my wife Rose I owe the deepest gratitude. Herself a symbol of courage, she has remained my chief source of strength.

Notes

1 Nnamdi Azikiwe, 'Pioneer Heroes of the Nigerian Press', lecture delivered in honour of the first graduating students of the Jackson College of Journalism, University of Nigeria, Nsukka, 31 May 1964. Text in *West African Pilot*, 3 June 1964; *Daily Express*, 2 June 1964.
2 Published Berkeley and Los Angeles, 1960. See pp. 184–6.
3 Published Cambridge 1960. See pp. 49–52.
4 *The Newspaper and Authority*, New York, 1923, p. 385 quoted in Jonathan F. Scott, 'The Press and Foreign Policy', *Journal of Modern History*, 4 December 1931, pp. 627–38.
5 *Lagos Times*, 18 November 1882.

1 The origins of the newspaper press

Newspapers conducted by Nigerians appeared for the first time in the 1880s. This development had a complex background. Not only was the indigenous newspaper movement a response to the social and political revolutions precipitated by the European Christian missionaries and the British colonial administration, it was also a continuation of earlier journalistic activity pioneered by philanthropic interests. Furthermore, a certain historical continuity exists between the modern newspaper and the indigenous systems of public communication. Although indigenous Nigerian society had no newspaper, it had agencies and institutions which in several respects served the same purposes as the newspaper or at least answered the contemporary needs of communication. The desire for information about local people and events, the satisfaction of news hunger stimulated by war or rumours of war, the necessity to spread information about political and religious decision as well as threats to security, the need to stimulate and strengthen the sense of identification with values and objectives of society, the need to strengthen awareness of the authority structure and to generate and identify loyalty to those in power – all these were answered by the indigenous media forms. A brief examination of these agencies and institutions, therefore, is an appropriate starting point for the discussion of the origins of the Nigerian press. Most African communities have their characteristic media but the focus of this survey will be limited to the southern parts of Nigeria where the flourish of newspaper activity confined itself until the fourth decade of the present century when newspapers began to emerge in the northern areas.

TRADITIONAL MEDIA OF COMMUNICATION

The agencies of public communication may be conveniently classified into two groups – the oral communication or informal transference media and the organised communication or formal transference media. The media in the first group operated through informal contact between individuals and persons and essentially did not go beyond the circulation or dissemination of rumours and 'unofficial' information. In this category, the primary example is family visiting .The African social organisation, characterised by a strong sense of kingship, community and neighbourliness, naturally increased the scope of news circulated in this way. It was virtuous then as now to visit relations and friends in their homes, 'eat from the same pot', and exchange the latest information. The sense of kinship and community did not exhaust itself in the individual town or village; on the contrary, it was manifested in a much wider sphere, in, for example, the attitude to relatives in other communities and the relatively harmonious relationship between people in one community and those in another. The extent of these connections and attitudes gives some idea of the scope of news circulation in indigenous society by informal contact.

Exchange of information was also promoted by means of the organised and spontaneous gatherings which are fairly frequent in the African society. Death and burial ceremonies always attracted large congregations which often included participants from neighbouring or distant places. These ceremonies often lasted quite long and while weeping and wailing characterised the particular moments of death and burial, the intervening periods were usually occupied with gossiping, story-telling and general exchange of information. Similar results were encouraged by town or village festivals, marriage and circumcision feasts, public meetings and trials, propitiatory assemblies, open quarrels and disputes, and several other aggregatory events which characterise the African way of life. In this respect, mention must be made of the popular moonlight gatherings which were dominated by folk-tales. Although anyone could be a folk-tale teller, some were highly proficient in the art. They knew what was interesting to an audience and had a gift for the exciting and the sensational. They could be seen as perhaps the prototypes of the modern news reporter.

Another prototype of the modern reporter was the masquerade.[1] Although it was essentially an impersonation of ancestors, the masquerade in some societies, like the Igbo, emerged in the night to gossip and expose scandals like a modern gossip columnist, except that the masquerade's freedom of expression knew no laws of libel and sedition.

News circulated with great rapidity through the various processes of trading. Most communities had markets which were not only centres of trade but also a principal means of communication, information and recreation;[2] they provided a most convenient forum to meet friends and kinsmen and exchange news and gossip. While bringing together large numbers of sellers, buyers and mere visitors, some from distant places, they created an atmosphere of festivity and entertainment in which gossip and the exchange of information flourished. Some markets were also the terminal points of trade routes connecting different parts of one area with one another and with foreign lands and civilisations. The caravans which plied these routes helped to distribute information. They 'gathered and relayed' news as they passed from place to place communicating with fellow traders and collecting information on resources and prospects of trade.

The view that traders were satisfied with spreading their wares on the ground and waiting for customers to make the first advance is entirely misleading.[3] The phenomenon of advertising which is so dear to modern newspaper owners has always been present in the African market. Traders called the attention of prospective customers to the excellent quality and quantity of their goods and sometimes coined slogans to give added effect to their usually exaggerated claims.

The second category of the traditional media – formal transference – was concerned with the more systematised dissemination of information not between persons and persons but between the government and the people. The objectives underlying this direction of communication have been stated in the opening paragraph of this chapter. The tools employed were recognised officials and recognisable sounds, signs and symbols. In the Old Oyo empire, for example, state messengers and intelligence officers (*Ilari*) carried information between the capital and the outlying provinces. But the most common of these indigenous officials was the town-crier or bell man. With his loud-sounding gong, he announced the promulgation of laws and regulations, meetings, arrangements for communal work and generally spread 'official' information in the community. The town-crier is very much a crucial part of village society today and can still be seen in autochthonous parts of urban centres with an established indigenous monarchy.

A measure of news dissemination was achieved through the

booming of guns to announce the death of important personalities and also to warn of imminent danger. Smoke was also used, different thicknesses having particular significances. Most extensively used of all was the drum. Several ethnic groups in the area covered by this survey have a rich heritage of drums. When some of these drums are expertly sounded, they are capable of conveying specific meaning; in other words, they 'talk'. The 'talking drum' is a most fascinating agency of organised communication and it is a pity that no serious study of Nigerian drums has yet been attempted. Exploratory investigations reveal some data which permit little more than a superficial survey of the subject. However, it is widely known that the Yoruba have an impressive array of talking drum-sets and probably possess the richest heritage of drums in our area. The *dundun*, a set of six drums, only one of which was 'non-talking', is said to be able to 'imitate all the tones and gibes in Yoruba speech'.[4] In addition to producing music for dancing, it directed the movements of dancers and, at social gatherings, announced the appearance and departure of important persons. The dundun's capacity for mischief is proverbial. Its 'freedom of the drum' enabled it to recite and multiply praise-names (*oriki*) and also to pour abuse as the occasion warranted. Apparently nobody in the kingdom was above drum criticism. Old Oyo had what can be called 'free-speech festivals' during which talking drums freely ventilated their opinion about the king and his government. For the drummers, who operated from outside the walls of the palace, it was one of the greatest events in their lives. In modern Yorubaland, the use of talking drums in political faction has often led to outbreaks of violence.

Some other ethnic groups have a variety of talking drums. The Igbo *Ekwe*, carved out of a cylindrical block of wood, was a diminutive variant of the much bigger *Ikoro* (*Ikolo*) which was set up permanently in market places, village squares or in shrines. The Ikoro and functionally similar traditional state-drums like the Yoruba *gbedu*, the Itsekiri *oji*, the Edo *okha*, the Isoko and Urhobo *ogri* were used to summon special meetings, proclaim the arrival and departure of important visitors to the palace, announce serious acts of sacrilege and disasters, alert the community against invasion and, in war, advertise the presence of war chiefs.

THE PLANTING OF THE NEWSPAPER PRESS

New communication needs in the preliterate era began to arise with the coming and expansion of European trade between the fifteenth and eighteenth centuries. A common vehicle of communication was needed and this emerged in the form of a 'trade language' hybridised from various European and African languages. It was widely spoken on the coast and at a later period came to be known as 'pidgin'. It is said that in the late eighteenth century, one Antera Duke, a leading Efik trader, wrote a diary in 'pidgin'.[5] However, a new situation arose when the circumstances of the slave trade abolition brought together large numbers of West African peoples to create a new society under British patronage. The founding of Sierra Leone in 1787 inevitably gave the English language a new functional importance in inter-African communication. Given the diversity of West African languages in the new settlement, English language necessarily had to become the *lingua franca* and to foster this need became a major object of British policy.

The *Sierra Leone Gazette*, published in Freetown during the first quarter of the nineteenth century, probably represents the earliest attempt to promote actively the knowledge of reading in the English language in West Africa. Founded in 1801 by officers of the Sierra Leone Company which administered the settlement before it became a British colony in 1808, it underwent alterations and restorations of name until 1827 when it was given up.[6] It is not too certain what considerations influenced the establishment of the journal ('at dinner', an employee of the Sierra Leone Company noted in his diary, 'the conversation turned upon having a newspaper – so a newspaper we must have')[7] but there can be little doubt that the gazette played some educational role. At its best in the second decade of the nineteenth century when it took the name *The Royal Gazette and Sierra Leone Advertiser*, it carried local news, advertisements, poems, letters and 'accounts of fashionable life in Freetown'.[8] Nothing is known about the circulation of any of its various series, especially among the rising but obviously small African literate public, but it is unlikely that many copies were sold in that quarter.

The decisive factor in the process which was to establish the English language as the *lingua franca* along the West Coast was the intrusion of European missionary enterprise. The missionaries were inspired by abolitionist idealism – whose greatest representative was Sir Thomas Fowell Buxton – which advocated the liquidation of the slave trade by means of evangelical Christianity, utilitarian civilisation and commercial development, and partially influenced by the ideas of the Rev. Henry Venn whose concept of a Native Agency argued the possible extension along the West Coast of an 'intelligent and influential' class of educated West Africans who would become the 'founders of a kingdom which shall render incalculable benefits to Africa and hold a position among the states of Europe'.[9] They embarked upon programmes of Western education and general enlightenment in Sierra Leone and subsequently in what became the colonies of Nigeria, Gold Coast and Gambia. Their most enduring weapon was the school but journalism played an important role. The newspaper had been established as an essential instrument of mission work outside Britain as a result of the effective use which the British humanitarian movement made of it in mobilising support for their programmes. The era of the humanitarian movement coincided with remarkable changes in British newspaper history: a technological revolution associated with Friedrich Koenig, the expansion of the reading public as well as the increased demand for self-education – all interacting one upon another and transforming the character of the newspaper which became a major agency of organised public campaign and enlightenment.[10] The prevailing situation evidently made a strong impression on British missionaries going to Africa and the emphasis which the humanitarians placed upon pamphlet and newspaper publicity and propaganda elevated the printing press into an important engine of missionary enterprise. It is not surprising, therefore, that printing presses and mission-inspired newspapers proliferated in West Africa during the first half of the nineteenth century.

The pioneer of this movement was Liberia where from 1836 to 1846, a bi-monthly journal, *Africa's Luminary*, was published by the Committee of the Missionary Society of the Methodist Episcopal Church in New York and printed by the Methodist Mission press in Monrovia.[11] In Sierra Leone, in 1843, the Wesleyan Missionary Society brought out the *Sierra Leone Watchman* and twelve years later associated themselves with the C.M.S. in starting *The African and Sierra Leone Weekly Advertiser*.[12] The *Watchman* was abandoned in 1846 in exaggerated deference to

Governor N. W. MacDonald who complained to the Wesleyan Society in London that the publication had become hostile to him.[13] *The Weekly Adviser*, printed by Moses Henry Davies whom the C.M.S. had sent to England to learn printing, would seem to have disappeared by 1861 when Davies started his own newspaper.[14] In the 1860s, the American Missionary Association started the *Early Dawn* in Bo. It appears to have been short-lived but was revived by the United Brethren in Christ in the 1880s. In the Gold Coast (Ghana) in the late fifties, the Wesleyans established a printing workshop and founded two newspapers, the *Christian Messenger* and the *Examiner*.[15] In Nigeria, the first printing press was installed by the Presbyterian Mission when they arrived in Calabar in 1846. Eight years later, the Rev. Henry Townsend fitted up a printing press and inaugurated a printing school in the mission compound at Abeokuta. In 1859, he founded the *Iwe Irchin* (Iwe Irchin fun awon ara Egba ati Yoruba) which appeared as a Yoruba-language fortnightly but became bilingual when an English language supplement was added from 8 March 1860. It came to an abrupt end in October, 1867, as a result of the *ifole*, the popular rising which led to the expulsion of Europeans from Abeokuta and the destruction of the mission printing press.[16]

The *Iwe Irohin* was unique in several respects. Selling for a hundred and twenty cowries, the equivalent of one penny, it was the best organised of the mission papers at the time (Townsend had some connections with newspaper work in Exeter where his brother was a newspaper publisher) and more importantly, it was the first to be published in an African language. This experiment was made possible by the exceptional nature of Abeokuta which was linguistically homogeneous and where greater progress had been made in reducing the Yoruba language into writing. The Yoruba part of the *Iwe Irohin* was entirely translated by Egba converts whereas the *Early Dawn* was translated from English by European missionaries.

It is impossible to estimate the influence which these publications exerted. Circulations were small and perspectives were limited. The general indifference to reading which the missionaries often remarked upon, the absence of promotive enthusiasm in publications that were essentially non-commercial and the fact that the newspapers, in putting emphasis on literary content, lacked sources of excitement – all these affected the influence of missionary journalism. Paradoxically, it was in the field of politics, which at

7

best occupied a secondary or merely incidental place, that the mission papers exerted the greatest identifiable influence. As we have seen, the *Watchman* of Freetown was forced to fold up because it had become a source of embarrassment to Governor MacDonald. The *Iwe Irohin* was Townsend's chief weapon in his ambitious political propaganda and shrewd manoeuvring for power in Egbaland. His eagerness to symbolise Egba hostility towards the Lagos government in the post-cession era reached a high point in December 1862 when Governor Freeman lodged a complaint against the *Iwe Irohin* with the Colonial Office.[17] Less than two years later, Freeman was to accuse the mission paper of aggravating problems of foreign policy.[18] Several times in 1863 the C.M.S. authorities, at the prompting of the Colonial Office, cautioned Townsend to exercise restraint.[19]

The missionary newspapers may not have exerted a very wide influence on West African society but there can be no doubt that they introduced the first generation of educated Africans to what had become an intrinsic part of enlightened society in Europe and other lands. Their example gave inspiration to African people who inherited the idea of the newspaper and came to employ it as the chief weapon by which they were to exercise their power of participation in the government of their land.

THE WEST AFRICAN BACKGROUND

In 1850 there was no newspaper in West Africa conducted by Africans but by about the end of the third quarter of the nineteenth century, a more genuinely indigenous African newspaper press had emerged in Sierra Leone as well as in the Gold Coast which contributed to stimulate the inauguration of popular newspaper activity in Nigeria and the Gambia in the 1880s. The movement began in Sierra Leone where, during the second half of the nineteenth century, there was a remarkable flourish of newspaper activity and the newspaper became popular as an important factor in colonial society and politics in West Africa.[20] The immediate audience of the newspapers was largely the expanding educated public in Freetown but their circulation was extended to the literate communities throughout West Africa. It is not known how many subscriptions they got, but we may guess from the small total sales – from about 200 to 300 in the 1850s and 1860s to about 500 to 700 in the 1870s and 1880s – that their outside subscriptions could not have been large. The possible numerical insignificance notwithstanding, the early newspapers distributed along the coast were an important influence on ideas, attitudes and outlook.

The earliest pioneer was the *New Era* launched on 31 March 1855 by William Drape, a West Indian. It saw its responsibilities as including 'an exposure of falsehood . . . and a vigorous enunciation of truth'. It quickly became the mouthpiece of a variety of interests opposed to the government's anti-smuggling and politically discriminatory policies. Its eventful career, marked by a major collision with the government which will be discussed presently, came to an end in 1859 when Drape died. The impact of the *New Era* stimulated the sprouting of a succession of newspapers in the sixties. In 1861, Moses Henry Davies established *The Free Press and Sierra Leone Weekly Advertiser*. A year later, A. C. Harleston, a black American and former government printer, brought out *The Sierra Leone Weekly Times and West African Record*. This collapsed in 1863 as a result of a libel suit initiated by Moses Davies with whom Harleston was locked in a press war. Moses Davies abandoned *The Free Press* in 1865 and bought out *The Day Spring and Sierra Leone Reporter* which underwent further transformations in a remarkable journalistic adventure which did not terminate until the late 1880s. A leading influence in the growth of the Sierra Leone Press in the 1860s was William Rainy, a distinguished lawyer of keen intellect and intense patriotism, whose opposition to government in Sierra Leone dominated African political activity. Among his newspapers were *The Sierra Leone Observer and Commercial Advocate* (1864), *The African Interpreter and Advocate* (1866) and *The West African Liberation* (1869). An interesting development at this time was the transfer to Freetown in 1868 of the *West African Herald* which Charles Bannerman had founded at Cape Coast in the Gold Coast. After four years in Freetown, the *Herald* migrated back to its original home.

The 1870s were distinguished by the appearance in 1872 of *The Negro*, edited first by Dr Edward W. Blyden and later by the Rev. (later Archdeacon) G. J. Macaulay. The inspiration behind *The Negro* was the Native Pastorate Controversy which had assumed a new proportion when certain Wesleyan opponents of the Native Pastorate idea, whose most ardent spokesman was the

9

Rev. Benjamin Tregaskis, mounted an intensive propaganda campaign with occasional journals and other publications. *The Negro's* impact unsettled the Wesleyan lobby to the point of entering the lists with a more regular newspaper, the *Independent* (1872–78). This counter-offensive apparently overwhelmed its opponent which disappeared in 1873. This period also saw the establishment of the *West African Reporter* in 1876 by William Grant, an influential businessman and politician. The advertised aim of the newspaper was to foster unity among English-speaking West Africans. Grant's death in 1884 led to the abandonment of the enterprise two years later. Among the important names associated with this venture were Edward W. Blyden and Samuel (later Sir Samuel) Lewis. James Bright Davies, destined to be a leading administrator and journalist in all the West African colonies except Gambia, was one of the editors.

Thus by 1880, the Sierra Leone press was twenty-five years old. During this period some fifteen to twenty different newspaper titles had advertised themselves, many of them with seemingly prestigious double names which contrasted significantly with the modesty of the newspapers' industrial establishments. The press had firmly taken root in society and was to be further consolidated with the arrival in the 1880s of Cornelius May's *Sierra Leone Weekly News*, which was to survive into the middle of the present century with a proud record of success and influence, and in the 1890s of the *Sierra Leone Times*, inaugurated by the Sierra Leone Printing and Publishing Company.

Developments in the Gold Coast did not attain a comparable level until the 1890s but the early growth of the press was nonetheless noteworthy. The *Accra Herald* was founded in 1857 by Charles Bannerman, eldest son of James Bannerman, a pioneer Gold Coast leader, but was later changed to the *West African Herald* and, as we have seen, transferred to Freetown for a while. The more important enterprise before 1880 was the *Gold Coast Times* founded on 28 March 1874 by James Brew, an uncompromising African nationalist.

Although these early newspapers in Sierra Leone and the Gold Coast had an obvious attraction for their readers in Nigeria, there were other presses in and outside West Africa that had an important influence in Lagos. The press of Liberia was quite familiar all along the coast. The *Liberian Herald* (1860), the *Liberia* (1863), the *Lone Star* (1867) and the *Liberia Sunday School Advocate*

(1874) were some of the pioneer newspapers with which the reading public in Lagos was acquainted. Outside West Africa, the London-based *African Times*, founded in 1861 as the journal of the African Aid Society and edited by Ferdinand Fitzgerald, the society's secretary, enjoyed considerable prestige in West Africa until its demise in 1884.[21] It succeeded in encouraging public discussion and debate by opening its pages to the free expression of opinion on a variety of issues and it also generated or intensified the development of a critical outlook in the vehemence with which it increasingly attacked various aspects of colonial administration. The journal no doubt helped to strengthen the foundations of radical journalism in West Africa.

What distinguished West African newspapers from the earlier mission newspapers was their high radical potentiality. This is not to deny that the popular newspapers followed the mission journals in embracing the principle of philanthropy and attached considerable importance to the need to promote literacy and general enlightenment by featuring short stories, didactic essays and other literary matter. (A Nigerian newspaper was to claim in the 1880s that an important objective of the West African press was 'the infusion into the minds of the community the fondness for reading for its own sake'.)[22] However, the early press was inevitably a political press. Because Africans were denied effective political participation in a situation of Crown Colony rule and sought to influence the trend of events and to achieve greater racial identity and dignity within the principles of free expression newly accepted in Britain, the pith of their anxiety was the demands of political and nationalist persuasion and propaganda. The educated Africans were therefore concerned not that people should acquire just any knowledge but that their knowledge should form the basis of a strong public opinion which the colonial government could not easily disregard. It followed that the press assumed the role of the opposition and sought to rival the government, encouraging political awareness and involvement by providing a means of criticism of the authorities and spreading dissatisfaction with official plans and policies.

In the nature of things, the tone of press criticism of government was bound to be vigorous and severe. Some of the factors which explain this phenomenon have been examined elsewhere and merit only a brief restatement here.[23] They include the position of the government as the obvious target in a situation where the absence of widespread literacy and sophistication focused public attention on politics; the political and social prestige which attached to anti-government activities and the advantages in sales and advertising.

The colonial administrators were human beings and, like all men who rule, sensitive to criticism. But by an inherent anomaly in the British colonial system, what could be dismissed as fair comment in Britain was likely to be condemned as damaging criticism in a colony. For although Britain believed in government by discussion for herself, and was inclined to assume that liberty of thought and speech was of universal validity, in governing other peoples outside her homeland she was inevitably autocratic. British colonial administrators in Africa, as local representatives of the 'imperial power' were more than doubly sensitive to criticism. In keeping with contemporary racial prejudices, they believed that the vast majority of African populations were barbaric and excitable and that, although reckless statements or misinformation might not be strictly seditious, they could mislead or inflame the people and undermine the basis of colonial power.

However, the administrators probably knew that strong executive action against newspapers appeared to the people more as a sign of weakness than of strength – an acknowledgement of press influence. Furthermore, to institute criminal action against a journalist was to confer honour on him, for he emerged from the court a nationalist hero, a symbol of freedom. The popularity and circulation of the relevant newspaper increased, and the journalist was encouraged to become more vigorous. A further problem was that the English laws of sedition and defamation were a museum of legal imprecision and confusion, and so did not provide the sort of precise authority which a colonial governor would want to exert in controlling newspapers. His problems would be solved if he had codified, unencumbered laws of the press, but this implied prior authorisation by the Colonial Office.

Those who took final decisions at the Colonial Office shared some of the prejudices of the colonial administrators: in particular, they subscribed to the myth that Africans were 'semi-civilised and excitable', and they naturally believed that the authority of the government should be sustained in principle. However, they could treat colonial matters with some detachment. What was more, they were exposed to the pressures of influential liberal and humanitarian groups, of which many of them had been members or with which many of them sympathised, who advocated the cause of Africans inside and outside Parliament. Apart from this, they were 'the heart' of the British empire, and well placed to profit by their experience, or by their predecessors' experience, of press legislation in other parts of the world. The use to which such experience or precedent was put ultimately depended upon the individual character of the Colonial Secretary, for the British Government laid down no clear principles to guarantee the freedom of the press in the colonies or to govern the attitudes of colonial secretaries and governors towards colonial newspapers.

As a result of these conflicting considerations, the Colonial Office was from time to time caught between sustaining the authority of a governor who introduced a controversial press law, and inflicting what amounted to a humiliation on him by rejecting such a law and thus conceding victory to the governor's critics and enemies. To uphold the decision of the governor in such a matter would invite attack from Africans and their British advocates who spared no pains to mobilise British public opinion against the measure. On the other hand, to reject a proposed law would not only strengthen anti-government forces and possibly encourage unscrupulous critics to become a law unto themselves, but also lead to unpleasant encounters with governors unwilling to accept defeat and therefore reluctant to carry out the directives of their superiors. It could be seen that the problem of the relations between African newspapers and the colonial governments were very complex: in the final analysis, colonial administrators had to adjust themselves to an unusual dilemma: to preserve a certain balance between expediency, local official necessity, and the supervisory uncertainties of the Colonial Office.

The press freedom dilemma is exemplified in the relations between the newspapers and the government in Sierra Leone and the Gold Coast in the nineteenth century. It was not until the first decade of the present century that Nigeria became involved. In Sierra Leone in 1857 Governor Stephen Hill moved to suppress the *New Era* which he accused of exhibiting 'abuse and slanderous publications'. Earlier, in October 1856, he had tried to intimidate the newspaper by withdrawing government advertisements which brought it £30 a year but, far from impairing its vigour, the action drove it to uncompromising opposition. Hill, an erratic and intolerant old soldier, saw the gauntlet thrown down, and he prepared to pick it up, drawing his weapon from the armoury of antiquated and repressive English press laws.

The Bill which came before the Governor's Council in May 1857 was entitled 'An Ordinance for preventing the mischiefs arising from the Printing and Publishing of Newspapers and Papers of a like nature by persons not known and for imposing certain regulations upon the Printers and Publishers of the same within the Colony of Sierra Leone and its dependencies'. Most of the clauses were not only as wordy as the title but also repetitive and vague. Several paragraphs stipulated that it was an offence punishable by a fine of £20 to print or publish a newspaper until a signed declaration specifying the names and addresses of the printers, publishers and proprietors had been delivered to the Registrar General. Clause 18 stipulated that it was an offence punishable by a fine of £50 to print or publish any newspaper for which recognizances in the sum of £200, backed by sufficient sureties in the same amount, had not been entered into before the Chief Justice. The names of such sureties were to be included only after approval by the Chief Justice. By two amendments, obviously designed to make the law more oppressive, the Governor replaced the Chief Justice as the judge of sureties, and the amont of the bond was increased to £300.[24]

In forwarding copies of the Ordinance to the Colonial Office for confirmation, Hill explained that the law was inspired by the need to check the *Era*, whose editor he disdainfully described as 'an adventurer from the West Indies without position or substance'.[25] For this reason at least, the Secretary of State could have taken steps to find out how the law would operate in practice. Labouchere did nothing of the kind, nor did he object to the principle of directing a law against a single newspaper in a small colony like Sierra Leone. He unhesitatingly sanctioned both the law and a minor amendment that soon followed it,[26] and thus created a monster, the consequences of whose activities were to be a source of embarrassment both to himself and to his successors.

Governor Hill's thrust was swift; although the general impression was that the law would come into force forty days from its confirmation, and not retrospectively from its passing (the words used in the Ordinance were 'On and after forty days after the passing of the act . . .'), the unsuspecting Drape was caught in a snare, prosecuted, and fined £30. And when a proposal was eventually submitted for the registration of sureties, the Governor rejected it and three other separate proposals as well. Drape decided to appeal to Caesar for reparation, and addressed a lengthy memorial to the Secretary of State.

Shaken from their uncritical acceptance of Hill's oppressive legislation by the force of Drape's arguments and also by the fact that a British Liberal newspaper, the *Daily News*, had published some strong animadversions on the Ordinance, the Colonial Office decided to enquire into the matter. Their investigators not only revealed that the Sierra Leone law was adapted from a mid-eighteenth-century English law, but also that it contained provisions which must have been considered too severe by framers of the English law. It was hardly surprising that Labouchere felt obliged to reconsider his earlier decision on the Ordinance. He informed Hill that it was essential that an Ordinance of such 'restrictive nature' should be executed with fairness; however, apparently aiming at striking a balance, he also brushed aside Drape's request for compensation, and directed only that the law be amended to make the Chief Justice the judge of sureties.[27]

From the point of view of Governor Hill, Labouchere's decision meant a return to the original draft Ordinance; but the Governor did not take kindly to the implied rebuke in the Colonial Secretary's despatch, not did he like the idea of conceding any measure of victory to Drape. So he forwarded to the Colonial Office a protest in which he claimed that Drape was, as he put it, 'the weak tool of a few characterless Europeans consisting of dismissed public officers, supporters of slave dealers and smugglers'. Their aim, he went on, was:

to excite to discontent the native population, in which evil cause they may succeed, as it is hardly to be expected that a semi-civilized people easily led by the discontented few, can clearly understand why this government allows the publication of slanderous attacks on its policy and intentions towards them, without contradiction, the uneducated native supposing the government he has hitherto respected, and the power of which he has probably always over estimated would naturally contradict untruth and punish the utterer of such falsehood, can only attribute its silence to acknowledgements of the allegations published against it, and be induced to believe that he is oppressed and therefore justified to offer opposition to constituted authority, and by such means a docile and contented people be made factious and troublesome to their own injury and that of the colony generally.[28]

By the time Hill's protest letter reached the Colonial Office, certain significant developments had taken place. Palmerston's first ministry had resigned, and Labouchere had been succeeded in office by Lord Stanley. At about the same time, the Aborigines' Protection Society had begun to build up strong pressure against the newspaper law. In a memorandum on colonial affairs, it condemned what it described as 'a corrupt and tyrannical abuse of power' in Sierra Leone. In Parliament, questions had been asked, and the new Secretary of State had promised to members all the relevant papers on the controversy. So explosive had the matter become, and so seriously did Stanley regard it, that, after consulting Labouchere, and totally ignoring the non-committal line advised by some officials, he made up his mind that the law should be repealed.[29] In a lengthy and scholarly dispatch, Stanley took strong objection to the policy of the Sierra Leone government, pointing out the absurdity of demanding sureties in such a small colony. It was his view that to impose vexatious restrictions on the freedom of printing was an unwise course and that whatever abuses that freedom may engender are best left to be corrected by the gradual operation of public opinion aided by appropriate judicial sanctions against personal injury. He charged the Governor with misdirection of authority and instructed that the Ordinance be repealed.[30]

The Governor had since allowed Drape to publish a new paper in his brother's name;[31] to inform him in addition about the amendment would result in a triumphant revival of the old paper, and to repeal the law altogether would be to inflict a great blow on the government. Faced with the choice of public humiliation or disobedience, Hill chose the latter. In the meantime, Stanley had been succeeded as Secretary of State by Bulwer Lytton, one of the leading spirits of the movement in England against newspaper taxes.[32] And to the Association for Promoting the Repeal of the Taxes on Knowledge, Governor Hill had become a marked man.[33] It is not surprising that when the dispatch arrived in which Hill politely refused to repeal the controversial Ordinance, it was greeted with cries of indignation; the only minute on the dispatch was the question: 'Shall the Governor be recalled?'[34]

Hill's desperate but unsuccessful fight to muzzle the freedom of the press in Sierra Leone had important consequences. In the first place, it apparently damaged his record at the Colonial Office and destroyed his chances of being awarded the honour which he had been seeking since 1855.[36] In the second place, as we shall see later, it made possible the development of an unfettered press in Nigeria in the nineteenth century.

Of interest also is the background to the Commission of Inquiry on the role of the Sierra Leone press in the 1898 Insurrection.[37] In explaining the causes of the conflict to the Secretary of State, Governor Frederick Cardew charged insistently that the Sierra Leone press 'had directly encouraged' the Mende and the Temne not to pay the imposed tax and that it had in fact incited the Protectorate communities to rebellion.[38] This impeachment was taken serious enough to warrant the setting up of an official inquiry undertaken by Sir David Chalmers. At the inquiry, government witnesses testified that Protectorate chiefs were acquainted with Freetown newspapers which were allegedly often read or retailed to them by clerks or creole traders or literate children. But Chalmers totally rejected their evidence. He found the press criticisms to be 'fair and moderate' and saw no tendency to incite to resistance and rebellion nor the possibility that any deliberate incitement in Freetown would necessarily have the desired effect in the interior. The press – consisting then of the *Sierra Leone Weekly News* and the *Sierra Leone Times* – was therefore cleared of responsibility for the outbreak of the insurrection and probably saved from the imposition of restrictive legislation. It seems probable that Governor Cardew would have gladly considered imposing restrictions if he had won the sympathy of the Colonial Office regarding the impeachment.

In the Gold Coast, comparable developments took place in the 1890s. During the previous decade, the vigour of the *Western Echo* had so unsettled Governor W. Brandford Griffith that he wanted to initiate a prosecution but was discouraged by his son who was then Acting Queen's Advocate.[39] There was, however, no thought of introducing a law until the *Gold Coast People* made certain serious allegations early in 1893.

On 2 January the paper carried a pseudonymous article which attacked some officials and went on to suggest that the Chief Justice bribed the Governor before he got his appointment. The paper also alleged that most members of the Gold Coast Bench, the district commissioners, took their seats in court three-quarters 'tipsy'. The Chief Justice was amazed at the allegation about himself, and he promptly took steps to find out who wrote the article and who owned and edited the paper. It was common knowledge that John Mensah Sarbah, then a Cape lawyer, was the owner-editor, but no one co-operated with the government and official inquiries proved fruitless. The Chief Justice even wrote directly to Sarbah, but the latter repudiated responsibility. Frustrated in his anxiety to initiate a prosecution, the Chief Justice drafted a Newspaper Bill which among other things would establish a register of newspaper proprietors.

The procedure was probably slightly irregular, and the judicial officer's report on the Ordinance after it had been passed seems to bear out this view.[40] However, the administration backed it; on 29 June the Newspaper Registration Ordinance was passed by the Legislative Council.

As a Whitehall official was later to point out, the law was taken almost verbatim from an Act passed in England in 1781, but the sections of the English Act which modified the severity of the law were left out, while restrictive provisions were taken from an earlier Act as well as from unfamiliar sources.[41]

The Ordinance contained three major provisions. The third clause provided that a month after the commencement of the Ordinance and thereafter annually in the month of January, every newspaper must submit to the government its title, the names of the proprietors with their respective occupations, places of business and places of residence, and, finally, figures for its total and average circulation during the year. The penalty for non-compliance was £25. The sixth clause dealt with false and misleading returns which carried a penalty of £100.

The ninth clause carried the common provision requiring printers to print on the first or last page of every newspaper their names and occupation and place of residence, but added that whoever violated this subsection and whoever sold or assisted in selling any newspaper which offended against the subsection should for every copy printed or sold be liable to a fine of £5.

The Colonial Office was uncompromisingly hostile to the measure. One official was surprised to learn that 'such an inquisitorial act' as regards registration of proprietors existed in England. He observed that 'inquisitorial' as the Act was in England, it could be tenfold more so 'in a small place like the Gold Coast'. In general, it was felt that most of the clauses went too far, and that the penalty for false and misleading returns was too high, and that it should be a maximum and not a fixed penalty.[42] The Marquis of Ripon agreed with these views, and disallowed the Ordinance.[43]

It seemed a double victory for the Gold Coast press: the *People* had embarrassed the Chief Justice with impunity, and now Whitehall had thrown out the vexatious regulation. But the end of the matter was not yet. Acting Governor Hodgson undertook to do precisely what Governor Hill had unsuccessfully done in Sierra Leone more than three decades earlier. In a tendentious dispatch, early in 1894, he presented a statement by the Chief Justice which rehearsed the already mentioned background to the proposed law, and he begged for permission to carry out certain amendments.[44] Probably because the Chief Justice's personal statement excited pity, the impact of the Acting Governor's dispatch was overwhelming. Those officials who had recently condemned the legislation now saw nothing wrong with it. Ripon was won over: the Secretary of State withdrew his earlier intimation, and instructed the Governor to re-enact the Ordinance 'in the same terms'.[45]

The registration law of 1894 undoubtedly made it dangerous for newspaper editors to evade identification again, but this was probably all the control which the government was able to exercise. The Ordinance did not stop the newspapers from castigating the administration in the following years. Of importance is the fact that the press in other parts of West Africa denounced the inquisitiorial law, and thus set a precedent for the multi-territorial attack which was to characterise press legislation in Nigeria.

TOWARDS THE BIRTH OF THE NIGERIAN PRESS

Strictly speaking, the history of Nigeria's indigenous press begins in 1863 when Robert Campbell founded the *Anglo-African* which he abandoned two years later. But judged by the dominant principle upon which it was conducted, it cannot be said to have formed part of the newspaper movement which began in the 1880s except as a source of inspiration. Campbell's aim was to exploit the growing interest in Western education and enlightenment in Lagos in the 1860s by providing cheap and accessible material which would educate, inform and entertain its readers. The establishment of the Lagos Grammar School in 1859 by the C.M.S. mission was indicative of future educational growth and Campbell's rich experiences as a printer and teacher entered into the execution of an experiment in literary journalism. Born in

Kingston, Jamaica, of a mulatto mother and a Scottish father (he playfully remarks that he combined in himself three elements 'in the proportion of one-quarter Negro, one quarter English and half Scotch'),[46] he worked as an apprentice printer for five years after he had acquired, as he put it, 'the rudiments of a plain English education'. He subsequently entered a teacher training institution where he studied for two years before becoming a schoolteacher in his home town. Circumstances compelled him to seek a more remunerative employment but he found insecurity dogging his every step. A victim of racial antagonism and discrimination in the United States, he served for a short time in 1853 as a compositor and two years later joined the Institute of Coloured Youth at Philadelphia, U.S.A., as a 'scientific teacher'. In 1859–60, in response to the philanthropic idealism which fired the imagination of many West Indians and Afro-Americans in their Back-to-Africa movement, Campbell joined Dr Martin R. Delany on a tour of Yorubaland with the aim of establishing a Negro colony. A treaty was contracted with the Alake of Abeokuta who subsequently repudiated it before Campbell arrived back in Lagos in 1862 on his way to Abeokuta which he thought would be his new home. Disappointed but undaunted, he decided to settle in Lagos. For the next twenty-two years, he was to distinguish himself as journalist, intellectual, manufacturer, merchant and adminstrator. Early in his career in Lagos, he established the 'Lagos Academy' where he gave lectures on human physiology. His literary achievements were to earn him the title of 'professor'.

Given Campbell's background and outlook, it is not surprising that he decided on a literary publication as a paying proposition and an educative medium. On 6 June 1863, he launched his journal, a $6\frac{3}{4}'' \times 8\frac{1}{2}''$ assortment of scraps culled from a variety of sources – books, novels, magazines, and overseas newspapers.[47] The closest modern comparison is *Read*, the Nigerian edition of the *Reader's Digest*. A weekly, it sold for threepence and was printed every Saturday evening at Campbell's printing school. From the outset, the venture proved a failure and it would seem that what kept it going was Campbell's determination to reject defeat and perhaps the evidently small proceeds from a few government and other advertisements which were inserted in the journal. The literary matter interested only a few subscribers and sales did not exceed about 30–50 copies a week. Some viability was claimed for the publication in mid–1865, but it died at the end of that year (last issue was 30 December 1865). Judging from the feeling of utter disappointment with which Campbell continually referred to the apathy of the public, it seems obvious that the enterprise was far from self-supporting.

The establishment of the *Anglo-African* was no doubt a noteworthy development in the history of Nigeria, but its fortunes and character demonstrated that its emergence was probably historically premature. The real founding of the press would take place fifteen years later, when certain social, political and economic developments interracted with the impact of local and external sources of inspiraton to create conditions which favoured the emergence of popular newspapers. For when to the frustration of educated Africans which had been gathering momentum from the 1860s, and the keen competition which became a feature of commerce from the 1870s was added the growing circulation of learning and the eruption of nationalist and intellectual fervour in the 1880s and after – all in an environment in which the newspaper had become a most familiar institution – the stage was set for the growth and development of the newspaper press.

In the 1860s the African intellectuals who had hitherto seen cooperation with the missionaries as the only means by which they could pave the way for the creation of a modern African nation were becoming disillusioned and frustrated. They were finding it increasingly difficult to reconcile missionary protestations of Christian ethics with evidences of glaring hypocrisy exemplified, for example, in Henry Townsend's desperate fight against Ajayi Crowther. When Robert Campbell charged in 1865 that Townsend's reputation for forthrightness and sagacity was a myth, he was saying about one missionary what many Africans were beginning to think about all missionaries. The strands of resentment stiffened in the 1870s and 1880s when contradictions to the principles of Christianity and democracy freely expounded by Europeans assumed new perspectives with the new European impact upon Africa. The Partition-of-Africa wave of European expansion which the missionaries applauded, combining as it did the loss of respect for African rulers with a sense of supremacy based upon the since discredited philosophy of racial superiority, produced a significant revulsion in the minds of the educated Africans. These not only began more than ever to demand recognition in both church and government but also to awaken interest in things African. A cultural nationalism was fostered which questioned the uncritical adoption of European culture and stimulated a new interest and pride in the African civilisation. These developments heightened the need for indigenous media for the effective ventilation of social and political grievances and for the inculcation of nationalist sentiment.

The way for the emergence of the newspapers was also paved by the growth of education and by the general expansion of literacy in Lagos. One source of this growth was the increasing consciousness of the value of Western education which was true of Lagos as it was of the main trading cities along the coast.[48] Primary schools became a popular source of education and a good foundation was laid for the establishment of secondary schools in the colony in the 1870s and after. The Lagos Grammar School had been founded in 1859. In 1873, the Female Institution for Anglican girls was established. Three years later, the Methodist Boys' High School was started, shortly followed by the Methodist Girls' High School. Another source of the growth of a literate class was related to the fact that as opportunities for trade improved from year to year, more educated Africans were attracted to Lagos from Sierra Leone and other parts of West Africa. This 'latter-day' emigration must have been given considerable impetus by the atmosphere of successful rivalry which characterised the economic life of Lagos in the seventies.

The trade of Lagos was characterised by what a newspaper was to call 'suicidal competitions among merchants'.[49] Business establishments which had begun to grow from the 1850s now proliferated and in the absence of local newspapers, a few of these advertised their wares in the London-based *African Times*. The importance of the commercial situation lies not only in the fact that it stimulated further emigration but also because it heightened the demand for the type of news (shipping intelligence and market conditions, for example) that had fostered newspapers in England and other European countries.

Another consideration was the growth of the printing industry. Initially, as we have seen, printing was part of the educational process initiated by the Christian missions. At a time when the missions were encouraging the growth of skilled labour, their presses produced indigenous printers, many of whom must have migrated to Lagos in search of employment. And it should be remembered that like Calabar and Abeokuta, Lagos quite early boasted a number of liberated and educated Africans who had learnt printing in Sierra Leone or in the New World. The printer population must therefore have been relatively significant when Robert Campbell brought in a printing press in 1862 and Richard Beale Blaize, a future newspaper owner, established the Caxton Printing Press in 1875. As the economic possibilities of the printing business became manifest, more printing houses were established and by the end of the 1880s, there were at least five printing establishments in Lagos. In this way, the personnel essential for the development of the indigenous newspaper press was not only trained but also afforded opportunities for greater experience. It was hardly surprising, therefore, that when the first indigenous newspaper came into existence it was only an extension of a printing establishment.

With the inauguration of the indigenous press in Lagos, a new era was to open in the history of Nigeria. Conflict between African opinion and the colonial administration would characterise political development and an impetus would be given to the evolution of a pioneer African industrial enterprise.

Notes

1 C. Xrydz Eyutchae, 'The Press in a one-party system', *West African Pilot*, 9 June 1965; Onuora Nzekwu, 'Masquerade', *Nigeria Magazine*, 1960, pp. 134–44. Also Ulli Beier, 'The Agbegijo masquerades', *Nigeria Magazine*, 82, September 1964, pp. 188–99.

2 For a general treatment of the non-economic functions of markets, see Caroline B. Sherman, 'Markets', *Encyclopaedia of Social Sciences*, vols. IX–X, New York, 1933; P. Bohannan and G. Dalton (eds.), *Markets in Africa*, Northwestern University Press, 1962.

3 Cf. G. T. Basden, *Niger Ibos*, London, n.d., p. 334; '. . . The goods are left to advertise themselves; there is no attempt on the part of the vendors to advocate their qualities. On the whole, the women sit mutely as if they had no interest whatever in the business, and wait for a prospective customer to make the first advance. . . . Usually, it is possible to wander throughout a market without a suggestion of being pressed to buy.'

4 Laoye I, Timi of Ede, 'Yoruba Drums', *Odu*, 7 March 1959, pp. 5–14. Also 'Yoruba Drums', *Nigeria Magazine*, 45, 1954, p. 4.

5 Kannan K. Nair, 'The Old Calabar Missionary Educated Elite, 1846–1896', paper read at postgraduate seminar on African history, University of Ibadan, 6 May 1965.

6 C. H. Fyfe, 'The Sierra Leone Press in the Nineteenth Century', *Sierra Leone Studies*, 8, June 1957, pp. 226–36.

7 *Ibid.*
8 *Ibid.*
9 J. F. Ade Ajayi, 'Nineteenth Century Origins of Nigerian Nationalism', *Journal of the Historical Society of Nigeria (JHSN)*, 2, 1961, pp. 196–210.
10 Francis Williams, *Dangerous Estate: The Anatomy of Newspapers*, New York, 1958; H. W. Steed, *The Press*, London, 1938.
11 E. U. Oton, 'Press in Liberia: a case study', *Journalism Quarterly*, xxxviii, 2, 1961.
12 C.O. 267/258, Hill to Labouchere, 17 December 1857, Encl. 1.
13 Fyfe, *op. cit.*
14 *Ibid.*
15 David Kimble, *A Political History of Ghana*, Oxford, 1963, p. 162.
16 Fred I. A. Omu, 'The *Iwe Irchin*, 1859–1867', *JHSN*, iv, 1, 1967.
17 C.S.O. 1/1, Freeman to Newcastle, 6 December 1862.
18 C.S.O. 1/1, Freeman to Cardwell, 9 June 1864.
19 Venn to Townsend, 23 March 1863 (C.M.S. Papers, University of Aberdeen library).
20 For a bibliographical survey of the early Sierra Leone press, see Fyfe, 'The Sierra Leone Press in the Nineteenth Century'.
21 Persons who constituted the butt of Fitzgerald's attacks succeeded in closing the Society and therefore the newspaper in 1866. But Fitzgerald took over the journal himself as proprietor and remained editor until his death in 1884 at the age of 77.
22 *Eagle and Lagos Critic.*
23 Fred I. A. Omu, 'The dilemma of press freedom in Colonial Africa: The West African example', *Journal of African History*, *(JAH)*, ix, 2, 1968.
24 C.O. 267/260, Hill to Labouchere, 26 February 1858.
25 C.O. 267/257, Hill to Labouchere, 22 May 1857.
26 C.O. 267/258, Hill to Labouchere, 17 October 1857; C.O. 267/260, Hill to Labouchere, 8 February 1857. The Amendment (No. 13 of 1858) was to supply a date which was found missing in the Ordinance.
27 C.O. 267/258, Labouchere to Hill, 22 January 1858.
28 C.O. 267/260, Hill to Labouchere, 26 February 1858. See also C.O. 267/260, Hill to Stanley, 16 April 1858.
29 Minute in C.O. 267/260, Hill to Labouchere, 26 February 1858.
30 C.O. 267/260, Stanley to Hill, 20 May 1858.
31 The *Sierra Leone Spectator and West African Intelligencer*. It was begun on 3 April 1858.
32 Harold Herd, *The March of Journalism*, London, 1952, pp. 147–59.
33 C.O. 267/263, Association . . . to Lytton, 9 September 1858.
34 C.O. 267/263, Hill to Stanley, 8 September 1858.
35 C.O. 267/261, Lytton to Hill, 16 September 1858. The repeal took effect from 11 October 1858. For a reprint of the repeal proclamation, see *Lagos Standard* 15 July 1903.
36 C.O. 267/255, Hill to Labouchere, 27 October 1856; Labouchere to Hill, 13 February 1857. Also C.O. 267/261, Hill to Stanley, 4 August 1858.

37 For a prospective study of the 1898 insurrection, see J. D. Hargreaves, 'The Establishment of the Sierra Leone Protectorate and the In-surrection of 1898', *Cambridge Historical Journal*, xii, 1, 1956, pp. 56–80. For Chalmers Report, see C.9388, Part I, 1899.

38 C.O. 267/438, Cardew to Chamberlain, 28 May 1898; 31 May 1898.

39 C.O. 96/172, Griffith to Stanley, 2 February 1886; Stanley to Griffith, 15 March 1886.

40 Queen's Advocate, E. Bruse Hindle's Reporton the Ordinance, Encl. No. 2, C.O. 96/236, Hodgson to Ripon, 5 September 1893.

41 Minutes in C.O. 96/236 cited.

42 *Ibid.*

43 C.O. 96/236, Ripon to Griffith, 2 November 1893.

44 C.O. 96/243, Hodgson to Ripon, 26 February 1894.

45 C.O. 96/243, Ripon to Griffith, 13 April, 1894. The Ordinance met with criticism from the unofficial members but was re-enacted as No. 8 of 1894 (13 August). C.O. 96/247, Griffith to Ripon, 31 August 1894.

46 For detailed biographical information, see Robert Campbell, *A Pilgrim-age to my Motherland*, London, 1860.

47 Fred I. A. Omu, 'The Anglo-African, 1863–65', *Nigeria Magazine*, 90, September 1966, pp. 206–12.

48 J. F. Ade Ajayi, 'The Development of Secondary School Education in Nigeria', *JHSN*, 4, 1963, pp. 517–35.

49 *Iwe Irohin Eko*, 5 April 1890. Also *Lagos Standard*, 29 August 1906.

2 Newspapers and Newspapermen

The early Nigerian newspapers did not have the impersonal character of their modern successors nor did they experience the competition of other vehicles of mass communication and public opinion. Owned and edited in the illiberal situation of the Crown Colony System mostly by persons of stature in society, the newspapers exercised a degree of influence which bore no relationship to their low standards of presentation and modest circulation. The newspapermen consisted of professional and vocational journalists who took a positive role in politics and were active in social life. What they published, whether written by themselves or contributed by other people, invariably represented their own policies and viewpoints which earned attention. It is essential therefore that the newspapers which flourished in our period should be presented against the background of the personalities of their owners, their life-experiences, aims, outlooks and aspirations. This will provide the necessary perspective for the analysis in a later chapter of the role of the newspapers in social and political development.

A total of fifty-one newspapers was established between 1880 and 1937. These consisted of eleven dailies, thirty-three weeklies, three fortnightlies and four monthlies. Excepting fifteen provincial weeklies, all these newspapers were conducted in Lagos which has remained the centre of the most developed newspaper industry in Africa. Newspapers did not begin to appear outside the island until the early 1920s. Between 1921 and 1937, provincial newspapers were established at Calabar, Aba, Onitsha, Enugu, Port Harcourt, Ibadan, Abeokuta, Ijebu-Ode and Oshogbo. The major factor responsible for the spread outside Lagos was the growth of urban centres. With the promotion of greater internal peace and security, the growth of communications, the spread of education, and the transformation from a restricted to a modern economy, the growth of pre-European urban centres was accelerated and the rise of new centres stimulated.[1] In the eyes of the urban dwellers in the post–1914 amalgamation period, Lagos was the centre of sophistication, the fountain of enlightened values and tastes. Because Lagos was so regarded, the newspapers produced there and distributed in several towns were seen as representative of greatness. This conception gave birth to the idea that any town worth a respectable name ought to have a newspaper. In other words, in the growing reading public outside Lagos a newspaper came to be seen as the key to status,[2] and upon this many early provincial newspapers were founded. A second reason for the rise of provincial newspapers was the quest for opportunities. The proliferation of newspapers in Lagos and the introduction of promotion wars which sharpened the competition in the newspaper trade in the 1920s and 1930s, faced small newspaper owners with a choice between a pathetic existence in Lagos and the search for new opportunities in the provinces.

The provincial newspapers are of little importance in the political evolution of Nigeria. They certainly contributed to inculcating the habit of reading and general enlightenment in various parts of the country but because of limitations of communication and distribution, they did not make any noteworthy contributions to the advancement of political ideas or to the resolution of political controversies.

A few of the newspapers were published in Nigerian languages. The new interest in Yoruba language and literature in the 1880s and 1890s found expression in Yoruba-language journalism which at first, however, relegated advertisements to the English-language supplement. It was a reflection of the triumph of the language campaign that during the first decade of the present century, a religious journal was able to carry advertisements in Yoruba. A short period of decline in cultural consciousness in the second decade was followed by a reawakening in the twenties which produced a sprouting of Yoruba-language newspapers. In fact, Yoruba-language newspapers came to acquire such popularity and prestige that they were seen by many established publishers as an essential addition to their establishments.

An important issue in a narrative of newspaper history is the motive of those who founded the newspapers. Because of the limitations of the resources available to the pioneer newspapermen and their accomplishments in spite of those limitations, it is

27

commonly assumed that they were inspired by a high sense of duty to establish newspapers for the purpose of enlightening and educating their countrymen as well as championing their causes. The newspapermen themselves helped in no small measure to create this tradition of sacrifice and philanthropy. They advertised themselves as motivated by a 'strong sense of obligation' which they owed to their country and as doing a public duty which the people did not appear to appreciate. If this were the real explanation one would have expected the newspapermen to be fairly wealthy or at least sufficiently stable financially to engage in a public service without regard to making a profit or not. A development of this nature would not have been altogether improbable at the time given the philanthropic overtones of educated African nationalist thought. A wealthy man such as Richard Beale Blaize, about whom we shall hear more presently, could afford to donate generously towards educational development[3] but such men were few. Although many people occasionally contributed to funds to sustain weak newspapers or to pay fines imposed on newspapermen by the courts, they did not have the resources for any substantial acts of philanthropy. Indeed, the majority of the pioneer news-papermen would seem to fall into two broad categories: those anxious to recover from financial ruin arising from the bankruptcy of European firms in or with which they were employed or associated or from the monopolistic practices of Europeans who came to dominate the profitable trade between Lagos and the River Niger; and those in want of employment owing to dismissals and resignations from jobs, prohibitions from legal practice and incapacitation by illness. In other words, the early newspaper press was the refuge open to many whose careers had been ruined. This explains why journalism continued to attract new practitioners in spite of its hazards and frustrations.

The frank assertion by one of the leaders of the early press that his venture was not 'a public benevolent institution (or) philan-thropic charity' but 'a private enterprise undertaken for profit',[4] underscores the role of economic self-interest in the origins of the newspapers. The newspaper business with a small initial outlay and regular even though modest income seemed best suited for persons waiting to recoup their fortunes gradually. Furthermore, it should be noted that journalism was about the only other occupation outside medicine and law in which African enterprise was not blocked.

Emphasis on the paramountcy of economic motive, however, could distort what was and has always been a complex situation. A few newspapers were established in the early twenties largely for reasons of elective propaganda and political rivalry and even those inspired by considerations of profit did not necessarily exclude the demands of political ambition and patriotic inclination. The desire to make money often blended with the desire to influence public opinion and advocate causes for personal and communal ends and economic ambitions were often intertwined with threads of philanthropy. The remark of the Royal Commission on the British Press that 'the ambitions that inspire those who own newspapers are commonly varied purposes are seldom single and motives seldom unmixed',[5] is illuminating as a general statement of the problem.

The forerunners

The establishment of the *Lagos Times and Gold Coast Colony Advertiser* on 10 November 1880 marked the beginning of the indigenous newspaper movement. The *Lagos Times*, was founded by Richard Beale Blaize, a wealthy businessman of Yoruba and Sierra Leonian origin. It appeared twice a month and sold for sixpence. Born in Freetown on 22 November 1845 to John Blaize (alias Daddy Ojelabi Olapajuokun) of Oyo and Maria from Abeokuta, R. B. Blaize had his primary education in Freetown, became an apprenticed printer and subsequently was employed in the public service of Sierra Leone. He came to Lagos in 1862 and was employed the following year as a workman in the office of the *Anglo-African* founded by Robert Campbell, the Jamaican printer and educationist. When this newspaper died in 1865, Blaize became a government printer; it is said that during the ten years he was in that job he saved £20 which he invested in business with encouraging results. About ten years later he was to become so prosperous that the administration would estimate his fortunes at £150 000.[6] Blaize's initial investment probably went into the purchase of a second-hand printing press in 1875. At that time the press was already becoming firmly established in Sierra Leone and the Gold Coast and their impact could not have been lost on Blaize. However, his hope to start a newspaper in 1876 was not to be realised until four years later.

In establishing the *Lagos Times* (the full name was in recognition of the marriage of Lagos with the Gold Coast Colony which lasted from 1874 to 1886), Blaize was at pains to point out that it was a philanthropic effort and not inspired by 'the hope of large pecuniary returns'.[7] However, it was financial problems which forced Blaize to suspend the newspaper in November 1883. The newspaper was printed by Andrew W. Thomas, a future newspaper owner, and edited by various people the most prominent of whom was Mojola Agbebi, the famed cultural nationalist. However, Blaize's own nationalism and in particular his deep consciousness of his Egba connection found strong expression in the newspaper.

The initial success of the *Lagos Times* stimulated the rise of rival newspapers which ultimately forced it into collapse. On 4 February 1882, the *Lagos Observer*, a fortnightly which sold for fivepence, was established by J. Blackall Benjamin, a Saro who had become an auctioneer following the collapse in 1880 of the firm of Walsh and Brothers Ltd, of which he was for nine years head book-keeper and assistant agent. His newspaper venture was supported by Dr N. T. King, a brilliant doctor and literary expert,[8] and Robert Campbell who functioned as the chairman of the Editorial Super-vision Committee. The deaths of King and Campbell in 1884 were a great setback to Benjamin but he carried on single-handed until July 1890 when the newspaper died. In terms of life-span, the *Observer* was the most successful newspaper in the nineteenth century. Its role in politics too was distinguished. More than the *Lagos Times* which made every effort to balance radicalism with decorum, the *Observer* emerged as one of the symbols of the intellectual aggression which characterised political developments in the two decades of the nineteenth century.

The *Observer* was followed by the *Eagle and Lagos Critic*, a sevenpenny monthly inaugurated on 31 March 1883 under the editorship of Owen Emerick Macaulay, a grandson of Bishop Crowther and brother of Herbert Macaulay. A printer and a student of Greek language and history, Owen Macaulay wanted his newspaper to be marked by 'the fearlessness and acute ob-servation characteristic of an eagle' but it had neither the attributes of an eagle nor the resources of a critic. It was largely a pro-government newspaper inspired by what Owen Macaulay saw as his need 'to balance opinions when they are in opposition'.

Typical of Owen Macaulay's notion of 'balance' was the *Eagle*'s attitude to the Ajasa Affair in 1884. Chief Ajasa, the *Apena* (spokesman) of Dosunmu was deported, with four others, to the Gold Coast in September 1884. Described as 'of tall commanding stature, the first of native orators and the most shrewd of native diplomatists', he had led the public campaign for the better recognition of Dosunmu and at one time had gone to England to interview the Secretary of State. His deportation for alleged treasonable activities provoked public agitation for his return. But the *Eagle*, while praising Ajasa's personal qualities, felt convinced that the government could not have taken the action it took without reasonable cause.[9] The *Eagle* was partially sustained by government advertisements inserted by the administration of Lieutenant-Governor W. B. Griffith, Moloney's predecessor. It disappeared finally on 31 October 1888.

The Lagos press of 1883 had its critics. While the existence of three newspapers filled some with 'indescribable delight and satisfaction', it appeared to others as an unnecessary dissipation of energy and misuse of opportunity. These latter group felt that at least one of the newspapers should have been in a Nigerian language so that by addressing itself to the masses, it could put itself 'in the pathway of real power'. This campaign of cultural nationalism found the clearest expression in an anonymous letter to the *Lagos Times*:[10]

> They all address themselves only to the comparatively small number of English reading people on the island . . . no thought is taken of the large bulk of people to be found in connection with every church on the island and in the interior who can only appreciate a vernacular newspaper . . . the very large number of Yoruba readers are all neglected and left to suffer from intellectual starvation as if they also are not in the country and as if their help is not needed for their own advancement and the building up of the Negro race. . . .

The call for a newspaper in Yoruba would be heeded five years later but before then, the weekly newspaper had been introduced by P. Adolphus Marke who brought out a tiny newspaper of two columns which he called the *Mirror*. Marks was the local agent of an unsuccessful European firm based in London and had previously worked as a printer for the *Gold Coast Times*.

Notwithstanding Marke's remark that 'small axes cut big trees', he had modest aims for his newspaper which died with the issue of 24 November 1888. Between 1888 and 1890, two newspapers appeared, the *Iwe Irohin Eko* and the *Lagos Weekly Times*. The *Eko* was a tiny Yoruba-language fortnightly founded on 3 November 1888 by the printer Andrew Thomas to exploit the growing interest in Yoruba language and literature. It sold for twopence and was characterised by features on Yoruba traditions and folklore. It expired finally in 1892.

The *Weekly Times* which came out on 3 May 1890 and sold for threepence was the new version of the defunct *Lagos Times* revived by John Payne Jackson, a Liberian-born businessman, in a special arrangement with Blaize. John Jackson, who rose to become one of the leading influences in Lagos in the nineties and after, was to found his own newspaper the following year and therefore his background will be examined in its proper perspective. It may, however, be mentioned here that by 1890 when he entered journalism, his capabilities and acute sense of nationalism were widely acknowledged and were to earn the esteem of Dr Edward Wilmot Blyden, the pan-African patriot, when he visited Lagos in 1890. The arrangement with Blaize ultimately broke up in circumstances of crisis and confusion with important consequences for the history of the Nigerian press.

The agreement between Blaize and Jackson provided that Jackson should revive the *Lagos Times* under the new name, have a free hand in managing the sales, advertisement and job-printing business and prepare a statement of account at the end of three months so that Blaize's share of the revenue which was fixed provisionally at £5 a month, could be definitely determined. The three-month period could also serve to reassure Blaize that Jackson was a different man from what he was eight years ago when his poor book-keeping and love of drink in the office of the *Lagos Times* led to his dismissal. Jackson's editorship of the *Weekly Times* was excellent but his financial management showed no signs of improvement. At the end of three months, he could not render any account, not even when he was given two more months. The relationship became strained and although Jackson eventually managed to submit an account, it failed to reassure Blaize that he had not made a mistake in yielding to Jackson's pressure for a new relationship. On 29 November, Blaize discontinued the *Weekly Times* and arranged to revert to the old name as from 6 December. Jackson at first acquiesced in Blaize's decision but soon changed his mind and in hand-bills began to dispute Blaize's right to discontinue the *Weekly Times*. When Blaize brought out the *Lagos Times*, Jackson countered with the *Weekly Times* which he printed elsewhere. By the third week of the month it seemed that Blaize might decide to take the issue to court but Jackson eventually climbed down, announcing that he would start his own newspaper the following year.

JOHN PAYNE JACKSON AND THE *Lagos Weekly Record*

The Blaize/Jackson quarrel, which was to poison the relations of the two families for a long time, had a significant effect upon the history of the *Record* for Jackson appears to have resolved not only to outsell the rival *Lagos Times*, drive it into a second and final collapse and force his former proprietor out of the newspaper trade, but also to father a newspaper organisation which would be commercially successful and possibly overshadow Blaize's financial prestige. There could be no doubt that the background of disagreement and dispute would give a new dimension to Jackson's editorial and propagandist competence with obvious popular implications but money was needed to establish the new venture. Assistance came from friends of which the most prominent was Dr John Randle, a medical doctor and a future political leader. Not much is known about Randle's precise relationship with Jackson and the condition of his assistance, but it would seem that the assistance was not in the nature of an invest-ment carrying shareholding influences. In any case, Jackson's initial capital could not have been large. He could not purchase his own printing press until the late nineties and had to rely on hired presses, first from Owen Macaulay, former owner of the *Eagle and Lagos Critic*, and later from J. Bagan Benjamin, formerly of the *Lagos Observer*. When he eventually purchased his printing press, he named it Samadu Press after the notable Mandingo leader, Samori Ture.

A Nigerian proverb which says that it is the wind that fetches firewood for the cripple[11] may be said to apply to the infancy of Jackson's enterprise. For in the uncertainty of tenuous finances, a source of assistance arrived in 1892 in the form of a government advertisement subsidy. In the aftermath of the Anglo-Ijebu War of 1892 in which John Jackson most exemplified the bellicose en-thusiasm of public opinion, Governor F. T. Carter arranged to pay him about £150 a year for a column of government notices in the *Record*. The arrangement survived Carter's departure from Lagos in 1896 and was not terminated until 1900. How important was the subsidy for Jackson's budget throughout the eight years?

33

This is difficult to ascertain but it must have been significant only at the beginning. It is estimated that advertisements brought a revenue of about £350 in 1895 and £400 in 1900.[12]

A government subsidy is a potentially restrictive measure but it does not necessarily succeed in its aim as the experience of William Drape of Sierra Leone indicates.[13] The Jackson subsidy, however, was somewhat unique in its motivation and implication. Did Carter, who arrived in Lagos late in 1891, recognise Jackson's potential power and seek to win his friendship? Did Jackson's weak financial situation make him a good bait? Or rather did the arrangement have its roots in Carter's friendship with Blyden who was a great inspiration for Jackson? In other words, was the subsidy the product of a mutual admiration which Jackson's dynamic role as propagandist and war correspondent help to strengthen? This would seem to explain Jackson's curious ambivalence characterised by support for Carter and stimulation of nationalism. The collaboration with Carter grew as Jackson became more involved in the mechanics of government as a respected adviser and reached a high point in 1896 when, at Carter's instance, Blyden was appointed as Agent for Native Affairs in Lagos. As we shall see, Jackson's acquaintance with the processes of government continued, albeit indifferently, to influence his attitude to government, but generally by the time of Governor McCallum in 1897, the impact of Carter's absence and the increasing rivalry of other newspapers had driven Jackson into a more positive realignment of policy, expressed in vigorous opposition to the government. Governor McCallum rode the storm but his successor MacGregor decided in 1900 to abolish the subsidy, a course of intimidatory action which drove Jackson into total opposition until his death in 1915.

When Jackson died, his contemporaries wished it to be proclaimed that 'a great king hath fallen in Israel'.[14] A Yoruba-language newspaper portrayed him ten years later as 'field-marshal, educationist, philosopher, evangelist, the praiseworthy and omnipotent'.[15] And ten years after his death, it was urged that his portrait be installed in the Glover Memorial Hall.[16] There is no doubt that his career most exemplified the important role played by the newspapermen in the history of Nigeria and West Africa. A dominant figure in newspaper and nationalist activity, he was for twenty-five years, from 1890 to 1915, the most outstanding journalist in the whole of West Africa. In protest politics, he was an acknowledged force, inspiring and directing movements of agitation. He was the author of most of the petitions which the people of Lagos forwarded to the local and imperial authorities during his lifetime. His newspaper, the *Lagos Weekly Record*, was not only the most successful among its contemporaries but also an arsenal of ideas from which opponents of the government took their weapons.

John Jackson owed his inspiration to a variety of influences. Born in Cape Palmas in the small Afro-American colony of Maryland which in the late fifties united with Liberia to its north, Jackson inherited his father's painstaking disposition and incisive intellect. The father, Thomas John Jackson, was an emigrant from Maryland in the United States of America who distinguished himself in Cape Palmas as town councillor, chief justice and local preacher and missionary of the Methodist Church. He died when John Jackson was only four years old, a tragedy which must have inclined the future African nationalist to a spirit of independence early in his life. As a young man, Jackson's ambition was to be a successful merchant and as soon as he completed his education at the Training Institute on the Cavalla River in Cape Palmas where he showed great capacity in liberal subjects and in printing, he embarked on a course of extensive travelling which took him to the Gold Coast and terminated in Lagos in the 1860s. Employed by the prominent merchant J. S. Leigh, he was posted to the Brass River in the seventies but he ultimately broke with Leigh and started to trade in palm produce on his own. However, he suffered successive setbacks owing to what he was later to describe as 'the cruel greed of European commerce' on the Lower Niger. He eventually abandoned trade and got employment as a book-keeper in the *Lagos Times* in 1882. John Jackson's misfortune had an important bearing on his future career, for it would seem to have convinced him as well as those similarly fated contemporaries, many of whom were also to find refuge in the press, of the determination of Europeans to elbow their Nigerian rivals out of all African trade. This conviction resulted in the greater stimulation and hardening of nationalist enthusiasm and in the generation of a crusade against European imperialism.

Certainly the most powerful influence on Jackson was Dr E. W. Blyden.[17] *His Christianity, Islam and the Negro Race*, published in 1887, was for Jackson a veritable bible. He quoted from it approvingly and had strong faith in its message. Blyden's visit to Lagos in December 1890 and his return there five years later

35

as a government official stimulated a closer relationship between him and Jackson. For Jackson, Blyden was 'an oracle on both sides of the Atlantic . . . recognised as the highest intellectual representative and the greatest defender and uplifter of the African race . . . a man of colossal intellectual abilities and of unimpeachable moral worth.'[18] For Blyden, Jackson was 'an able man' with 'strong race feelings'.[19]

John Jackson's habits and qualities cannot but capture the imagination of the modern professional journalist. Although he was fond of drink and tended to lack organisation in his personal affairs, he read widely and was able to speak with confidence on practically every current subject. In particular, he was acquainted with works on British history, politics and law and subscribed to a variety of foreign newspapers and journals. His journalism was scholarly, marked by quotations and references, and its quality would seem to indicate how severely standards have fallen over time.

His legacy was personified by his son Thomas Horatio Jackson who succeeded to the editorship in 1915 and under whom the *Record* was to attain fresh heights of influence and inspiration.

GEORGE ALFRED WILLIAMS AND THE *Lagos Standard*

The impressive career of the *Record* has so captured the limelight that it has nearly driven the *Standard* into obscurity. And yet there is considerable evidence that the *Standard* was the powerful rival of the *Record* for more than twenty-five years. Founded on 16 September 1894, and edited with virtually unbroken success, it outshone the *Record* on a number of issues even after the latter had begun to establish its leadership at the turn of the century. The only occasion on which it failed to come out was the week of 30 September 1914 when its offices were closed as a consequence of its failure to pay heavy damages awarded against it in a libel action.[20] When the anomaly of John Jackson's collaboration with the government irritated many important Lagosians in the early nineties, it was the *Standard* which became the major focus of anti-government activities. Because those opposed to Jackson had their advertisements withdrawn from the *Record* and inserted in the *Standard*, the latter became the major beneficiary of African advertising for a long time.

The owner and editor of the *Standard* was George Alfred Williams, a former businessman who had turned to the newspaper field initially as a freelance journalist after European competition had forced him out of the Niger trade. Born in Freetown on 11 October 1851 to parents of Egba origin, and educated at the Sierra Leone Grammar School where he learnt printing, his life's experience compares with that of John Jackson. Employed by J. S. Leigh when he came to Lagos in 1871, he was posted to the Lower Niger (at about the same time as John Jackson was sent to the Brass River) where he eventually established an independent enterprise which soon collapsed due to European trading operations. Williams's Egba connections stimulated in him a fervent affection for Egbaland whose interests he enthusiastically defended and whose aspirations he did so much to inspire. The commercial disillusionment which he experienced was also an important stimulus to the acutely nationalist persuasion which he most clearly manifested in being one of the nine founders of the United Native African Church, a prime foundation of the African Church Movement. The motto of his newspaper, 'For God, the King and the People' (which he borrowed from *The Independent* of Freetown) exemplified his belief in what he called the 'inseparableness of African nationalism and Christianity'.

George Williams was no doubt one of the outstanding nationalists of his time. His assertive and fearless opposition to the colonial government as well as his cultural zeal most exemplified in his vigorous campaign for the rebirth of Yoruba language suggest that he was a man of vision and character, a man who, in the words of Dr Akiwande Savage 'never learnt to play a given tune'.[21] However, the circumstances in which the *Standard* was founded are rather curious and would tend to indicate an initial pro-government inspiration. Its two chief backers were Kitoyi (later Sir Kitoyi) Ajasa, a Nigerian lawyer of decidedly moderate opinions, and Frank Rohrwerger, a government official who at one point in the 1890s was Acting Colonial Secretary and Acting Administrator of the Lagos Colony. These two men severed their connection with the *Standard* when it had hardly started on the ground that George Williams had deviated from the agreed policy of the newspaper. Apparently it had been agreed that the *Standard* should have a pro-government bias but while Ajasa was away to Accra on business, its maiden issues appeared with robust declarations of courage and independence and pungent criticisms of the administration. Pressure was brought to bear on George Williams to cool his enthusiasm but this failed woefully. Ajasa's break with Williams was final and twenty years later would lead him to found his own newspaper to give expression to his conservative opinions but the nature of Rohrwerger's reaction is not very clear. He continued for a long time to enjoy publicity in the *Standard*, which suggests that he did not become *persona non grata* as Ajasa did. However, there is no trace of Rohrwerger's influence on the political attitudes of the *Standard* and the relationship was probably on a more personal level. Williams' about-face could be variously interpreted – it might have been the result of outside pressure or an attempt to resolve a personal crisis of conscience or a premeditated dishonest manoeuvre. Whatever its cause, his change of allegiance resulted in the development of a newspaper which was financially successful and which played a key role in politics in the pre-democratic election years. After George Williams died on 18 May 1919, the *Standard* was suspended for five weeks and resuscitated under the management of one James A. White and the editorship of Williams' son, A. R. Williams. But Alfred Williams lacked the drive and resourcefulness of Thomas Jackson with fatal consequences for the *Standard* which expired after the issue of 28 January 1920.

OTHER NINETEENTH-CENTURY NEWSPAPERS

The *Standard* comes after the *Record* in importance but not in time of appearance. In fact, two publications preceded its establishment. The first was the *Lagos Spectator* which was founded on 1 July 1893 and apparently collapsed soon afterwards. No copy seems to have survived. The other was the *Lagos Echo* established on 1 September 1894 by a group headed by J. S. Leigh 'to stimulate patriotism and manly independence'. They floated the Lagos Printing and Publishing Company (LPPC) with a share capital of £500 some of which were offered to the general public. The company, the first of its kind in Nigeria, was managed by a Board of Directors consisting of the Rev. James Johnson, J. Egerton Shyngle and C. H. Savage. J. Bagan Benjamin, formerly of the *Lagos Observer*, was the first editor of the *Echo*. Among his successors was Victor P. Mason who later founded his own newspaper. The view of a critical observer that the newspaper was conducted by 'controversial and polemic writers and hot-headed editors' throws light on its life.[22] The editorial staff was reshuffled repeatedly and also there was persistent controversy between the shareholders and the Board of Directors over mismanagement of funds. The resignation in December 1894 of Shyngle and Savage who were solicitor and secretary respectively was caused by disagreement over policy. This confused state of affairs reduced the effectiveness of the *Echo* and caused its final collapse on 16 July 1898.

With the death of the *Echo*, Victor Mason brought out the *Lagos Reporter* on 12 September 1898. It was a failure and was suspended in July 1899. It was revived on 17 March 1900 under the pseudonym of Sydney Graye and renamed the *Wasp*. But like its predecessor, it had no sting and was poorly produced. In August 1900, a libel action instituted against it by Samuel Percy Jackson, Chief Registrar of the Supreme Court, drove it into swift collapse.

'NIGERIAN' NEWSPAPERS

The emergence of modern Nigeria in 1914 was conceptually anticipated by the introduction of the word 'Nigerian' in the place identification of newspapers during the first decade of the present century. This was inspired by the administrative arrangements of 1906 which established the Colony and Protectorate of Southern Nigeria as well as by reports of a projected North-South amalgamation. These helped to widen the horizon of the educated Lagosians with consequences which found expression in the naming of new newspapers.

The first of these was the *Nigerian Chronicle* founded on 20 November 1908 by two brothers – Christopher Josephus Johnson and Emmanuel T. Johnson. Christopner Johnson, who was born in 1875, studied economics at the University of Liverpool where he was admitted in 1905. His brother Emmanuel was ordained a Methodist minister in 1898, taught at the Wesleyan Boys' High School from 1898 to 1900 and served variously at Lagos, Ijebu-Ode and Ibadan between 1903 and 1909. Christopher Johnson was the brain behind the venture and the editor of the newspaper. Apart from his desire to anticipate the final amalgamation, he was anxious to change the focus of newspapers by shifting their bias from the mere purveyance of news and information to a more analytical and academic approach to problems. This was a bold and ambitious experiment but although the *Chronicle* came to be distinguished by a high academic tone, it failed to influence the orientations of its contemporaries. Its high level of scholarship had limited appeal. The newspaper expired in 1915, whereupon Christopher Johnson turned to produce trade for a while and later qualified as a lawyer.

Two years after the *Chronicle* was established, James Bright Davies, a remarkable West African journalist, patriot and administrator, brought out the *Nigerian Times* on 5 April 1910. In its purity of diction, its spasmodic existence, its changes of name and proprietorships, it was one of the most intriguing newspapers in our period. A few lines of an obituary acrostic on Davies by E. A. Akintan, a newspaper columnist, indicate how much the newspaper and its owner and editor were admired.

> James – a journalist and patriot of high repute
> A man of talent in literary dispute
> Be not sorrowful, ye house of the dead,
> Rest in the Lord, your genius is not dead.[23]

James Bright Davies, one of the great figures of the early nationalist movement in West Africa, played a key role in the establishment of the newspaper press in Sierra Leone, Ghana and Nigeria. In Ghana, he was dismissed from the public service because of his clandestine anti-government journalism; in Nigeria he was convicted twice in one year and was the first newspaperman in the country to serve a term of imprisonment.[24] Davies alternated active journalism with public administration. One of the earlist Africans to attain high office in the colonial civil service, he distinguished himself as a talented administrator in Sierra Leone, Ghana and Nigeria. In the context of West African nationalism, his combination of attributes was unique. Born in Waterloo, Sierra Leone, on 20 June 1848 to parents of Ibo origin, he received his education at the C.M.S. Grammar School, Freetown, where he was admitted as a foundation student with a C.M.S. scholarship in 1864. He had an impressive career in the Sierra Leone public service, rising in a few years from a clerk in the Treasury Department to chief clerk in the Adult Department and Financial Secretary to Governor Samuel Rowe. Rowe's peremptory methods annoyed Davies out of government service into private employment in 1878. He took over the management and editorship of the *West African Reporter* owned by William Grant.

Earlier, between 1873 and 1875, he had been a regular contributor and leader-writer for the *Independent* of Freetown. Davies eventually secured employment as chief clerk in the colonial secretariat in Accra on a salary of £200 per annum and once acted as Colonial Secretary. Discrimination in the refusal of the Accra government to raise his salary to £300 which was being paid to his European counterpart in the Treasury increased his distrust of the colonial government and intensified his desire to fight for the emancipation of his fellow Africans. He now contributed more frequently to the opposition press and sought every means to embarrass the government. This line of action reached a crisis in 1886 when Davies joined in signing a farewell address to an Inspector of Police (Walter Higgwison) which appeared to the government to have reflected injuriously and libellously on the police officer's predecessor in office and on the police in general. The government, which had all the time suspected Davies of being a regular contributor to the anti-government *Western Echo*, saw in the Higgwison address a good opportunity to get rid of him. He was called upon to substantiate all the claims made in the address but he was defiant; he bluntly refused to answer the query, whereupon he was suspended from office on the ground that he signed a petition animadverting of government and for disobedience to orders.[25]

Forced once again into private life as a result of the fervour of his patriotism, he entered full-time journalism and joined in founding the Gold Coast Printing and Publishing Company which brought out the *Gold Coast Independent* in 1895. He was manager of the venture and editor of the newspaper until he resigned three years later after disagreements caused by his financial difficulties with the Liverpool firm of Walter D. Woodin for whom he was agent. He was subsequently an editor for the press in August 1899, but history was to repeat itself: at the end of that year, Davies left the Gold Coast to assume an administrative post in Northern Nigeria as chief transport clerk in the administration of James Wilcock. On the birth of the proctectorate of Northern Nigeria in 1900, he became one of the pioneer African officers under Frederick Lugard. He was chief transport clerk at Jebba and senior marine clerk at Burutu. In 1906, he retired finally from the administrative service and settled in Lagos to pursue his newspaper trade.

Thus by the time James Bright Davies inaugurated the *Nigerian*

Times, he was already a man of wide experience, an acknowledged patriot and a renowned journalist. His life in Lagos further enhanced his reputation, for apart from his contribution to the growth and development of the Nigerian newspaper, he played an active part in local politics. Displeased by the extent of the stranglehold which European firms had on the Nigerian economy, he inspired the establishment in 1909 of the Nigerian Shipping Corporation with a share capital of £20 000 which aimed at establishing regular transport service by steamers between Lagos, Forcados and Lokoja. The chairman of the enterprise was A. W. Thomas and members included T. H. Doherty, S. H. Pearse, W. F. Lumpkin and Prince Ladapo Ademola. Davies was secretary. Shortly afterwards, he became the 'Corresponding Secretary' of the Lagos Auxiliary of the Anti-Slavery and Aborigines' Protection Society founded in 1910. In this office, he was to play a leading role in the agitation against Britain's attempt in 1913 to subvert the system of land ownership in southern Nigeria.

The career of James Bright Davies exemplifies the devotion to the cause of nationalism for which many pioneer newspapermen were known. He was a man of inflexible courage and boundless energy dedicated to the elevation and political education of his fellowmen.

In launching the *Nigerian Times*, Davies declared that he was determined to express opinion and pass judgment on government measures 'freely and frankly and with open candour'. He denounced what he saw as a growing tendency in Lagos newspapers towards sensationalism and 'scurrilous and scandalous attacks' on individuals, pointing out that it was more rewarding in the long run to promote high moral standards than debase them. To Davies, public opinion was sadly lacking and it was his desire to create in Nigeria 'a strong, healthy and vigorous' public opinion. These declarations were not the empty promises of an opportunistic journalist but the sincere pledges of a patriot who, as one admirer put it, 'lived for the truth and was prepared, if need be, to die for the truth'.[26]

The *Nigerian Times* was an influential newspaper, so popular indeed that some admirers made unsolicited donations to it. In 1910, for example, four anonymous subscribers gave a total of £12. However, sales as well as small mercies did not meet the cost of production and so on 30 October 1911, after eighteen months, the newspaper was suspended. When the 1914 amalgamation took place, Davies revived the newspaper on 13 January, renaming it *Times of Nigeria*. He finally abandoned it in 1915, again after eighteen months, and two years later sold it to Adamu Idrisu Animashaun, leader of the Jamat faction of the Lagos Muslims, in whose hands it expired in 1924. Davies himself had died four years earlier on 17 January 1920, an old and resolute man, an important symbol of intellectual resistance to foreign domination.

KITOYI AJASA AND THE *Nigerian Pioneer*

Few Nigerian newspapers have invited greater reproach than the *Nigerian Pioneer*. Founded in 1914 by Kitoyi Ajasa, its policies aroused the wrath of opponents which consistently pounded at it with abuse. It was often dismissed as 'the official' (sometimes 'unofficial') organ of Sir Frederick Lugard's administration. A contemporary charged it with being the 'guardian angel' of a 'reactionary and inquisitorial' oligarchy who saw nothing but the dissemination of disloyalty and discontent in any form of public protest.[27] The *Weekly Record* grieved for its 'phenomenal and ex-cruciating chronic ignorance' in local and world problems. In this newspaper's view, the *Pioneer* was consistent to the extent that it was 'a thorough-going lick-spittle journal – sworn to the blind defence of governmental policy whether right or wrong, good or bad – the greatest enemy and traitor of its race'.[28] The denunciation of the *Pioneer* reflected upon Ajasa whose personality did not escape censure. Typical was this denunciation of his consistent support of government.[29]

> That any man in Lagos, African by birth, race and descent . . . should be so wholly devoid of race consciousness and utterly oblivious of appreciation of the duties, obligations and responsibilities devolving on him . . . and lacking a correct interpretation of the needs of his country and the aspirations of his people, is a misfortune to his people and a calamity greatly to be deplored.

The impression created by these and many similar remarks has been passed on uncritically from generation to generation and today constitutes the basis for the incorrect appreciation of Ajasa's place in Nigerian history. However, the familiar view of him as a disreputable reactionary is unlikely to stand a serious study of his life in politics, in the Church, the legal profession and the press. The necessary research is seriously inhibited by the fact that his private papers are not yet available. But we have some useful information on his legal practice which, viewed together with a dispassionate study of opinions expressed publicly in the *Pioneer* as well as in the Legislative Council, indicates that the stereotyped appraisal of him would need to be revised.

Already, two eminent Nigerians have revised their opinions of him. Chief Obafemi Awolowo in his autobiography describes Ajasa as well as his two most prominent friends – Sir Adeyemo Alakija and Dr Henry Carr – as 'patriotic but misunderstood Nigerians'.[30] Dr Nnamdi Azikiwe in *My Odyssey* acknowledges Ajasa's inspiring interest in his spirit of adventure and concludes, 'I admired the dignity and gentility of Sir Kitoyi Ajasa but reading the attacks launched against him and in keeping with the prevailing sentiment among the young men of my time, I thought that his leadership was not dynamic enough for Nigeria. In later years, I learned to appreciate him as a great man.'[31] These informed testimonies urge the need to reassess Ajasa against the background of the school of thought which he represented and the realities of political experience in Nigeria. For his belief that social and political stability depended upon a process of slow and gradual growth rather than upon rapid and hasty development is not likely to be considered entirely unpatriotic in the Nigeria of the seventies.

Kitoyi Ajasa was born in Lagos in 1866 with the original name of Edward Macaulay. It is not known for certain when and for what reasons he changed his name but it would seem that he was one of those who dropped their foreign names under the influence of the cultural nationalism of the late nineteenth century. Ajasa's father, Thomas Benjamin Macaulay, belonged originally to the Mahi ethnic group in northern Dahomey. He was sold into slavery, recaptured and resettled in Sierra Leone. In the 1860s, he migrated to Lagos where he lived until his death on 8 February 1899. Very little is known about Ajasa's earliest years. At about 14, in 1880, he was taken by an apparently philanthropic European to England for his post-primary education. He played cricket for his grammar school and eventually rose to be captain of the cricket club from whose members he claimed to have exacted obedience. These sporting activities had a lasting impact on Ajasa. As he himself occasionally claimed, his management of a popular club in a British school gave him early training in responsibility; he had to efface the obvious disadvantage of his skin colour by exhibiting much tact and integrity. He became convinced that these and similar qualities must be the chief weapons in Africa's struggle for social and political equality with Europeans. In later life, he was to lament the lack of sportsmen on Nigeria'a political scene.[32] After Ajasa left school, he studied privately until he joined the Inner Temple where he was called to the Bar in June 1893. He held his first brief in a case in the Lambeth County Court, in south London, in which he distinguished himself, winning his case with costs. He returned to Nigeria that year.

The period and length of time of Ajasa's sojourn in England are of critical importance in the attitudes that he displayed in this country. Initiated into adult life in an environment markedly different from that in which he was born, and deeply exposed to British cultural influence for over thirteen years, Ajasa acquired patterns of behaviour which made him probably the most celebrated 'Black Englishman' of his time. In Lagos, he cultivated the friendship of Europeans who reposed so much confidence in him that most of the merchants among them employed him as their counsel. This relationship must have made him one of the richest lawyers in Nigeria at the time.

Saturated in the British tradition and deeply conscious of the fact that this tradition was crystallised after a long period of experimentation and in circumstances that were different from those in Nigeria, Ajasa was inclined towards a Fabian philosophy in his attitude to local political problems. He spoke of the 'process of evolution' which 'must slowly work its way to a proper organisation' of the entire West African political system.[33] He was genuinely apprehensive of what he felt was the rapid pace of social and political development in the country, believing that with the low level of literacy throughout the country, movement was being achieved at the expense of future stability. 'If you feed a threshing machine too rapidly,' he was known to say, 'you may choke it and smash it, even though you feed into it nothing but good grain.'[34] For Ajasa, peaceful persuasion was a better way of getting the government to redress grievances than 'violence and vituperation' which displeased those in authority and destroyed all chances of success.[35] He strongly asserted that he was not an advocate of abject humility or 'acquiescence to injustice'; he only wanted his contemporaries to eschew 'unbridled personal vilification or deliberately hostile effusions against authority'.[36] There should be a greater dignity and moderation in the expression of opinion and 'a saner charity to all men'.[37] In certain respects, Ajasa could be compared with the Afro-American educator and leader of the nineteenth and early twentieth centuries, Booker Taliafero Washington whose attitudes of moderation and policies of accommodation established for him the 'Uncle Tom' image which research and rethinking on the part of scholars are beginning to weaken. Like Washington, Ajasa preached moderation and at the same time exerted his influence behind the scenes to achieve change and reform. His campaign for the improvement of opportunities for Africans in the Civil Service exemplify the paradox of his character. Generally speaking, he was in agreement with his more progressive contemporaries in their basic objectives; where he tended to differ was in the method of action. Indeed, an objective study of Ajasa's relationship with his more progressive contemporaries discloses an interesting evolution in time. Before about 1914, Ajasa associated with them; between about 1814 and 1923, differences of opinion, not totally absent in the earlier period, came most forcibly to the surface and in certain instances caused a cooling off of relations; from about 1923 when party politics began, Ajasa parted company with his old friends. In parting company, however, Ajasa was not turning his back on progress or on the nationalist movement. On the contrary, he embarked with men like Dr Henry Carr as co-travellers on a different and what he considered a cleaner and surer road towards the goal of African emancipation.

When all this has been said, however, it must be conceded that Ajasa had many weaknesses which his enemies deliberately and sometimes cruelly exploited in order to smear his reputation. He was too wedded to the British connection and seemed unable to imagine a Nigeria free of British tutelage. Out of his great love for Britain grew his overwhelming confidence in British officials and Europeans generally. He rather naively believed that they were in sympathy with African aspirations and would introduce reforms in the absence of vigorous agitation. He lacked flexibility and tended to judge the moral conduct of other people by the very high standard which he set for himself. Occasionally he carried his moderation to almost ridiculous extremes and failed to realise that in the public mind over-moderation often connotes boneless compromise and spineless diffidence. This apparent diffidence appeared to many to have been confirmed by what Thomas Horatio Jackson described as Ajasa's habit of retiring 'into inglorious silence before the finale of any discussion he may have . . . provoked'.[38]

But even in his areas of weakness, Ajasa commanded respect in the way he stuck courageously to his convictions. It is certainly clear that for courage he was rarely equalled among his contemporaries. And for Ajasa, this quality was the paramount ingredient in patriotism. As he himself put it,[39]

> Love of one's country, when that love is limited to what you can get out of that country, is false patriotism. True patriotism is that which resolves to do its duty faithfully and manfully, never mind whether you are cursed or despised, so long as you are convinced that that duty is being done in the best interest of your country.

Such a man could not have passed unnoticed by the colonial administrators. Indeed, as early as 1894, he had started to attend dinners at Government House. When in May 1896, he married Miss Lucretia Cornelia Layinka Moore, there was hardly any European administrator, not to mention the merchants, who did not honour the couple with an expensive wedding present.[40] In February 1902, he was appointed a member of the Board of Health and shortly afterwards became secretary of the Lagos Institute, the body founded by Governor MacGregor to promote discussion of public questions, in succession to the Rev. J. H. Samuel (Adegboyega Edun) who resigned to take up the post of secretary of the Egba government. At about the same time, Ajasa was appointed 'temporarily and provisionally' member of the Legislative Council. Four years later, in November 1906, he became a full member in succession to the late C. J. George. All this time he had enlisted in the Lagos Volunteers and in 1909, he was promoted from Sergeant to Quartermaster. When Lord Lugard inaugurated the Nigerian Council in 1914, he was appointed to a seat as representative for the African community of Lagos Island and the colony. On the reconstitution of the Legislative Council in 1923, Ajasa was nominated to a seat as member for Colony Division. In June the following year, he was awarded the O.B.E. and in 1929, he was knighted. He died eight years later in 1937.

Ajasa's enemies alleged that his newspaper was conducted with money provided by the British administration under Lord Lugard. According to the *Weekly Record*, Lugard was the *Pioneer*'s 'journalistic godfather and political patron'.[41] Unfortunately no private papers are available to throw light on this important matter but it is possible to draw certain tentative conclusions from the available evidence.

In heated exchanges in May–June 1914 between Ajasa and James Bright Davies the latter made certain disclosures which attracted much public attention. He claimed that it was he who started the *Pioneer* as assistant editor and manager (surprisingly, he was at the same time editor of his own newspaper, the *Times of Nigeria* which he had revived only five days earlier). According to him, he prepared the matter for the first issue and wrote the maiden editorial. Ajasa allegedly took him into full confidence and allowed him into secrets that he was unprepared to disclose. Davies dared Ajasa to deny that he (Ajasa) sent copies of the first issue of the *Pioneer* to Lugard who was then in the North and the Governor-General acknowledged the papers with a telegram in which he congratulated Ajasa on his achievement.[42] Ajasa strongly denied these claims, ignoring Davies's challenge but condemning his statement as 'obviously and foolishly false'.[43]

Six years later in 1920, Allister Macmillan, in his *Red Book of West Africa*, added a new dimension to the allegation. He claimed that the *Pioneer* was inspired not only by Lugard but also by his predecessor Sir Walter Egerton. According to Macmillan, Egerton endeavoured to get Ajasa to start a newspaper that would voice the opinion of both whites and blacks. Ajasa hesitated for a long time but Lugard eventually persuaded him to establish the journal.[44]

Given the above account, it may not be entirely unreasonable to imagine that Lugard probably assisted Ajasa in some way. However, it is significant, in spite of Davies's closer insinuations, that neither of the accounts claims that Lugard helped Ajasa with money. Even if Ajasa did send the first issue of the paper to Lugard as Davies alleged, there was nothing unusual about this as the two of them were good friends and the gesture could not reasonably be taken as evidence of some financial commitment on Ajasa's part. If such a claim were made, it would even be difficult to reconcile it with Lugard's endeavour in 1915 to get a European friend of his to start a pre-government newspaper. Margery Perham, in her biography of Lugard,[45] points out that in October of that year, Lugard wrote to his friend, Mr A. A. Cowan (Director, Miller Brothers of Liverpool Ltd) lamenting the abusive, seditious and libellous character of the Lagos press and regretting that there was no means of explaining in sober language the real objects and motives of reforms and the reasons for any especial piece of legislation. The public, including the schoolboys in the south,

Lugard alleged, were being brought up on race-hatred and contempt for government and it was impossible to counter with the truth all the misleading journalism they read. He therefore wanted a really high-class and rational but interesting weekly newspaper published in England with affiliated papers in each British West African territory, and edited by an Englishman with a sense of humour. Lugard realised that a newspaper subsidised by the government could be accused of being partisan, but he felt that papers such as he suggested, started with the support and the advertisements of the firms interested in West Africa, would meet the urgent need for public enlightenment. Cowan was sympathetic to the proposals but did nothing.

This letter would tend to suggest, if we ignore Lugard's usual misrepresentations of the critical character of the Nigerian press, that by October 1915, less than a year after the *Pioneer* came out, Lugard had become disappointed with its role and would not as much as allude to the paper in his letter. Indeed if the Governor expected the *Pioneer* to be a consistent purveyor of official opinion, countering and harassing anti-government newspapers from week to week, he should rightly have been disappointed for although the paper supported the administration from the outset and throughout its life, it was by no means remotely comparable with a medieval court gazette. While it did not compete with its contemporaries in the expression of radical opinion, it nevertheless maintained much independence of thought. However, it seems obvious from Lugard's character that if he had subsidised the *Pioneer* and had found it unsatisfactory, he would have bent it to his will. Moreover, Ajasa was a man of strong principles and was unlikely to have disappointed a friend to whom he was committed financially.

All this points to the view that in establishing his newspaper Ajasa did not depend on any government subsidy. Lugard himself, as the letter to Cowan shows, did not favour such a subsidy. He as well as Egerton must have given their moral encouragement to Ajasa with differing success and it is possible that by late 1915 Lugard had found the *Pioneer* not reactionary enough for his needs. The Governor's contemptuous views about African capability make one doubt if he would have placed such faith in even a friendly black editor. It is instructive to note that by 1914, Ajasa was already a fairly wealthy man and that he had been involved in the establishment of the *Lagos Standard* twenty years before. The impression he gives is not that of an indigent or unscrupulous lawyer capable of manipulation by means of government subsidies but rather of a rich and highly-principled professional man eager to indulge his interest in journalism and capable of running a newspaper, if not by his own resources, at least by relying on the keen support of his European merchant friends. The *Pioneer*, first printed on the C.M.S. press for six years and subsequently on Samuel Pearse's Awoboh Press until the early thirties when Ajasa purchased his own printing plant, was one of the best organised newspaper enterprises at the time. Until 1936, when it was given up, it never failed to appear. And even when the introduction of daily newspapers in the mid-twenties substantially reduced the volume of advertising in all the weekly newspapers, Ajasa, unlike some of his contemporaries, carried on until it was physically impossible for him to continue. Every aspect of his life reveals a tenacity of purpose and resolution of will which had few parallels.

THOMAS HORATIO JACKSON AND THE *Lagos Weekly Record*

The *Lagos Weekly Record* survived the death of its founder in 1915 and subsequently emerged as a re-animated force which for fifteen years dominated political activity in Lagos and stimulated important developments in the growth of the Nigerian newspaper industry. It became the pivot of the inter-war nationalism and the symbol of enterprising journalism. This achievement was owed to Thomas Horatio Jackson who followed his father as manager and editor of the newspaper. Thomas Jackson was one of the most colourful personalities in the history of the Nigerian press. A man of marked abilities and a versatile genius, he achieved fame as a journalist, politician, musician and sportsman.[46] He was born in Lagos in 1879 and educated at the Sierra Leone Grammar School where he distinguished himself in the classics and was reputed to be a prodigious reader. Among his contemporaries were E. J. Alex Taylor, and Eric O. Moore, who became leading lawyers in Lagos. After leaving school in 1898, he worked as a clerk in the Elder Dempster Agencies and in the Railway Department until 1904 when he entered into private business. In the Railways, he led a strike of clerical staff in 1904 in protest against a new form of agreement for staff contracts which, it was alleged, discriminated against African employees. Notwithstanding his public service and business engagements, he assisted his father in the *Weekly Record* and was also a regular contributor to the *Liberian Recorder* of Monrovia, Liberia.

Thomas Jackson's early interest in journalism and his association with his father in the conduct of the *Weekly Record* undoubtedly put him in tune with the movement of African nationalism and also exposed him to the journalistic style of John Jackson. A chip off the old block in many respects (including the love of drink), Thomas Jackson came to personify his father's patriotism and dynamism in politics and his rhetoric and scholarship in journalism. Wherever there was a fight to uphold the right of the underdog, he was always at the centre of the fray. He continued what had already become a family tradition of writing public petitions and organising protest activity. With the introduction of elective representation, he founded with Herbert Macaulay Nigeria's first Nigerian National Democratic Party. He was the party's secretary for many years and the party owed its fifteen-year dominance of Lagos politics partly to his newspaper's propaganda. In journalism, he distinguished himself as a prolific, astute and versatile writer, with an extraordinary aptitude in the effective use of complex words.

Other influences also helped to shape Jackson's attitudes. An admirer of Japan, he was inspired by the spectacular achievements of Japanese nationalism, which in the nineteenth century set in motion the processes that transformed the country from an Asian backwater into a modern state strong enough to beat Russia in the 1904–1905 War. The dynamism of Japan was a source of inspiration to the African nationalist movement in general, but it had a particularly great impact upon Thomas Jackson, raising his hopes in the future of Africa and apparently strengthening his resolve to usher a similar revolution into Africa by propaganda. It is remarkable that when in 1904 Count Cassini, the Russian ambassador in the United States, in an article reproduced by the *International Economist* for March that year, launched a bitter attack against Japan, warning against 'the perils of Japanese success' in the Russo-Japanese war, Thomas Jackson wrote a number of keenly pro-Japan articles in the *Weekly Record*, extracts from which were published in the British journal *Public Opinion* alongside opinions of *The Times* of London on the same subject. These extracts were reproduced by several newspapers in Britain, Europe, America, India and Japan. Thomas Jackson continually and proudly referred to these events, remarking that to him belonged 'the signal honour in which the opinions of a West African journal were quoted side by side with the opinion of *The Times* on a question of purely international importance'.[47]

Thomas Jackson's admiration for Japan was matched by his love for the United States of America. He prided himself on his American connections through his grandfather Thomas John Jackson of Liberia and admired America's ideals of liberty and traditional aversion to imperialism. His father's uncompromising opposition to imperialism was passed on to him but this was further strengthened by his identification with America. He seized every opportunity to attack imperialism and to plan for resistance against it. When he visited England in 1918, he took a leading part in the formation of the African Progress Union and was elected the Organising Secretary for the whole world. It is not without significance that when the fortunes of *Weekly Record* were at their lowest ebb in 1930, Thomas Jackson announced his withdrawal from local political controversy to devote himself to 'doing research work of sociological and imperial importance affecting the African race'.[48]

Another important influence on Thomas Jackson was the British newspaper magnate Alfred Charles William Harmsworth, the 'giant of Fleet Street' who later became Lord Northcliffe. Northcliffe rose from humble beginnings to make a lasting impact on the history of the British press. He built a newspaper empire unprecedented in its vastness which was the envy of many a newspaperman. He launched advertisement and promotion campaigns and made circulation battles a regular feature of the newspaper business. Thomas Jackson aspired to be the African Northcliffe. Until his death early in 1936, nothing was closer to his heart than the desire to produce a West African chain of flourishing newspapers. He dreamed of an ambitious commercial venture entailing the establishment of a chain of newspapers in all the capital towns throughout West Africa, with a co-ordinating centre for all of them in London. As he himself put it,[49]

> We hope . . . to be able to publish simultaneously with the local edition, Gold Coast, Liberian and Sierra Leone editions of the Weekly Record and also a London edition as a clearing house for West African press opinions. . . . .

The objective of the London edition was to 'disseminate native West African opinion throughout the British Isles and so correct where the British nation has been misinformed on West African matters and to inform them on points where they are ignorant'.[50] In furtherance of this plan, Thomas Jackson established a monthly journal, the *African Sentinel* at Byron House, 85 Fleet Street, London, in 1920. It is not clear who edited this publication and whether copies of it have survived. However, the scheme was apparently a dismal failure. Allister Macmillan's assertion that 'separate editions of the newspaper were issued in the Gold Coast Colony and Sierra Leone'[51] would seem to be misleading in view of the silence of Gold Coast and Sierra Leone newspaper records on what naturally should have been acclaimed.

In Lagos, however, Thomas Jackson was more successful. After he returned from his more than seven months' visit to England from 29 May 1918–17 January 1919, he re-organised the *Weekly Record* and introduced a new spirit of competition and enterprise into the Nigerian press. In London, he had bought a modern printing plant and secured the services of W. C. Wright, a former C.M.S. printer in Lagos, who became the Works Superintendent of the Samadu Press. Wright was an able and conscientious man and under him the Samadu Press became the best equipped private printing house in Lagos. The typography of the *Weekly Record* was improved considerably and the volume of job-printing expanded enormously. Given these improvements in production, Thomas Jackson introduced Northcliffe's methods of promotion and was able to double the circulation of the newspaper in a short time. By 1925, however, Samadu was in decline and it was probably in an attempt to stave this off that Thomas Jackson founded a Yoruba-language newspaper, the *Irohin Eko Osose*, in 1925. A cultural revival in the 1920s was giving a new popularity to Yoruba-language publications which found keen proprietors. The *Osose* appeared irregularly and was finally abandoned in 1927. On 1 January 1930, Thomas Jackson again experimented with a daily supplement but it lasted for only eight months, expiring after the issue of August 27. Its death heralded the collapse that same year of the *Weekly Record*, which had become a shadow of its former self, a collection of unenthusiastic commentaries, scattered advertisements and cartoons from foreign newspapers.

The swift decline and eventual collapse of the *Weekly Record* can be attributed in part to the introduction of daily newspapers in the late 1920s but it is perhaps best seen in the larger context of Thomas Jackson's personal weaknesses which explain the failure of his newspaper empire scheme. A contemporary lamenting the 'tragic wrecks of so many uncompleted hopes' summed up Thomas Jackson's faults as 'an uncontrolled imagination, incapacity for concentration and sustained application, a too light and joyous outlook and unrestrained optimism'.[52] His short-lived Lagos agency, established in 1903 for the European firm of Pearson and Company, shippers and importers; his subsequent business partnership with a Mr Silva under the name of Silva and Samadu (1907) which collapsed soon after it was started; his commission agency for the firm of the Anglo-Nigerian Company which traded in palm products and also proved a failure in 1908 – all those are variously cited in his disfavour.[53] We know very little about these events and therefore hesitate to endorse the implied charges against Thomas Jackson; however, they provide a noteworthy background for the fiasco of the Samadu empire project. Only a dreamer could plan such an ambitious venture and proceed immediately to implement it without first consolidating his base.

The establishment of a newspaper in London when the parent venture had only just been reorganised and needed to consolidate itself indicates that he was hardly a man of deliberation. The dissipation of energy and resources consequent upon the pursuit of fanciful dreams was bound to undermine the stability of the *Weekly Record* and to bring about the collapse of what promised to be a most profitable enterprise. Perhaps Thomas Jackson's drinking habits, in which he took after his father, played some part in shaping his character. Those who knew him recollect that whenever he published a particularly impressive editorial, full of six-syllable words and rhetoric, admirers would mob him in his office and he would regale himself with drink.

But serious as were Thomas Jackson's weaknesses, he was nevertheless the most outstanding journalist during the inter-war years. A kind-hearted, generous and affable man, his mind reeled at news of injustice to the ordinary man and he fought for redress of grievances with passion. His patriotism knew no bounds. During the scramble for shipping space which marked the post-war period, he took a leading part in the formation of a Federation of Native Shippers which succeeded in protecting the interests of African traders and shippers against the power of European commercial firms. His nationalism and journalism made him an important influence on many of the architects of Nigeria's independence. Nnamdi Azikiwe, in *My Odyssey*, attributes his interest in journal-

ism partly to the influence of the *Weekly Record* editorials.[54]
Anyone familiar with the *Weekly Record* and with Azikiwe's
West African Pilot, founded in 1937, will have little difficulty in
identifying Jacksonian phrases and expressions. It is not surprising
that when Azikiwe founded the University of Nigeria at Nsukka,
he established a Jackson College of Journalism.

ERNEST SESEI IKOLI AND THE *African Messenger*

The entry of Ernest Sesei Ikoli into journalism was significant in
two respects. First, he was the first newspaper editor produced by
a Nigerian educational institution and secondly, he was the first
man outside Yorubaland to emerge into prominence in Lagos
society and politics. Born in Brass in 1893, he was educated at
Bonny Primary School, where he won the 'John Miller' Silver
Medal presented annually to the most versatile pupil, and at
King's College, Lagos, where he was Senior Prefect in 1913 and
assistant master in science and mathematics later that year. A
display of European racial arrogance at his expense in 1919
launched him into a career of journalism and politics in which he
was to play a distinguished role until his death in 1960. On 19 May
1919, a football match was arranged between a European group and
the Old Boys of King's College. Ernest Ikoli, who had been
assistant master for about six years and was one of the organisers of
the match, got a football from the principal's office. The acting
principal, a Briton, was annoyed that Ernest Ikoli did not ask his
permission first and in the open field, in the presence of students
and guests, he rebuked him for his action. Ernest Ikoli was later to
remark in a letter to the Director of Education, Southern Provinces,
'this was most aggravating to me as a personal insult and disgrace
for which my pride and honour have compelled me to seek redress.
By addressing me as he did in the presence of boys, I felt my
authority undermined and my influence with the boys minimised.'[55]
The day after this humiliating experience, Ernest Ikoli sent in his
resignation. Two months later, he took up employment as assistant-
editor of the *Weekly Record*.

The manner of Ikoli's departure from a school which he had
helped so much to build as a student leader and schoolmaster
showed that he was a man of principle unprepared to tolerate his
being subjected to racial prejudice even if his reaction was to cost

him his job. It is not surprising that Ikoli became a nationalist celebrity overnight and was invited to join the *Weekly Record* by Thomas Horatio Jackson.

Ikoli's association with Thomas Jackson came at a time when the cause of Nigerian nationalism was receiving major impulses. The First World War had only just ended, bringing with it an intensification of political and nationalist awareness. The *Weekly Record* played a central role in the trend of events and afforded Ikoli the opportunity to understand the pressing issues of the time and to cultivate a style of radical journalism which was to distinguish his editorship of newspapers from the 1920s to the 1940s. He eventually became a member of the Lagos branch of the Garveyite movement, the Universal Negro Improvement Association, and was to be one of the founders of the Nigerian Youth Movement.

On 10 March 1921, Ernest Ikoli brought out his own newspaper, the *African Messenger*, which he printed at the Awoboh Press and published every Thursday at 24, Odulami Street. The necessary financial backing came principally from his close friend F. B. Mulford, a leading European businessman. The aim of the *Messenger* was to act as a third force between the then existing newspapers, the *Weekly Record* and the *Nigerian Pioneer*. Ikoli was eminently progressive and outspoken but it was characteristic of him to exercise restraint even in face of provocation and to seek a middle course in a controversy. Even when circumstances forced him to take sides, he always tried to be objective. It is not surprising that when party politics began in the 1920s, he inspired the formation of the Union of Young Nigerians, which was a sort of party of the centre between the Nigerian National Democratic Party led by Herbert Macaulay and the Reform Club led by Ajasa. Ernest Ikoli disliked what he called 'profitless feuds' between political groups in Lagos and often pleaded for unity: 'Let us settle our differences and let us unite our forces in serving this great country of ours'.[56]

The early period of Ikoli's career is chiefly important for his break with Herbert Macaulay. Ikoli was an admirer of Macaulay, of whom he wrote on 22 September 1921 that he 'must be recognised as a great factor in all political movements in Nigeria . . . a man of outstanding merits . . . a great force in the country'.[57]

Ikoli was on Macaulay's side on various important issues, but as a result of a quarrel the former comrades-in-arms became sworn enemies. The disagreement came in November 1921 when Ikoli refused to publish an article by Macaulay because he feared he might go to gaol for it. Macaulay had begun to write for the *Messenger* in August soon after he returned from England and there had been no problems. Now he felt insulted and would not forgive Ikoli.[58] The breach soon became final and Ikoli's newspaper became one of the major organs of opposition to Macaulay. The *Messenger*'s view in 1926 that Macaulay was 'a perfect blend of unscrupulosity, cunning, vanity and malignity, combined with a flair for intrigue and mischief' revealed how far apart Ikoli and Macaulay had drawn.

The *Messenger* was a respected newspaper and was able to pay its way. But by 1925 it had begun to collapse owing to financial problems. Events, however, saved it from tottering to inglorious death. The demand in many quarters for a daily newspaper in Lagos had led to regular discussions between Ernest Ikoli, Adeyemo Alakija, a lawyer and politician, and Richard Barrow, the chairman of the Lagos Chamber of Commerce. They decided to launch a daily newspaper and succeeded in winning the support of certain expatriate firms. The Nigerian Printing and Publishing Company was founded and in 1926 began to publish the *Nigerian Daily Times*. By agreement, Ernest Ikoli became the editor of the *Daily Times* on a salary of £300 per annum while his paper was taken over at a fee of £500.[59]

The *Daily Times* was a pro-government paper and its relationship with government was in the pattern of *The Times* of London. In conducting a paper with such an obviously conservative outlook, Ernest Ikoli must have experienced a crisis of conscience. Certainly, for a man who in the early 1920s was a prominent member of the Lagos Branch of the Garveyite movement, the editorship of the *Daily Times* must have been severely trying. Apparently, it was his financial problems and his break with Herbert Macaulay which drove him to occupy the same bed with reactionaries and opponents of African nationalism. Nevertheless, his connection with the *Daily Times* was relatively brief and he was to resign in 1929 and to start a rival newspaper, the *Nigerian Daily Mail*, the following year. After the *Mail* collapsed in June 1931, he was to continue his journalistic career as editor of the *Nigerian Daily Telegraph* founded by H. Antus Willams in 1927, and editor of the *Daily Service*, the organ of the Nigerian Youth Movement.

ADEOYE DENIGA AND *Eko Akete*

The twenties witnessed important developments in the growth of the Nigerian press. Nigerian language newspapers sprouted in response to a revival of cultural nationalism; new newspapers emerged to answer the needs of electioneering and daily newspapers and newspaper companies arose with unhappy consequences for the survival of the weekly newspapers. The cultural revival, which the post-war political ferment must have helped to stimulate, found one of its greatest embodiments in Adeoye Deniga, a remarkable journalist and author whose greatest achievement was *Eko Akete*, a Yoruba-language weekly which he founded in 1922. Deniga was a resourceful and tenacious patriot devoted to the cause of African nationalism to the extent that he was selected as a delegate from Lagos to the inaugural meeting at Accra of the Congress of British West Africa in 1920. In an age when newspapermen added to their income by engaging in small-scale trade, Deniga devoted his full attention to writing and publishing and was the founder of various news sheets and author of many publications in both English and Yoruba languages.

Born in Lagos on 9 April 1881 to parents of Ondo origin, Adeoye Deniga was originally named Gabriel Adeoye Thomas, a name he dropped in 1908 in practical demonstration of his cultural nationalism. After his education at St Peter's Anglican School and the C.M.S. Grammar School, Lagos, he entered the Civil Service in 1901 as Express Delivery mailman in the Lagos Post Office. After a year he resigned to become a teacher in which profession he rose to the position of headmaster of the Wesleyan Tinubu School in 1910–11. The course of public events during the first decade of this century persuaded him that he would be more effective as a journalist and so started a new career destined to be marked by a succession of failures.

In 1909 he had launched the *Lagos Astrological Mercury* which circulated among a small circle of people and was written by hand. The following year, he had founded a monthly journal *The New Age Herald* which dealt with 'the laws of higher life and kindred subjects of interest'. A leading library and a bookstall were provided to promote interest in the journal. Nevertheless, it was short-lived and on 27 March 1913, Deniga brought out a bilingual monthly called the *Harald Alore* which also had a brief existence and had disappeared by the end of 1914. In 1918, he became sub-editor of the *Weekly Record* and took charge of the newspaper when Thomas Jackson went to Britain between May 1918 and January 1919. In 1921, he planned to publish a magazine to be called *The New Nigeria* but later abandoned the idea. That same year he became editor of Ojo Cole's *African Herbal Messenger Health Review* whose aim was to educate public opinion on the study of the efficacy of African herbs. The journal died a quick death.

Thus by 1922, Deniga, even though a talented and energetic journalist, had not made a name for himself in the newspaper business. The turning point came with *Eko Akete*. Launched on 7 July 1922, it survived until 6 April 1929, when it was suspended. It was revived on 4 March 1937 but was abandoned finally on 14 October that year. It was, at least in the early twenties, a successful newspaper, easily overshadowing its rivals, *Eleti Ofe* (1923), *Iwe Irohin Osose* (1925), *Eke Igbehin* (1926) and *Akede Eko* (1928). Its support of the Nigerian National Democratic Party in the political strife of the twenties helped to increase its circulation from 500 in 1922 to 1800 in 1924.

In editing the *Eko Akete*, Deniga employed not only the resources of his rich journalistic experience and unrivalled mastery of the Yoruba language but also the sense of objectivity with which he assessed evidence for his biographical researches on West African leaders which resulted in a number of pamphlets as well as his *Who's Who* published in 1934.[60] Deniga was a man of great self-confidence unruffled by difficulties. He believed that God had a special purpose for him in life, an attitude which led him to form the Lagos Theistic Union in December 1913. He saw his work principally as a service to the public and therefore did not hesitate to appeal for public support whenever he was in financial difficulty. In 1913, for example, he made an urgent public appeal for £25 to sustain the *Herald Alore*. For the *Eko Akete*, whenever the need arose Deniga would usually summon a public meeting and invite donations towards what he called a Sustentation Fund. Sometimes he would merely address his appeal in the newspaper to 'those who appreciate the paper's further services and continued usefulness'. In 1925, he inaugurated an *Eko Akete* Annual Dinner, the first of which took place at the Bonanza Hotel. Public response to Deniga's appeals did not always solve his financial problems but he was always thankful for small mercies.

Adeoye Deniga died in 1934 a poor man, but he will always be remembered as the man who, spurred by the desire to promote the exchange of ideas, published a newspaper which he wrote by hand. He will also be remembered as the first indigenous Nigerian, different from the Saro, who made his mark on Nigerian journalism and intellectual life.

ELECTIONEERING NEWSPAPERS

The introduction of democratic elections on the basis of the Clifford Constitution of 1922 was bound to add a significant dimension to the role of the newspapers which would now become outlets for electoral policies and propaganda. This consideration led some Nigerians to found newspapers to give effective expression to their political opinions. The most famous of these newcomers was the *Nigerian Spectator*, founded by Dr Richard Akinwande Savage, a medical doctor and journalist, on 19 May 1923. Akinwande Savage was one of the most renowned vocational journalists in the nineteenth and early twentieth centuries. It has been said of him that 'his was a facile pen . . . a style peculiarly engaging . . . a rich and copious vacabulary which he used with the deft hand of a perfect master'. In politics, however, his record was less distinguished. Although he attended the 1900 Pan-African Conference as one of the delegates of the Afro-West Indian Literary Society of Edinburgh and played a leading role in initiating the practical implementation of the National Congress of British West Africa scheme, he acquired a reputation as one of those who wrecked the Lagos branch of the Congress movement. Indeed, he was an unsuccessful politician particularly embittered by failure to be named as the representative of Egbaland in the new Legislative Council. His enemies thought that his most serious fault was his inability to see the point of view of the other man. The view of an observer that it was impossible for 'a savage to abandon his savage disposition and ferocity' was perhaps a pun inspired by political enmity but he was in fact an intemperate, self-assertive and self-satisfied man with a penchant for mud-slinging and abuse. His character did not endear him to many people and added little to the popularity which he seemed so anxious to win.[61]

Born in Lagos on 22 January 1874, the son of Josiah Alfred Savage, a prominent merchant of Sierra Leone and Egba origins, Akinwande Savage was educated at the C.M.S. Grammar School and the University of Edinburgh where he studied medicine from 1895 to 1900. His acquaintance with journalism began at Edinburgh as sub-editor of *The Student*, the magazine of the Students' Union, and joint editor of the *Edinburgh University Hand Book* for 1899–1900. His medical career began in the Gold Coast where he alternated government service with independent practice during the years 1900–11. In that country, he wrote regularly for the newspapers and in later years (1912–13) actively collaborated with his friend J. E. Casely Hayford in regular contribution to the *Gold Coast Leader*. In Nigeria, he contributed to the *Standard* for many years before he founded the *Spectator* which ran for seven years (last issue was 27 December 1930).

The other newspaper inspired by the events of 1922–23 was the *Nigerian Advocate* established by S. H. Braithwaite on 1 August 1923. Braithwaite, an Oyo man, was the representative in Nigeria of the 'Central News', an organisation that served the British and American newspapers. Unlike Savage, he was a man of moderate opinions and must have been inspired largely by the commercial possibilities of electioneering readership. His opening statement that his newspaper would not declare any policy but would content itself with leaving everything in the hands of God indicates his limited ambitions in politics which found expression in a mediatory role.

The Nigerian Daily Times

The greater popularisation of the newspaper as a result of the political ferment of the early twenties, demonstrated by the rise in the overall weekly circulation from about 3 000 in 1920 to over 7 000 in 1925, and the significant expansion in advertisement patronage stimulated by post-war economy, increased the attraction of the daily newspaper as a sound commercial proposition. Some enthusiasm for daily newspapers was also provoked by Governor Clifford's lament of the absence of such publications in the country in his famous address to the Nigerian Council in 1920:[62]

> . . . the absence of a daily press prevents the wide dissemination of news throughout the country which is customary in the West Indies, and which, for example, is effected in Ceylon by the publication in Colombo of two morning and two evening newspapers on every week day. . . . .

61

Clifford's pronouncements, which were given considerable publicity in the press, contributed to whet public appetite for daily newspapers and gave strength to a current rumour that S. H. Pearse, a prominent businessman, was planning to launch the first daily newspaper. Pearse abandoned his plans owing to lack of partners and it was not until 1925–26 that daily newspapers were born.

The Nigerian Daily Times, launched on 1 June 1926, was a milestone in Nigerian press history. Although it was not the first daily newspaper, the formation of its proprietors, the Nigerian Printing and Publishing Company Ltd, in 1925 represented the first concrete expression of opinion in favour of establishing a daily newspaper in Nigeria. As well as stimulating the growth of daily newspaper ventures, the *Daily Times* encouraged the development of a new journalism which was to attain new heights at the end of our period. However, from the point of view of political development, the newspaper was not of much importance. Founded as a partnership between certain Nigerians of moderate views and European businessmen, its reactionary role as a supporter of the colonial government was circumscribed by the demands of commercial realities. According to one of its founders, the title of the newspaper was adopted because it was considered that the journal should serve the same function as *The Times* of London ('like our great London contemporary . . . our policy is to support Government as far as possible')[63] but its conservative intervention in politics had little public impact, partly because it was inconsistent in its studious endeavour to safeguard its image of independence.

The establishment of the Nigerian Printing and Publishing Company Ltd (NPPC) was partially accidental. For some years before 1925, the Government Press published every weekday afternoon a sheetful of cabled messages from Reuter's Agency and wireless news broadcast from Rugby. This publication was distributed initially at an annual rate of £2 to government departments and private subscribers, chief among whom were the European Commercial Community. In 1925, the subscribers rebelled against the government's proposed doubling of the subscription on the grounds that costs had risen. As a way out of the deadlock that ensued, the government proposed to run the service as a business undertaking (by taking in advertisements) but it was quick to recognise that such an undertaking properly belonged to private enterprise.

All this time, sporadic opinions in favour of establishing a daily newspaper were being crystallised in regular discussions between Ernest Ikoli, whose *African Messenger* had begun to collapse, Adeyemo Alakija, a lawyer and politician, and Richard Barrow, Agent of Jurgen's Colonial Products Limited and Chairman of the Lagos Chamber of Commerce. These saw the solution to the Reuter's news crisis in the establishment of a daily newspaper which should embody Reuter's and wireless news. The idea gained the government's approval and the support of a large number of powerful expatriate commercial interests. These included V. R. Osborne, Manager, John Holt; L. A. Archer, Manager, Elder Dempster Agencies; W. E. Becker, District Manager, British Bank of West Africa (now Bank of West Africa); P. D. Doe, General Manager, African and Eastern Trade Corporation; H. Scott-Taylor, Manager, Gottschalk and Company. As a result of the combined efforts of these interests, a private limited liability company with a nominal share capital of £3 000 was founded to publish the *Daily Times* and, in addition, take over Ikoli's *Messenger* under an agreement by which the latter was to be the editor of the new venture. The company had a six-member Board of Directors whose Chairman was Adeyemo Alakija, the only African on the Board. Ikoli was editor until 1929 when he was succeeded by A. A. C. Titcombe, an Egba who had risen from being a correspondent at Abeokuta to assistant editor. Titcombe was editor from 1930 to 1938.

The Nigerian influences in the *Daily Times* were bitterly opposed to Herbert Macaulay. Ikoli had broken with him in 1921 and Alakija was a close friend of Kitoyi Ajasa and Henry Carr. Therefore, Europeans and Nigerians who had feelings of hostility towards Herbert Macaulay found an outlet in the newspaper. But criticisms of Macaulay and of the nationalism whose leading spokesman he was, were sporadic and widely disregarded.

The foreign-capital factor in the *Daily Times* assured for it a position of uncontested dominance for at least ten years. Its virtual monopoly of European commercial advertising, its ability to attract experienced technical staff who introduced popular techniques of presentation and general improvements in typography and distribution, enabled it to achieve a wide appeal and to undergo a process of expansion which led to the fusion in July 1936 between the NPPC and the West African Newspapers Limited of London and Liverpool. This was the first step in the developments which culminated in the enterprise coming under the Daily Mirror Group of London twelve years later. The popularity of the *Daily Times*, notwithstanding that its policy was pro-government, may be regarded as an index of its relatively insignificant role in Nigeria's political development in our period.

HERBERT MACAULAY AND THE *Lagos Daily News*

In 1927, Herbert Macaulay, in association with Dr J. Akilade Caulcrick, a Sierra Leone-born surgeon and politician, purchased the *Lagos Daily News* from its original founder, Victor Babamuboni, a bookseller. Babamuboni had founded the newspaper two years earlier in a frantic attempt to find alternative means of livelihood in view of crushing competition by the C.M.S. Bookshop. At that time arrangements for the inauguration of the *Daily Times* were nearing completion; Babamuboni, apparently believing that the earliest bird catches the worm, hurriedly came out on 9 November 1925 with a tiny daily news sheet which he proudly proclaimed as 'West Africa's First Daily'. It was an amateurish and ludicrous venture which managed to survive for 67 days (until 14 January 1926). The following year, both the newspaper and its printing plant (Tanimola Press) were sold as mentioned above.

Although Caulcrick was co-proprietor of the *Daily News* and J. A. Olushola was editor for a while, the newspaper was the stormy mouthpiece of Macaulay, who was designated 'Controlling Editor and Joint Proprietor'. Under his direction, it became a firebrand and assumed the sub-title of 'the paper with a punch'. It quickly rose to prominence, becoming the most popular as well as the most ridiculed newspaper in Lagos. Enemies and political opponents of Macaulay called it 'The Penny Lagos Rag' while his admirers referred to it as 'Lagos Penny Pepper'. As a matter of fact, the paper combined the qualities of Rag and Pepper, for Macaulay could not do much to improve the wretched appearance of the original *Daily News*, partly because the paper relied solely on sales for its revenue. Anxious to avoid any compromising influences, he refused to take in advertisements even though his sales revenue was hardly adequate to pay his staff. By 1934, the *Daily News* was virtually defunct. It would disappear for long periods and suddenly re-emerge to the pleasure of Macaulay's friends and the displeasure of his enemies. He was then seventy years old but his journalistic energy seemed inexhaustible.

Macaulay's journalism was an important factor in his rise to political dominance in Lagos. He wielded the most deadly pen in Nigeria's press history. A man of unusual literary gifts and an historian, he carefully assembled and marshalled his facts and figures which added force to his arguments and conclusions. Macaulay had trained as a civil engineer in England, but his impatience with the inadequacies of British colonial rule drove him to seek to influence government policy through the medium of the press. His stay in Britain from 1890 to 1893 had the familiar impact on his political attitude except that his extensive reading of British and European history helped to deepen his knowledge of the British system and to increase his impatience with colonial misrule.

It is possible that Macaulay wrote secretly for the newspapers while he was in the Civil Service. However, it was from about 1900, two years after he resigned from the Civil Service to become an independent licensed surveyor, architect and civil engineer that he truly emerged as an outspoken newspaper critic of government. The *Daily News* assumed its new form when the political tensions of the preceding quarter-century were abating into relative quiescence, but Macaulay's role in the controversies of that period, and as co-founder and leader of the influential Nigerian National Democratic Party, found active expression in his numerous contributions to the press. There was hardly any respectable newspaper at the time which did not carry at least one of his articles. However, by 1927 he had quarrelled with almost all the newspaper owners in Lagos. Whoever expressed reluctance to publish for any reason whatsoever faced instant quarrel. This was true, for example, of John Payne Jackson in 1908 and Ernest Ikoli in 1921. Macaulay was a man of strong convictions and once he had completed an article nothing could stand in his way of publishing it. If newspapers expressed reluctance, he promptly arranged to print the article privately and to publish it as a pamphlet. A good many of his numerous pamphlets came into being in this way.

Anyone interested in the contribution of journalists to the intellectual history of Nigeria is not likely to find the *Daily News* very rewarding. Unlike John Payne Jackson, Thomas Horatio Jackson, George Alfred Williams and James Bright Davies, Macaulay was not full of ideas. He was more a man of action, a practical politician who believed that the most effective way to carry out agitation was to continue to cry out. At the least provocation, he hit out ferociously at government, even though he revealed his basic acceptance of Nigeria's colonial connection with Britain by ending his tirades with the words 'God Save The King'.

Macaulay's style of journalism made him many enemies. A newspaper columnist remarked in 1932 that 'The Lagos Daily News had developed a most unenviable taste for the bellicose and, in tune with popular relish for something exciting, something emotional or ludicrous, it has made the habit of attacking people its chief means of living'.[64] Macaulay did not show any reserve in the way he flayed his African critics. Men like Kitoyi Ajasa, Dr Henry Carr, Dr Obasa and Dr Randle who disagreed with him were subjected to scathing criticism which left deep wounds.

Macaulay's opponents were never able to mount effective counter-propaganda and their only weapon was press legislation and prosecution. By the early thirties, however, there must have been a few broad-minded enemies of his who felt that, his weakness notwithstanding, he had done a lot for his country and that the Grand Old Man should be left alone to enjoy his journalistic game even at their expense. Macaulay was a great journalist but the wounds which his pen inflicted cannot be said to have been completely healed even after his death in the forties.

DUSE MOHAMMED ALI AND *The Comet*

Although the post-Clifford era was one of relative tranquillity, the novelty of daily newspapers stimulated further expansion of the newspaper press. On 12 November 1927, H. Antus Williams (lately Akin Fagbenro Beyioku) started the *Nigerian Daily Telegraph* which he sold three years later to a company established by T. Adebayo Doherty, I. A. Ogunlana and Victor Babamuboni with nominal share capital of £5000. The *Telegraph* was a vigorous newspaper but the instability of the editorship (five editors in seven years) had an unwholesome effect on it. In January 1928, I. B. Thomas started the Yoruba-language weekly *Akede Eko* and on 1 June the following year, he added the *Nigerian Evening News* which ran for five months. Two newspapers were started in 1930 – the *Nigerian Daily Mail* by Ernest Ikoli and the *West African Nationhood* by J. C. Zizer, secretary of the Lagos branch of the National Congress. The *Nationhood* began as a daily (October 1930 to December 1931) and subsequently declined into a monthly (November 1932–September 1933). A Sunday edition, the *West African Sunday Digest*, appeared irregularly between 1931 and 1934. In 1931, H. Antus Williams re-emerged with the *Nigerian Daily Mail* which was ostensibly edited by his friend Miss F. Ronke Ajayi. All these newspapers played noteworthy parts in political development but the most important of them all was *The Comet*, founded in 1933 by Duse Mohammed Ali, the Egyptian-born African nationalist.

Duse Mohammed Ali came to settle in Lagos in 1930 ten years after his first visit. By this time, he had acquired considerable experience in the newspaper business as well as in pan-African journalism. He was well-known in many parts of the world either through his many travels or through his widely-circulated newspapers and other publications. Born on 21 November 1866, in Alexandria, Egypt, Duse Mohammed Ali had been sent to Britain as a boy to learn English. He lost his parents at the age of sixteen in the 1882 British bombardment of Alexandria, which set the stage for the British occupation of Egypt. Left in London without support, he had to eke out a meagre existence as actor, playwright and journalist. Provoked by some careless statement on Egypt by the American leader Theodore Roosevelt, Duse Mohammed Ali early in 1911 wrote *In Land of the Pharaohs*, a book which was favourably received in British newspapers and magazines. In July 1912 he founded the *African Times and Orient Review*, which appeared monthly until October 1918. In January 1920 the *African Times and Orient Review* was revived as *The African and Orient Review*, which ran for twelve months. The *Reviews* penetrated into all the continents in the world but they were commercial failures. In an effort to improve his poor financial position, Duse Mohammed Ali left Britain in 1920 and settled in the United States where for ten years he was a produce trader.

When Duse Mohammed Ali arrived to settle in Lagos in 1930, he turned to journalism. His first appearance was as a contributor to the *Daily Times*, at a guinea for each article published. The following year he served as editor of the *Nigerian Daily Telegraph*, founded in 1927. In 1933, he launched *The Comet*.

Duse Mohammed Ali brought to *The Comet* a wide experience in journalism, a sense of detachment and the goodwill of his many readers and admirers throughout the world. In explaining the background to the *Reviews*, a Nigerian newspaper had remarked in

1920 that Duse Mohammed Ali 'burnt like a patriot with zeal to work out the salvation of his kinsfolk' because he was 'impressed with the tremendous disadvantages and disabilities, political and social, under which the peoples of Africa and the Orient are forced to exist by their foreign overlords'.[65] In the 1930s, the picture remained unchanged. *The Comet*, which appeared as a weekly from 21 July 1923 until it was turned into a daily in the forties, was a resurrection of the *Reviews* in its outlook and temper. It attracted a team of brilliant contributors like Obafemi Awolowo, Dennis Osadebay, Fred Anyiam, A. K. Ajisafe and others. It was a brightly written and attractive weekly which sold for only one penny instead of the usual threepence. The features of the paper included a front-page column entitled 'Men and Matters' in which Duse Mohammed Ali discussed mainly international affairs. The object of the column, according to him, was 'to deal with the large issues affecting West Africa rather than the minor issues of Nigerian politics'.

The focus of Duse Mohammed Ali's thinking was international and his reputation as an eminent journalist in Nigeria rested on his abiding interest in and understanding of world affairs. *The Comet*, like its London predecessors, became an influential organ of international politics and a source of inspiration and challenge for the emerging new leaders of Nigeria who had visions of an independent nation which would occupy a proud place in the international community.

'THE CURTAIN RISES'

In November 1937, Nnamdi Azikiwe started the *West African Pilot* which immediately became the major forum of the increased nationalist consciousness which had been awaiting a potent outlet and stimulus. The *Weekly Record* had died in 1930, the *Daily News* had ceased to attract serious attention by 1934 and *The Comet*'s focus was international. By the mid-thirties, therefore, no newspaper existed to crystallise and canalise the growing nationalist influences of the late inter-war years. The *West African Pilot* stepped into the void and with Azikiwe's admission to membership of the Nigerian Youth Movement and his election to the Central Executive Committee of the Movement, a new era of politics and nationalism was born.

Azikiwe, an admirer of Thomas Horatio Jackson, brought into Nigeria a new idealism of nationalism as well as new techniques of political and journalistic propaganda learned during his training and experiences in the United States. His initial platform was the *African Morning Post* which he edited in Accra for two and a half years until he resigned on 1 April 1937, a week after the West African Court of Appeal allowed his appeal against the judgment of the Supreme Court which the previous year had convicted him for sedition. His influence developed in Lagos with the incorporation of the Zik Press Limited on 5 August and the launching of the *Pilot* on 12 November. The opening address entitled 'The Curtain Rises', described the editorship as 'sentinels of popular liberty and guardians of civilisation' whose 'supreme task' was to make assertions in unequivocal terms.

The curtain had risen for a new drama of nationalism in which the *Pilot* would be the star. An introduction was made in 1937 but the real unfolding of the drama belonged to the future.

This survey of the pioneer newspapers and newspapermen demonstrates that although the press was generally a place of refuge for a variety of distressed people, it nevertheless attracted many people of intellectual competence and quality. Indeed, the early press provided the most distinguished intellectual forum in Nigerian history. The high standard of debate and discussion and the quality of thought and expression cannot fail to fascinate the modern reader. This will be appreciated when we examine the role of the newspapers in the development of politics and nationalism. However, what the newspapers accomplished politically bore no relationship to their weak economic situation. They functioned under severe financial limitations most vividly illustrated by the unprepossessing appearance of many of the newspapers. In the next chapter, we shall investigate the economic background of the political press and inquire into the significance of the newspaper trade for the political attitudes of the newspapers.

Notes

1 J. S. Coleman, *Nigeria, Background to Nationalism*, Berkeley and Los Angeles, 1960, p. 72.
2 See letter of 'A Patriot Abroad' to Ijebu people, *Nigerian Advocate*,

23 October 1930; Also, *Nigerian Eastern Mail*, 31 August 1935; *Egba National Harper*, 26 September 1926: 'There is no town or country throughout all the Yoruba speaking land in Nigeria which could boast of an earlier civilization than Egbaland . . . whilst Lagos is able to boast today of about 10 local newspapers and Ibadan at least one, Abeokuta could boast of none . . . It is time we remove the stigma with which we are daily branded as an unfortunate people in an unfortunate clime. . . .'

3 In the nineties Blaize gave the C.M.S. £1 000 for an industrial department at the Lagos Grammar School. When after ten years the money was not used, he withdrew it but left £3 000 in his will to the Egba government for what became the Blaize Memorial Institute at Abeokuta. See J. B. Webster, 'The Bible and the Plough,' *JHSN*, ii, 4, 1963, pp. 418–34. Also J. F. Ade Ajayi, 'The Development of Secondary Grammar School Education in Nigeria,' *JHSN*, ii, 4, 1963, pp. 517–35.

4 John Payne Jackson in *Lagos Weekly Record*, 21 April 1894.

5 Francis Williams, *op. cit.*, p. 184.

6 C.S.O. 1/3/3, Denton to Chamberlain, 24 November 1896. Blaize died on 21 September 1904 reportedly of 'enterocolitis' leaving his six children a fortune of nearly £90 000. (Report of proceedings, Mrs Obasa vs. Oluyemi Blaize, 1934.) *Nigerian Daily Telegraph*, 29 May 1934.

7 *Lagos Times*, 10 November 1880.

8 Dr N. T. King; born on 14 July 1847 in Freetown, Sierra Leone. Came to Abeokuta in the 1860s when his parents were transferred there in the service of the Yoruba mission. Sent to Sierra Leone for further studies in 1866. Went to England in 1871. Back in Lagos in 1876 holding the degrees of M.B., C.M.; M.B.C.S. Died on 12 June 1884. In perpetuation of his name, a memorial in the form of a stained glass window was erected in Christ Church, Lagos.

9 *Eagle*, 25 October 1884.

10 'A Native' to *Lagos Times*, 22 August 1883.

11 A proverb of the Isoko people in Midwest State of Nigeria.

12 See Chapter 3.

13 See Chapter 1.

14 Tribute by Dr Orisadipe Obasa of Ikija (1863–1940). See 'Kekere Ilu' (Adeoye Deniga), *Eko Akete*, 1 August 1925.

15 *Ibid.*

16 *Nigerian Advocate*, 5 August 1925.

17 For a scholarly appraisal, see Hollis R. Lynch, *Edward Wilmot Blyden, Pan-Negro Patriot, 1832–1912*, Oxford University Press, 1967.

18 *Lagos Weekly Times*, 29 November 1890.

19 Hollis Lynch, *op. cit.*, p. 231.

20 See Chapter 5.

21 'Scrutator', (Dr Savage) *Lagos Standard*, 9 July 1919.

22 Samuel Murray Harden in 'Lagosian On Dits', *Lagos Standard*, 6 February 1895.

23 For a more detailed appraisal of Davies, see Fred I. A. Omu, 'James Bright Davies, West African Nationalist and Administrator', *Lagos Notes and Records.*

24 See Chapter 6.

25 C.O. 96/134, Griffith to Kimberley, 11 February 1881; Kimberley to Rowe, 23 March 1881; C.O. 96/145, Griffith to Kimberley, 20 December 1882; C.O. 96/175, Griffith to Stanhope, 29 October 1886.

26 See *Times of Nigeria*, 23 February 1920; *Nigerian Times*, 5 April 1910.

27 African Messenger, 19 May 1921.

28 *LWR*, 21–31 December 1921.

29 *The Times of Nigeria*, 6 October 1919.

30 Chief Obafeui Awolowo, *Awo*, Cambridge, 1960, p. 114.

31 Nnamdi Azikiwe, *My Odyssey*, London, 1970, pp. 67 & 75.

32 See speech by Ajasa at the opening of the pitch of the 'Yoruba Cricket and Recreation Club' of which he was President, at the Race Course on 20 June 1908. *Lagos Standard*, 8 July 1908.

33 *Nigerian Pioneer*, 29 May 1914.

34 See Solade Solomon, 'Some reminiscences and observations', *Nigerian Daily Times*, 17 August 1937.

35 *Nigerian Pioneer*, 12 May 1916, Also 29 May 1914; 31 May 1918.

36 *Pioneer*, 12 May 1916.

37 *Ibid.* For Ajasa's views on standards of journalism, see also *Pioneer*, 31 May 1918; 10 October 1919; 16 February 1923. In 1923 he refused to congratulate the *Eleti Ofe* on its first appearance because he considered that the standard of its articles was low. (*Pioneer*, 16 February 1923.)

38 *LWR*, 31 December 1921.

39 Nigerian Council minutes, 29 December 1920. C.O. 657/11.

40 A commentator remarked that 'the quality, variety and costliness of the wedding presents' showed how popular the couple were. See *LWR*, 23 May 1896.

41 *LWR*, 21–31 December 1921.

42 See *Times of Nigeria*, 2 June 1914.

43 *Pioneer*, 29 May 1914.

44 Allister Macmillan, *Red Book of West Africa*, London, 1920, p. 128.

45 Margery Perham, *Lugard, The Years of Authority, 1898–1945*, London 1960, pp. 598–9.

46 An excellent cricketer, he was a member of the Essex County Cricket Club and Afric's Athletic Club of London. In music, he was author of *Vespers, Hymns and Chants*, London, 1900, published by the Guild of Church Musicians of London of which he was a member. Other publications were 'The match got broken or misunderstood' (a comic song), 'Lula' and 'Advance, Nigeria'.

47 *LWR*, 21 June 1930; 15 August; 29 October; 5 November; 19 November 1904; 25 December 1905.

48 *LWR*, 21 June 1930.

49 *LWR*, 7 June 1919.

50 *Ibid.*

51 *Red Book of West Africa*, p. 109.

52 See *Nigerian Daily Telegraph*, 27 January 1936.
53 *Nigerian Daily Telegraph*, 27 January 1936; Eko Akete, 6 October 1923.
54 Azikiwe, *My Odyssey*, p. 67.
55 23 May 1919. See *LWR*, 28 June 1919.
56 *African Messenger*, 22 September 1921.
57 *Ibid.*
58 At the height of their quarrel, Ikoli accused Macaulay of having attempted to employ the *Messenger* for his 'little personal grudges'. According to him, Macaulay was deliberately planning to involve him in libel actions 'by making sweeping allegations against prominent individuals in Lagos without any foundation.' *African Messenger*, 7 February 1924.
59 Annual Report of the NPPC Limited, 1928.
60 Deniga's works in English include the pamphlets *What is Religion?*, *Necessity for a British West African Conference*; *Defence of Native Customs*; Also the poems *Ode to Lagos*; *Memoirs to the Crowned Heads of Lagos* (a poem); *Aribiloso* (described as the Egba national poet). His publications in Yoruba include the poems *Aiye Loso* (Hasten Slowly); *Odunlami* (an account of the influenza epidemic of 1918); Kilopo (Why Worry?).
61 *Nigerian Daily Telegraph*, 3 October 1935.
62 Nigerian Council, Address by Governor Clifford, 29 December 1920, pp. 224–5.
63 Ernest Ikoli, 'Our Works', Christmas Number, *Daily Times*, 1933. Also *Daily Times* 31 August 1927.
64 'Mee' in *Daily Times*, 28 April 1932.
65 *Times of Nigeria*, 16 July 1920.

3 Evolution and organisation of the newspaper industry

By the beginning of the last quarter of the nineteenth century, the scope of modern African enterprise in Nigeria was to a large extent limited to the training opportunities provided by the Christian missionaries who undertook programmes of industrial workshops. Printing occupied a dominant position and, as we have seen, the Abeokuta printing school produced many skilled printers who were to be associated with the growth of the early newspaper press in Lagos. The rise of the newspaper industry, therefore, was an important development in Nigeria's economic history. It marked the rise of the first indigenous industrial enterprise and thus paved the way for the development of an institution which was to play an important part not only in the growth of newspapers but also in the rise of the Trade Union movement.

Printers dominated the contemporary artisan class and were some of the earliest promoters of Trade Unionism in Nigeria.[1] In this chapter, we shall survey the changes in the pattern of the newspaper industry from an individual or family organ to a corporate institution and also examine the pattern of newspaper trade.

Down to the second decade of the present century, the pattern was small-scale sole proprietorships, the editor as a rule determining the outlook and policy of the newspaper. The greater popularisation of the newspaper and the increasing cost and complexity of production brought about transformations which began with the expansion of the individual organs and culminated in the formation of newspaper companies. The greater popularisation of the newspaper can be attributed to a variety of factors – the political impact of the newspapers particularly during the first two decades of the present century and in the aftermath of the First World War;

the expansion of the newspaper market as a result of the amalgamations of 1906 and 1914; improvements in communications, and the introduction of prize competitions in the competitive warfare generated by Thomas Horatio Jackson. These will be examined in greater detail later. It is sufficient here to draw attention to the increasing drive during this period to establish distribution agencies in all parts of the country. This reflected a positive response to new opportunities which in turn demanded a corresponding enlargement in the newspaper organisation.

Production costs were influenced by the growth and development of the printing industry. We saw in the first chapter the rise of mission and commercial printing presses before 1880. More private printing houses sprouted in the eighties and nineties, among them Andrew Thomas's General Printing office, John Payne Jackson's Samadu Press and the Karaole Press, established in 1898 by C. C. Cole, a leader of the African Church movement. The growth of the printing industry reached a milestone when Akintunde Adeshigbin, a former apprentice-printer with the Samadu Press, founded the Tika Tore Press in 1910. Adeshigbin, popularly known as the Nigerian 'Caslon' (William Caslon was a famous British typographer in the eighteenth century), was so successful that Tika Tore came to exemplify the enterprising genius of pioneer Nigerian entrepeneurs. It became a proud monument to African industry and resourcefulness, and was a great source of inspiration to contemporary and prospective printing proprietors. As a young man in 1901, Adeshigbin became acquainted with printing in the office of the *Weekly Record*, and thereafter worked in the Government Press from 1906 to 1910, when he set up on his own. In 1918, he carried out a thoroughgoing reorganisation of the business, enlarging it and installing new equipment. By the middle twenties, Tika Tore ('Evil has its own reward') had established a position of dominance in the printing industry which was to last into the era of independence.

Thanks to Tika Tore, printing presses of comparable advancement began to proliferate in and outside Lagos. For example, the Awoboh Press was founded by Samuel Herbert Pearse, a prominent Egba merchant, in 1920. Three years later, V. A. E. Babamuboni, a bookseller, set up the Tanimola Press. The same year, I. W. Oshilaja established the Ife-Olu Printing Works, P. J. C. Thomas, the Ekabo Press and Dr Akiwande Savage, the Akibomi Press. By the end of the 1920s, Lagos had become an important printing

centre, and it was significant that in 1933 the government considered it necessary to enact the Printing Presses Regulations
Ordinance. This law required owners of printing presses, on
pain of a £50 fine or six months' imprisonment or both, to swear to
affidavits before magistrates to the effect that they were engaged in
the printing business. And in 1936, printing types which had been
classified among duty-free articles were held taxable on the ground
that they contained lead which was taxable! These measures were
apparently designed to control the rapid growth of printing presses
and protect the Government Press which was in competition with
them from the 1920s. The government's action does not appear to
have had any negative effect on the subsequent development of the
printing industry; if anything, it only served to demonstrate how
serious commercial printing had become. Antiquated and cheap
second-hand equipment gave way to new and more modern
machines which implied greater investment of capital and attracted
serious participation by outside interests in newspaper management.

By the end of the second decade of this century, the pattern of
organisation was basically unchanged, but certain tendencies
which were to become conspicuous later were becoming more
visible and it was possible to distinguish the one-man business of
the nineteenth century from that of the post-war period of the
twenties. The newspaper enterprise was becoming a more substantial business, in some cases having companions or associates
and undergoing important changes in the scale of operations which
in the middle twenties led to a significant transformation of the
structure of the press. Given the problem of increased capital cost
which assumed new proportions with the emergence of daily
newspapers in the late twenties, the need arose for the establishment of limited liability companies to own and manage newspapers.

PATTERN OF NEWSPAPER TRADE

The early newspapers in Nigeria were very weak economically, as
the editors themselves were quick to point out. The *Observer* once
remarked: 'All along this coast, ever since the earliest endeavours
were put forth in the direction of a newspaper, this has been the
one sad experience of many a heart-broken journalist; it does not
pay'. The *Reporter* asserted that journalism was 'by no means a

paying venture', rather it was 'a thankless task, a risk of time and talent to individual disappointment and popularity'.[2] Other West African newspapers had similar experiences. The *Gold Coast Times*, for example, spoke about the 'trials and troubles' of conducting a newspaper and confessed that their hopes had been 'most rudely shattered'.[3] The newspapers were poorly capitalised and proprietors were expected to meet the cost of production and other charges from proceeds from sales and advertisements. But sales were handicapped by a variety of factors and advertising was dominated by a few leading newspapers. In general, therefore, profits were small and consequently left newspaper-owners little margin for reinvestment in expanded markets or in improved equipment.

The relevant statistical data for the newspapers of the period are virtually non-existent. Newspaper publishing was usually only one of several business interests which were operated together. Only a few large newspapers may have kept separate account-books but are unlikely to have survived. Nevertheless, it is hoped that the limited evidence available from the newspapers as well as from other sources will provide a modest basis for some appreciation of the economic organisation of the newspaper industry.

THE RISE AND FALL OF THE NEWSPAPERS

Tables 1 and 2 summarise the fluctuations in the establishment and duration of the newspapers in the period under review. As revealed in Table 1, the initial enthusiasm in starting newspapers did not maintain its momentum, particularly during the first two decades of the present century. The explanation could be found in the adverse realities of the newspaper trade and the restrictive registration law of 1902–3 which provided for the payment of caution money. These factors would seem to have lost their significance in the ferment of political and socio-economic developments which followed the end of the First World War. Of major importance in these developments was the introduction of democratic elections and the revival of cultural nationalism. The increase in the numerical strength of the newspapers in the inter-war period was remarkable; the overall number tripled, rising from 18 in 1920 to 51 in 1937. Weekly newspapers preponderated, although with the advent of daily newspapers, the weeklies were able to survive only outside Lagos.

Table 2 shows that the infant mortality of the newspapers was high: 33 per cent died before they were one year old; 23 per cent died in their third year; 4 per cent in their fifth year and 10 per cent in their seventh year. Thirty per cent of the newspapers (including those which continued outside our period) had a life-span of up to ten years. Their lives, though short, were intensely patriotic, full of energy and action. Only a few disappearances were openly predictable.

TABLE I

Newspapers per decade of establishment

Papers	1880 to 1890	1891 to 1900	1901 to 1910	1911 to 1920	1921 to 1930	1931 to 1937	Total
Daily	–	–	–	–	7	4	11
Weekly	3	5	2	2	13	8	33
Fortnightly	3	–	–	–	–	–	3
Monthly	1	–	1	1	1	–	4
Irregular	–	–	–	–	–	–	–
Total	7	5	3	3	21	12	51

TABLE 2

Variations in the duration of the newspapers

Duration of newspapers	Frequency of publication					
	Daily	Weekly	Fort-nightly	Monthly	Irregular	Total
Under 1 year	6	10	–	–	–	16
Up to 3 years	1	7	2	2	–	12
Up to 5 years	–	11	–	1	–	12
Up to 7 years	–	4	1	–	–	5
10 years and above	4	11	–	–	–	15

RECURRENT EXPENDITURE

A useful background for the discussion of the sources of revenue is the pattern of recurrent expenditure. In every newspaper budget, the most expensive item is usually newsprint. We have no statistics

77

of newsprint purchases in our period but a statement by the *Pilot* in the 1940s provides an interesting insight into the cost of newsprint. The paper claimed that before the Second World War broke out, the price of newsprint fluctuated between £10 and £17 per ton. In wartime, the price varied between £36 5s and £52 10s per ton.[4] A newsprint shortage and the consequent rise in the price of the commodity has very frequently been the cause of the collapse of newspapers.[5] This was to a certain extent demonstrated by the way Nigerian newspapers reacted to the newsprint crisis during the First World War. It was said that paper had risen 500 per cent in price and that that warranted a steep increase in the price of the newspaper. The *Standard*, for example, increased its price by 100 per cent (from threepence to sixpence). The *Pioneer* resorted to using thicker low grade paper and as this led to increased postage, it raised its annual subscriptions outside Lagos by 14 per cent (from 19s to 21s 8d).[6]

The other major item in running costs was salaries and wages. The following salaries were paid by the *Daily Telegraph* in the thirties:[7]

Editor	£150 per annum
Circulation Manager	96 ,, ,,
Manager	200 ,, ,,
	£446

The figures should be higher for the *Daily Times* which paid the editor £300 at least during its first ten years.[8] However, the familiar type of newspaper paid wages only, for the proprietor was also the editor. Some idea of the wages of compositors, printers and proofreaders may be obtained from the following staff disposition of the *Daily News* in 1928:[9]

4 compositors at 80s, 70s, 60s, 60s per month		
1 distributor (compositor)	50s ,,	,,
1 machine man	25s ,,	,,
1 printer	40s ,,	,,
1 proof reader	60s ,,	,,

The staff thus earned £22 5s a month or £267 a year. Some newspapers, particularly those established in the nineteenth century, spent much less. For instance, the *Weekly Times* in 1890 paid out £8 10s a month or £102 a year to the 'printers'.[10] This compared with the £7 which the *Gold Coast Independent* paid its printing staff in January 1895. However, some newspapers in the 1920s and 1930s ran expenditure on salaries and wages which exceeded £400 a year. For example, the *Times of Nigeria* and the *Eastern Mail* each disbursed £540 and £420 respectively.[11]

The gathering of news and distribution of newspapers were items of recurrent expenditure, but they did not represent any considerable proportion of expenditure. Newsgathering underwent very little development during our period of study. A newspaper editor was generally his own reporter. Correspondents were fitfully employed on a part-honorary basis.[12] Newspapers could not afford the necessary expenses. That this was also true of other parts of West Africa can be seen from the lament of the *Gold Coast Independent* in 1927: 'Newspaper proprietors have not the funds to employ paid correspondents scattered throughout the country . . . and it will be a considerable time before they are in that lucky position.'[13] Distribution expenses covered commission to provincial agents and transport charges. Very little is known about rates of commission but in the circulation campaigns of the twenties, agents were offered 5 per cent for weekly sales of ten copies and 12½ per cent for sales above 40. With regard to carriage, the contract rate of £15 4s 8d (£182 16s annually) which the *Pilot* paid the Nigerian Railway from 1937 to the early 1940s,[14] possibly illustrates the highest level in our period. Road transport by lorry was the alternative but because the charges were relatively high, it was less patronised. The development of newspaper delivery fleets of transport lorries was very much in the future.[15] Distribution by post was quite common, but expenses incurred on stamps could not have been light.

Other financial requirements in newspaper production include rents and rates. Rents did not become a problem where the editor worked in his own premises as many of them did. For those who rented premises, charges varied from place to place and from time to time. Herbert Macaulay, in the late twenties and early thirties, paid £6 monthly for three offices.[16] Rates apparently fluctuated greatly also. No data exist to illustrate their nature.

Payment of fines imposed by the courts was an important though irregular item of expenditure. Hardly any newspaper in our period was not involved in lawsuits and some of the fines were relatively heavy. For instance, in 1900, the *Wasp* was mulcted of £100 in a libel action.[17] In 1914, the *Standard* was ordered to pay £350 for libelling C. A. Sapara Williams. Six years later, the sum of

£131 10s was awarded against the *Chronicle* in a libel action instituted by a European official.[19] Other remarkable cases included the amount of £250 for damages paid in 1921 by *Times of Nigeria*, and £150 for contempt of court paid by the *Daily Telegraph* in 1931.[20] These examples and many others in the range of £30 to £50 fine, demonstrate the extent of the financial handicaps to which newspapermen were exposed. It is true that some fines or damages were paid through public contributions but it is common knowledge that more libel claims are settled out of court than are actually determined in court.[21]

SOURCES OF REVENUE

In addition to sales and advertisements, there were two other comparatively insignificant ways by which newspapers were financed. One was through donations. Sometimes money was sent to the newspapers anonymously or editors took the initiative and openly campaigned for what was known as Sustentation Fund. Anonymous donations appear to have commenced in 1882 when the *Lagos Times* announced that some 'anonymous people' had donated money to the establishment.[22] In 1895, the *Record* received the sum of £10 from an unidentified person.[23] In 1910, the *Nigerian Times* got a total of £11 10s 6d from four anonymous individuals.[24] The lucky recipients of these gifts gave much publicity to the patriotic gesture and often appealed to readers to emulate the example. These open solicitations for donations were given new colour by Adeoye Deniga of the *Eko Akete* whose practice of calling public meetings in which he launched Sustentation Funds was copied by a number of newspapers, among them the *Ijebu Weekly News*.

The other source of revenue outside sales and advertising was job-printing. No precise information exists to throw light on the scale on which this supplemental service was carried out. However, it could be guessed that jobbing brought a sizable revenue to the newspapers. The contracts which newspaper establishments accepted from many places along the West Coast[25] and the efforts in the twenties and thirties to popularise the printing works of the various newspapers testify to the importance with which newspapers held commercial printing. It is significant that in their Report for the year 1928–29, the Nigerian Printing and Publishing

Company announced that the job–printing department was 'a very valuable asset to the Company'.[26]

Before we go on to analyse newspaper circulation and advertisement, certain points must be noted. The problem of delinquent subscribers and advertisers was one with which newspapermen constantly battled in vain. For instance in 1887, the *Observer* castigated subscribers who were unwilling to clear their debts which were from one to four years old.[27] In 1895, the *Record* lamented that out of a total subscription of £13 due from Abeokuta, the agent was only able to collect ten shillings.[28] In 1910, the *Standard* spoke of 'the callousness of defaulting subscribers whom prayers and threats of exposure' had failed to move.[29] Striking similarities existed at this time in other parts of West Africa. The *Eastern Echo* (Freetown) declared in 1885 that it was not prepared to receive any subscriptions. Readers were requested to purchase their papers from newsvendors or agents, 'Past experience in journalism', the newspaper explained, 'justify and warrant a resolution of this nature.'[30] The *Gold Coast Independent* was caustic; it commented in 1928 that the reading public in West Africa was 'mostly a curious blend of thoughtful and unintelligent people and an incongruous mass of irresponsible individuals. Irresponsible because while fully aware of the influence of the Press... most of them are yet reluctant to pay for what they get. ...'[31]

No doubt because the newspapers depended upon advertisers for their survival, delinquent advertisers were not as openly and bitterly scolded as were delinquent subscribers. At worst, the newspapers announced they would demand that advertising contracts be paid in advance.[32]

Circulation

Up to the middle of 1919, no newspaper could have realised as much as £500 from sales.[33] The greatest circulation during the period was 700 a week attained by both the *Record* and the *Standard* in the first half of the second decade of the present century.[34] At the beginning, sales amounted to the merest handful, about 200 copies being sold every fortnight. At 3d a copy, this fetched £65 a year. In the 1890s, circulation fluctuated between 300 and 500 a week. The corresponding proceeds thus varied from £195 to £325 a year. With a circulation of 700 a week, the receipts from sales stood at £455 a year. Three factors explain the limited circulations. In the first place, communications were backward. Until the beginning of the present century, travelling between Lagos and the outlying areas was primarily on foot. The roads, no better than forest paths, were in addition rendered unsafe as a result of the intermittent Yoruba succession wars. The completion of a railroad which linked Lagos and Ibadan in 1900 and Lagos and Kano in 1911, indicated improved communications but the possible effect of this development was counteracted by other considerations.

In his *Report on the Amalgamation of Northern and Southern Nigeria, 1912–1919*,[35] Lord Lugard pointed out that in Southern Nigeria in 1913, only one in every 180 children of school age 'had any sort of education whatever'. This meant that more than 99 per cent of the children were receiving no instruction at all. This illustrates the degree of illiteracy of the population at the time.

The third consideration was the indifference to newspaper reading. The apathy of the educated classes towards the reading of newspapers was a phenomenon to which newspaper proprietors alluded from time to time. As early as 1864, the *Iwe Irchin* commented: 'we are afraid but very few Africans here make a practice of reading to acquire knowledge . . . we do not think the cause is the want of time or money, but rather the want of interest'.[36] In the following year the paper observed, 'they (the educated Africans) don't like to spend money to buy newspapers, and if newspapers are lent them it is too much trouble to read them . . .'[37] The apathy towards foreign-owned news-sheets was carried over to the eighties and after when the indigenous press was being developed. In 1887, a columnist of the *Observer* complained that the literate community of Lagos did not understand 'the philosophy of newspapers'. If newspaper readership was a yardstick for determining 'the average intelligence of people with pretensions to civilisation', he observed, Lagos 'would fall grievously below the mark', for whereas in Europe the poorest beggar would be happy to spend his penny in order to be informed on current events, 'in Lagos and other portions of the (West African) coast, many men in affluent circumstances, be it said to their everlasting shame, would be most unwilling to subscribe to local periodicals'.[38] In 1915, the *Times of Nigeria*, disputing the then popular claim that Lagos had no reading public, pointed out that there was a good number of educated persons which could comprise "a fairly reading public" if only they became subscribers . . .'[39]

How do we explain the attitude of the non-newspaper-patron-ising educated Africans? Two reasons could be given. Firstly, the community of Lagos, which had the bulk of circulation, was relatively small and local news got as quickly circulated by word of mouth as through the medium of a newspaper. Secondly, some of the newspapers not only were dull in appearance but also involved themselves in personal feuds to the annoyance of responsible people. A further consideration was related to the social structure. The communal system of life and the sense of mutual inter-dependence characteristic of African people made the practice of newspaper borrowing inevitable. According to the *Nigerian Times* in 1915, a single copy was borrowed 'in succession' by 'three or four or more'.[40] Estimates of how many African people on the average read a single newspaper copy have varied from three to more than ten.

Between 1919 and 1937, the new tone of nationalist thought and activity coupled with exciting political events created a widespread eagerness for information and kindled enthusiasm for the reading of newspapers.

As the wave of popular agitation unleashed by the Eleko question swelled into intense electoral rivalries in the wake of the introduction of the Clifford Constitution, politics increasingly became the idiom in which the people spoke and it was small wonder that the twenties and thirties witnessed a proliferation of new newspapers.

Parallel to these developments were the rise in literacy and further improvements in communications. The table below illustrates the growth in literacy.[41]

	School		Pupils in attendance	
	Primary	*Secondary*	*Primary*	*Secondary*
1912	150	10	35 716	67
1926	3 828	18	138 249	518
1937	3 533	26	218 610	4 285

The improvements in communications can be seen in the fact that by 1926, 6 000 miles of roads had been constructed. And by 1936, a railway network of 2 178 miles covered the country.[42]

The expansion in circulation was also helped by the fact that newspapers were getting cheaper. Before and after the arrival of daily newspapers, readers paid an average of threepence for a weekly newspaper. From 1925 when daily newspapers were started, one penny fetched a newspaper. The arithmetic of this would make the point look absurd for a regular buyer of a daily newspaper paid sixpence a week. (The only Sunday newspaper in our period appeared irregularly between 1931 and 1943.) But human habits do not always lend themselves to such cold rationalisation. It appears less burdensome to spend one penny four times than threepence once.

A consideration that cannot be over-emphasised was the promotional expedients employed by the editors, foremost among them the prize competitions. The weapon of prize competitions to increase circulation was first used and subsequently popularised by the *Record*. In 1915, the paper announced a short-story contest which was limited to subscribers to the *Record* or to those who had purchased at least any four copies of the paper within a stated period. Probably because the 'innovation' did not yield results as expected, prize competitions were not exploited again until 1919. In that year, Thomas Jackson launched an ambitious Great Sales Campaign which featured prize competitions and precipitated an exciting circulation war.

Thomas Jackson's aim was to reach a circulation of 10 000, that is, about 15 times its original figure. To this end, he established the Weekly Record Scholarships as rewards to hardworking newsvendors and advertised a variety of bribes for ardent subscribers. Included in the offers were fountain pens, watches, bicycles, etcetera.[43] Six months after the launching of the campaign, the *Record*'s circulation rose by 150 per cent. Obviously pleased with the results, Thomas Jackson conducted similar campaigns in 1920, 1921, 1922 and 1923.

These promotional successes stimulated other newspapermen to similar action. For example, the *Messenger* in 1921 announced a prize of £4 4s for the most successful sales agent.[44] The *Eko Akete* organised competitions in Yoruba language from 1922. At Calabar in the twenties, the *Dawn* ran a form of lottery.[45]

Publicity tours were also embarked upon for the purpose of increasing circulations. The editors toured various parts of the country establishing agents and generally making themselves known to as many people as possible. In 1922, Ernest Ikoli travelled extensively in the then Eastern Nigeria 'in the interest' of the *Messenger*.[46] I. B. Thomas toured the same area in 1929 and when he returned, his paper, the *Akede Eko*, observed that the tour had 'helped a great deal to increase . . . circulation' and that several agencies had been established.[47] Representing the enthusiasm with which editors sought to boost sales was Antus Williams's 'touring trip' to the Gold Coast (now Ghana). At Accra in 1934, Williams addressed secondary schools and sought to popularise his *Daily Herald*.[48]

The table below reveals the readership expansion between 1913 and 1923:

TABLE 3
Growth in circulation[49]

Year	Total weekly circulation	Estimated revenue per annum (in pounds)
1913	2 000	1 300
1918	2 100	1 820
1919	3 700	4 810
1920	3 000	3 900
1921	4 200	5 460
1922	4 700	6 110
1923	7 800	10 410

During the years under review, the *Record* increased its circulation from 600 in 1918 to 1 500 at the end of 1919. The figure rose to 2 000 in 1923. In terms of income, the rise was from about £390 a year to about £1 950 and £2 700. The *Messenger*, the second leading newspaper at the time, sold an average of 1 200 copies a week, the estimated revenue being about £1 560 annually. Indeed, the only newspaper that did not benefit from the sales expansion was the *Pioneer* which sold under 500 copies in the twenties as it had done in the pre-war years.[50]

The year 1923 represented the zenith of the growth of weekly newspapers. The next four to five years saw a fairly widespread stagnation in sales and from about 1927, a decline set in. The records do not provide any guide for the nature of the decline[51] but it seems to have begun in 1926 following the enthusiastic public response to the establishment of the first serious daily newspaper. As the daily press grew, the decline gathered momentum and by 1929 had become evident even to the least observant.[52] It is significant that of the six weekly newspapers that witnessed the birth of the daily press, only one continued to 1931.[53]

There were nine daily newspapers between 1926 and 1936.

Only a third of these were steady journalistic ventures. Of these, the *Daily News* and the *Telegraph* could be considered together, for their circulations illustrated what was considered fairly remunerative at the time. The *Daily News* sold from 1 000 to 2 000 copies between 1927 and 1933, after which period it became very irregular and ceased to answer to the name of a daily newspaper. Its figure of 2 000 at 1d per copy was worth about £2 400 per annum. The circulation of 1 000 credited to the *Telegraph* for the period 1927–29 is unlikely to be reliable because the newspaper was then only a shoddy sheet in a dreary season. It was after it was reorganised in 1930 that it became popular. From that year to 1937, the newspaper sold about 3 000 copies every day, realising about £3 800 per annum.

Whereas the *Daily News* and the *Daily Telegraph* averaged from 2 000 to 3 000 in circulation, the *Daily Times* reached a peak of 6 000. The records of this paper have been found to be reasonably accurate and show that between 1926 and 1930, the paper doubled its sales, rising from 1 500 to 3 000. The subsequent performance of the paper is indicated in the table below.

TABLE 4
The growth of the Daily Times, *1930–7*

Year	Sales	Estimated income per day	Estimated annual income
1930	3 000	£12 10s	£3 800
1931	4 000	£16	£4 800
1932	4 500	£19	£5 700
1933	4 500	£19	£5 700
1934	5 200	£22	£6 600
1935	5 700	£24	£7 200
1936	5 700	£24	£7 200
1937	5 900	£24 10s	£7 300

How do we account for the popularity of the paper, particularly as it was not only pro-government in its policy but decidedly hostile to Herbert Macaulay, the idol of the general public? A preliminary point must be made here: the *Daily Times* was never pro-government to the extent of being the mouthpiece of the government nor did it compete with the *Daily News* in hurling volleys of abuse at political opponents. Circumspect in its tone. it was capable of appealing to many shades of political opinion.

Because the paper was highly capitalised, it was able to expand its distribution organisation. In 1929, for instance, the paper had about thirty distributing centres covering all parts of the country.[54] But the most important explanation was that it introduced new techniques of journalism which appealed to the rising literate classes. Departing from the tradition of nineteenth-century British and Nigerian newspapers which gave the front page over to advertisements, the *Daily Times* withdrew advertisements to the inside pages, thus putting an entirely new face on the newspaper. Another important contribution of the *Daily Times* to the advancement of newspaper techniques was its popularisation of headlines. In place of the traditional simple label which roughly indicated the nature of the news which the paragraph below it contained, the newspaper introduced the single-column three-tier or three-decker headline in bold type. In addition, there were significant improvements in typography brought about by the acquisition of a more modern printing press (the cylinder flat-bed) which was mechanically operated.

The changes pioneered by the newspaper marked a turning point in the technical development of the Nigerian newspaper. They gave rise to a new outlook upon techniques among newspapermen who became eager to lighten the pages of their newspapers as much as possible. Henceforth, the trend was towards the introduction of fresh journalistic devices, a development which entered a new phase when the *Pilot* emerged in 1937 with its formula of banner or multi-column headlines, robust features, display of photographs and sensationalism.

The circulation supremacy of the *Daily Times* was terminated in 1937 by the *Pilot* which had an instant public success with a circulation of 9 000, an increase of over 3 000 over the former. Thus while the *Daily Times* derived about £25 a day from sales, the *Pilot* got about £37 10s. The desire of the *Daily Times* to resume its dominance, and the determination of the *Pilot* to hold on to its lead, explain the bitter circulation feud which characterised the two newspapers in the late thirties and forties.[55]

ADVERTISING

The recognition of the importance of commercial advertising was one of the chief phenomena of the development of the early

Nigerian press. This was exemplified in the amount of space which the newspapers generally devoted to advertisements. At the start, this fluctuated between fifty and seventy-five per cent of the printed area of the newspaper. In the 1920s, some newspapers averaged between ninety and ninety-nine per cent. There were two principal sources of advertisement revenue: government publicity and commerce. For our purpose, we will break down the latter source of revenue into indigenous advertisements and advertising by European traders.

A study of the movements of all these advertisements reveal patterns or a conflict of patterns which show the nationalist flavour in indigenous advertising and also illustrate the dilemma inherent in a situation whereby the medium of advertising was employed against the best interest of those who patronised it most. The commerce and industry of Nigeria were controlled, as they are today, by European business interests and these inevitably dominated advertising in the Nigerian newspapers. The dictates of economy led them to patronise the leading anti-government newspapers which had relatively large circulations. At the same time, however, the European traders disliked certain features of the anti-government newspapers, for the newspapers not only displayed hostility to European domination in general but were also highly critical of the policies of the colonial administrations to whose good will the merchants owed their economic survival. If the expatriate firms supported the anti-government newspaper, they indirectly financed their chief critics, but to back the less popular pro-government newspapers made nonsense of the principle of 'commercial effectiveness' in newspaper advertising.

The examination of government advertising must begin from 1862. That year Governor Freeman suggested to the Colonial Office that there should be allowed in Lagos a single newspaper, in which would be inserted government notices and which would thus be a pro-government paper. The proposal was turned down,[56] but it is significant that when the *Anglo-African* was established the following year, it was reasonably supported by government advertisements which might explain the newspaper's pro-government leaning. Other newspapers which enjoyed government advertisement support were the *Eagle and Lagos Critic* and the *Record*. In the last chapter, we suggested the inspiration behind the pro-government *Critic* and examined the circumstances of the subsidy arrangement with the *Record* in 1892 as well as of its termination nine years later. For the *Record*, the evidence indicated that the subsidy as such did not have any implications for the newspaper's nationalism. Its collaboration with the administration of Governor Carter had its basis in the friendly relationship which the subsidy probably contributed to strengthen. The *Record*'s dissociation, in spite of the subsidy from the government after Carter's departure, indicated that the subsidy did not affect the newspaper's policy.

After Governor MacGregor cut off the *Record*'s subsidy in 1900, government patronage of newspapers ceased for the next quarter of a century. Not even the *Pioneer* had such favour. It is not clear why government advertisements were absent from the *Pioneer*, but it might be that Lugard only favoured support by foreign firms as his private correspondence would seem to indicate.[57] Government advertisements returned to the newspapers in 1926 when the *Daily Times* was founded. Between 1926 and 1931, a few Post Office notices appeared in that newspaper alone but in the latter year, Governor Cameron decided to distribute official notices among the leading daily newspapers. Ernest Ikoli was to charge later that the Governor proceeded on the 'crafty and unscrupulous' principle that 'everyone had his price' and that to this end, he had corrupted the press and rendered it 'dumb'. Certainly, the *Daily Telegraph* which Ernest Ikoli then edited and which also benefited from Cameron's generosity, did not appear to be dumb. Whether the accusation has substance is not clear from the available records but it is possible that Cameron's action was merely designed to cloak his support for his friend Herbert Macaulay. Cameron and Macaulay were good friends and the wretched finances of the *Daily News* may have attracted the sympathy of the Governor. The friendship, like that of Carter and Jackson, possibly had its political implications. The *Daily News*, like the *Record*, avoided critical references to the government and tended to concentrate upon local political differences and power struggles.

Advertising by indigenous traders and businessmen was relatively unimportant in our period. This can be explained by the small number of big African trading organisations and partly by the limited finances of African merchants. A practical evidence of the latter consideration was the fact that local advertisements were invariably short both in size and in the number of times they appeared. It would seem that up to the end of the First World War hardly any paper derived as much as £100 per annum from local advertisements. The estimated annual figures provided below illustrate the small volume of advertising carried.[58] They have been obtained by counting up the advertisements in the leading newspapers of the period.[59]

	Record	*Standard*
1895	£90	£80
1900	£40	£82
1905	£15	£60
1910	£35	£80
1915	£25	£90
1918	£25	£60

It is possible to see that African advertisers patronised one paper more than the other. In 1895, the *Record*, which was already five years old, had about the same patronage as the *Standard* founded in late 1894. Over the years, however, the former gradually lost most of its local advertisements to the latter which, in addition, attracted new patrons. Among the losses of the *Record* in 1895, for example, were J. P. Haastrup and A. W. Thomas, both auctioneers. E. A. Alder advertised with the paper between 1891 and 1893. In 1894, it switched over to the *Standard*. It is noteworthy that almost all the indigenous dealers in quack medicines advertised with the *Standard*. Chief among these were E. A. Caulcrick's Family Dispensary and C. V. O. Taylor's Oba Dispensary, Cole Brothers, W. N. Mason and Alex M. Williams. In fact, the patent medicines dominated indigenous advertising in the *Standard* between 1894 and 1919. They must have contributed about fifty per cent of the income the paper derived from local advertisements.

How do we explain the popularity of the *Standard* among African advertisers? The *Record*'s pro-government policy seems to have been the primary factor. When the paper was the only weekly in existence between 1891 and 1894, African advertisers apparently had no choice but with the emergence of the then more radical *Standard* in the latter year, it became fashionable for Africans to advertise with the paper. The result was that a tradition was established which portrayed the *Record* as an inappropriate medium for indigenous advertising.

The years between 1919 and 1937 witnessed increased activity in indigenous advertising. This development was of a piece with the bustling activity in advertising generally which characterised the inter-war years and which will be explained presently. However, the rise in indigenous advertising was not reflected in the pages of all the papers. For instance, the *Pioneer*, for reasons that should by now be obvious, must have derived less than £30 per annum from local advertisements.[60] Several other papers in the twenties and thirties were also indifferently supported because the advertisers had no confidence in their ability to thrive. Strictly speaking, only the *Record* and the *Messenger* enjoyed some notable support, the one publishing an average of 17 local advertisements a week between 1919 and 1930, and the other an average of 22 a week between 1921 and 1926.[61] The estimated revenue in each case was £170 and £400 per annum. The last figure was the highest attained by any weekly paper in our period and it is remarkable that it was the *Messenger* and not the older and more popular *Record* that was most substantially supported by African advertisers. This could reasonably be explained in terms of the old prejudice against the *Record*.

Conscious of the slow development of indigenous advertising, the Nigerian press tried various methods to kindle enthusiasm in the practice. They appealed to national sentiment, haranguing the people to demonstrate their support for African enterprises.[62] Much more successfully, they made indigenous advertising less burdensome by introducing cheap 'Wanted' advertisements in the form of classified advertising. Begun in 1919 by the *Record*, classified advertisements became a common feature of the news-paper trade, in the hands of various newspapermen giving rise to such adaptations as were calculated to enhance the ends for which they were introduced. [63] The *Daily Telegraph*'s Directory Scheme,[4] for example, probably yielded from about £30 to about £40 per month at the rate of one shilling per line per insertion.[65] This meant that certain categories of newspapers in our period were capable of getting upwards of £500 per annum from indigenous advertising.[66]

From the birth of the Nigerian press to the end of the First World War European advertisers can be said to have advertised in newspapers on the basis of their circulation. In the 1880s, the *Lagos Times* and *Observer*, the leading papers, were evenly patronised. In the 1890s and after, the *Record* and the *Standard* received the same treatment. The following table gives some idea of the revenue derived by each of the papers from expatriate merchant firms.[67]

	Record	*Standard*
1895	£260	£202
1900	£340	£235
1905	£290	£310
1910	£300	£360
1915	£350	£360
1918	£350	£350

Although the practice was for advertisers to advertise with a single paper at a time, a reasonable number of firms distributed their patronage among two or three newspapers. In this category were the Bank of British West Africa (B.B.W.A.), John Walkden and Company of Manchester and Elder Dempster and Company. These firms between them accounted for about thirty per cent of the European advertising in the two newspapers.

At this time, the *Pioneer* was occupying a distinct place in the scheme of things. In part because the European community was naturally inclined to support a newspaper founded to counter the increasingly militant nationalist press and in part because the proprietor of the paper was on intimate terms with a large number of Europeans, the establishment of the *Pioneer* occasioned an abundance of foreign advertisements unprecedented in the history of the Nigerian press. While in 1914 the *Record* with a circulation of 700 realised about £350 from European advertisements, the *Pioneer* with a circulation of 500 probably got between £900 and £950.

The *Pioneer*'s large patronage did not overwhelm the support which its leading contemporaries had hitherto enjoyed. Its significance was not in the withdrawal of advertisements from existing newspapers; rather, it was in the enthusiastic response of fresh advertisers. Notable among these were Paterson, Zochonis and Company (Manchester), Pickering and Berthoud Limited (Manchester), G. Gottschalk and Company (Manchester), Grace Brothers and Company (London), Rylands and Sons Limited, Edwards Brothers Limited (Liverpool), and Miller Brothers (Liverpool).

From about September 1919, European advertising witnessed a phenomenal rise. The extent of this rise may be appreciated simply by comparing the average number of European advertisements per issue by two leading papers in mid-June and at the end of the year:

	June 1919	*Dec. 1919*
Record	22	42
Pioneer	29	56

In terms of estimated revenue, the *Record*'s amounted to about £900 and the Pioneer's to about £1 300.[68] These figures fairly illustrate the volume of advertising by European firms carried out by the two newspapers during the greater part of the twenties.

What circumstances contributed to the signal growth in European advertising in the post-war years? In the first place, increased advertising was a logical response to the post-war economic situation in Nigeria. The end of the First World War was followed by an increase in import trade and the European commercial houses strove to reach as wide a market as possible. In the second place, it reflected the keen rivalry between the European trading organisations. This rivalry, which dated back to the 1870s, had been halted by the outbreak of war. The termination of war sharpened the old competition and consequently stimulated greater activity in advertising. In the third place, the newspapers exerted all effort to build up large advertisement patronages. As was pointed out earlier, the post-war period was marked by a promotional warfare and not only did newspapers seek to increase circulations; advertisements were also an enormous cake out of which it was the chief purpose of each newspaper to appropriate the largest possible slice.

Although the boom in European advertisements continued up to the end of our period, the weekly newspapers ceased from about 1930 to derive substantial amounts from that source.[69] The drop in patronage could be attributed to a number of factors, the most notable of which was the consolidation of the daily press.

During the first two years of the emergence of daily newspapers, foreign advertisements did not yield much revenue as far as these newspapers were concerned. The fact that daily newspapers did not quote advertisement rates coupled with the fact that their advertising was for the most part arranged by third parties,[70] makes it impossible to estimate their advertisement revenue. However, there can be no dispute that the newspapers were poorly patronised. The *Daily News* and the *Telegraph* each published between two and three small European advertisements a day. The *Daily Times*, supported by only a handful of firms which included G. Gottschalk and Company (a shareholder), Q. B. Coates and

Company, Bartholomew and Company and the Niger Company Limited, was a disappointment to its owners.[71]

The poor advertisement revenue of the *Daily Times* in its first two years creates a puzzle, for the newspaper had everything to qualify it for the type of support that greeted the establishment of the *Pioneer* twelve years before. What then was responsible for the reluctance of European firms to advertise with the newspaper? Three reasons could be given. One was that the management of the newspaper did not canvass for advertisements, having unwarrantedly assumed that the newspaper itself was sufficient attraction for advertising clients.[72] Another reason was that the European merchants were variously committed to the long-established weekly newspapers and therefore needed some time to terminate their advertising contracts. It would seem also that the expatriate traders were at first doubtful of the wisdom of supporting the enterprise established by a combination of their commercial rivals. But with sustained canvassing for advertisements and the increasing interest which advertisers in England were beginning to take in the newspaper,[73] European firms began from 1928 to pour their advertisements into the *Daily Times*. From that year to the end of our period, the *Daily Times* virtually monopolised foreign advertisements, inevitably deriving huge profits.

The *Times* had a serious rival in the *Telegraph* which, after it was reorganised in 1930, engaged in fierce competition with it. In 1931, for example, the *Telegraph* averaged 11 inches of European advertisements a day while the *Times* averaged 17 inches. In the years that followed, the ratio varied from 2:3 to 1:5 but it is important to note that while the United Africa Company alone accounted for about 20 per cent of the total advertising space of the *Telegraph*, it hardly ever advertised with the *Daily Times*. There is no ready explanation for this, but it might be that the UAC wanted to demonstrate its interest in the development of African enterprise in such a way as not to expose itself to the charge of collusion with nationalist agitators. This might help to explain the company's choice of the *Telegraph* in preference to the fiery *Daily News*.

Viewed as a story of small initial financial outlay, sales competitions and increases, and radical changes in the tempo of advertising, the trade of the Nigerian newspapers before the Second World War would seem to present a picture of general prosperity.

Such a picture, however, would be misleading because we have little knowledge of actual revenues and expenditures and, more importantly, only a few newspapers could have been profitable ventures judging by the length of their lives as well as the quality of their technical standards. The majority of the newspapers only managed to eke out a brief existence and their appearances were unprepossessing. These limitations may have disappointed the financial hopes of many a newspaperman but they did not affect their political aims and aspirations. Conscious of their influence as the major source of public opinion and political pressure, the newspapers exerted themselves in the public interest, making sacrifices which were to earn them the acclaim of future generations.

Notes

1 The journalist and printer, J. A. Olushola, was the first known Trade Union leader in Nigeria. In 1922, he founded the Nigeria Labour Corporation and two years later, established a monthly publication, the *Labour Bulletin* as its organ. Both Corporation and newspaper wound up that year. In February 1930, Olushola, an energetic and venturesome man from Iperu in Yorubaland, and W. H. Biney, a prominent businessman of Gold Coast origin, launched a Labour Bureau and revived the *Labour Bulletin* as a daily (it lasted for fourteen weeks).
2 *Lagos Observer*, 5 February 1887; *Lagos Reporter*, 12 July 1898.
3 29 February 1884.
4 *West African Pilot*, 29 October 1942. Cf. London market price of newsprint per ton, 1929–38:

Year	£	s	Year	£	s
1929	13	15	1934	9	15
1930	14	0	1935	10	0
1931	13	15	1936	10	0
1932	12	10	1937	10	0
1933	10	10	1938	11	10

See *Report on the British Press, op. cit.,* pp. 182–9.

5 See Emery, *op. cit.,* p. 521; *Report on the British Press, op. cit.,* p. 44.
6 *Nigerian Pioneer*, 17 May 1918, 6 September 1918. Also *In Leisure Hours*, March 1918.
7 *Nigerian Daily Herald*, 29 April 1931.
8 Annual Report of the Nigerian Printing and Publishing Co. Ltd, 1927/28. *Nigerian Daily Times*, 15 April 1929. Also Report for 1928–29 in issue of 24 February 1930.
9 Macaulay Papers.

10 See *Lagos Weekly Times*, 20 December 1890.
11 Animashaun papers; Interview with J. V. Clinton, formerly editor, *Eastern Mail*. Now writer and journalist, 10 Bello Street, Ladipo Estate, Shogunle, near Ikeja.
12 It was something of an honour for people outside Lagos to be recognised as correspondents of Lagos newspapers. It carried a social status which was seen as sufficient compensation.
13 See *Nigerian Spectator*, 22 & 29 January 1927.
14 See *West African Pilot*, 31 October 1942.
15 The first fleet of lorries to be run by a newspaper was first launched in 1949 by the *Daily Times*. In 1958–59, the newspaper put its cost of distribution at £57 444. See I. Coker, 'The Nigerian Press, 1929–1959', *Report on The Press in West Africa*, *op. cit.*, pp. 73–133.
16 *Moses da Rocha v Macaulay* (1932), Macaulay papers.
17 *S. P. Jackson v Wasp* (1900). The newspaper folded up soon after this case was tried in April.
18 *C. A. S. Williams v G. A. Williams and J. B. Benjamin* (1913). This was the famous Watchman Libel Case precipitated by a series of polemical articles written by J. B. Benjamin under the *nom de plume* of 'Watchman'. The articles insinuated that Sapara Williams was involved in the mysterious death of Otonba Payne (1839–1906), Chief Registrar of the Lagos Supreme Court from 1867 to 1899. See *Nigerian Chronicle*, 26 January 1914.
19 *H. S. Hewitt v Chris Johnson* (1910). See Chapter 6, note 109.
20 See African Messenger, 28 April 1921. *Nigerian Daily Times*, 30 June 1931.
21 For a remark on the British situation, see Steed, *op. cit.*, p. 179.
22 See *Lagos Times*, 25 January 1882.
23 See 30 November 1895. Also 10 June 1893.
24 The cash gifts were 2 of £5, one of £1 and one of 10s 6d. See *Chronicle*, 20 December 1910.
25 See example, *Lagos Weekly Record*, 21 February 1920.
26 See *Nigerian Daily Times*, 24 February 1930.
27 5 February 1887.
28 27 July 1895.
29 14 September 1910. For other instances of reactions to delinquent subscriptions, see *Iwe Irchin Eko*, 2 November 1889; Sunday Digest, September 1931.
30 *Western Echo*, 18 November 1885.
31 See *Nigerian Spectator*, 26 May 1928.
32 See, for example, *Lagos Weekly Record*, 22 January 1921.
33 Although special subscription rates were paid by regular readers and commissions were paid to agents, estimates of sales revenue will, for obvious reasons, be based on the stated cost prices.
34 Our main source of circulation figures is the Government *Blue Books*. With the exception of the era of Lord Lugard, the *Blue Books* in our period carried statistics of circulation. We do not know how the figures were obtained, whether they were based on actual returns or whether they were estimates. However they were obtained, they are not en-

tirely reliable because evidence from a variety of sources indicates that some of the figures are grossly exaggerated. Nonetheless, we shall employ the figures, calling attention to exaggerations wherever possible.

35 F. D. Lugard, *Report on the Amalgamation of Northern and Southern Nigeria, and Administration, 1912–1919*, London 1920, p. 59.

36 5 August 1864 (appendix).

37 22 June 1865 (appendix).

38 2 and 16 April 1887.

39 1 and 15 June 1915.

40 15 June 1915. See *Lagos Times*, 22 August 1883. Also *Lagos Weekly Record*, 7 June 1919: 'Whenever three or four literate men are gathered together in Nigeria, the *Weekly Record* shall be in their midst, not by borrowing one man's copy but by each and every one of them providing himself with his own copy.'

41 Coleman, *op. cit.*, p. 134.

42 *Ibid.*, pp. 55–6; Tamuno, Ph.D. thesis, *op. cit.*, p. 365.

43 The Scholarship Scheme provided that any boy or girl engaged in selling the *Weekly Record* was entitled to the following benefits:

   (a) Free tuition in any Primary School for one year – 10 copies weekly or 400–500 copies per annum.
   (b) Free tuition in any secondary school for one year – 25 copies weekly or 1000–1500 per annum.
   (c) Free tuition in King's College for one year – 50 copies weekly or 2000–2500 per annum.

   Agents were entitled to commissions ranging from 5 per cent for weekly sales of 10 copies to 12 per cent for sales above 40.

44 The first agent to raise his sales to 100 a week.

45 The paper numbered its title pages and from time to time called for copies bearing certain numbers. Holders of these numbers each won one guinea.

46 *African Messenger*, 25 May 1922.

47 2 May 1929. Also *Daily News*, 24 April 1929.

48 *Daily News*, 13 June 1934.

49 The statistics on the estimated annual revenue are calculated on the basis of the following newspaper prices: In 1913, 3d; 1918, 4d; 1919–1923, 6d. The notable exception to this price structure was the *Times of Nigeria*. It sold for one shilling between January and June 1921; for ninepence between June and December the same year.

50 The *Times of Nigeria* observed in 1921 that 'the journalistic outlook' was 'somewhat bright' and that great interest in journalism was being displayed (14 February 1921). Also *African Messenger*, 5 May 1921.

51 The records would seem to indicate that the newspapers maintained their circulations in spite of the competition by the dailies. Misleading evidences such as these account for the conflict in the circulation figures for the *Akede Eko* in 1919. While the relevant *Blue Book* quotes 800, the newspaper itself puts the figure at 500. See issue of 31 October 1929.

52 See *Lagos Daily News*, 1 May 1929.

53 This was the *Pioneer*.

54 The centres included Kano, Zaria, Kaduna, Jos, Minna, Ekwuanga, Lokoja, Oshogbo, Ilesha, Ibadan, Ife, Abeokuta, Ondo, Shagamu, Ijebu-Ode, Epe, Sapele, Warri, Asaba, Onitsha, Enugu, Umuahia, Aba, Imo River, Port Harcourt, Calabar, Opobo.

55 According to Azikiwe, the news that he was going to start a newspaper in Lagos struck fear into the minds of the *Daily Times* proprietors. R. B. Paul of the West African Newspapers Limited flew to Lagos from the United Kingdom. The *Daily Times* was promptly reorganised by the appointment of H. A. C. Bate, an experienced British journalist, as editor. Bate allegedly was armed with 'secret instructions' to do his utmost 'to checkmate Zik and his newspaper venture'. Bate improved the literary and technical production of the *Daily Times* and provoked press battles with the *Pilot*. The Bate-Azikiwe conflict culminated in a libel and slander action in which Azikiwe claimed £10 000 and £5 000 respectively. But Bate fled the country before the case went to court. See 'Zik', 'Political Reminiscences 1938–48 (2)', *West African Pilot*, 6 July 1948. Also *Awo, op. cit.*, p. 134.

56 C.S.O. 1/1, Freeman to Newcastle, 6 December 1862; C.O. 147/1, Newcastle to Freeman, 28 January 1863.

57 See Perham, *The Years of Authority*, pp. 598–9.

58 The advertisement rates during these years were as follows:

> Every 12 lines and under 4s
> Every additional line 6d
> Every Birth or Marriage 2s 6d
> Death 2s

The above 'secured' one insertion and half the price was charged for every subsequent insertion. Marriage, birth and death announcements were rare at this time and advertising was characterised by unvarying insertions – the advertisement typography in 1895 was basically similar to that in 1918.

59 It is difficult to estimate a newspaper's income by simply counting up the advertisements. In the first place, it is not always clear which advertisements are 'independent'. Many newspapermen were agents of European firms whose advertisements were inserted free of charge. In addition, advertisements were inserted free by people who contributed to finance the papers. Even when 'independent' advertisements are known, the problem is not solved. Advertisement rates varied from advertiser to advertiser. Some enjoyed preferential rates and others had quite arbitrary assessments. Nevertheless, it is possible to make rough estimates. The method adopted in this study is to ignore known 'dependent' advertisements like, for example, the National Bookshop of Nigeria advertisements which were inserted in the *Daily Telegraph* by its owner. Furthermore, temporary advertisements, like Removal Notices, notices announcing business liquidation, change of address, etc, have not been taken into consideration. Advertisements which ran into considerable lengths of size and time

have been reckoned at half their face value. The estimated amounts are the averages for the months of January and June.

60 When the paper was established in 1914, it carried no single indigenous advertisement although it proudly claimed to be the 'unrivalled medium for advertising purposes in Nigeria'.

61 The African advertisements in the *Messenger* were not transferred to the *Daily Times* when the former was discontinued in 1928. As a matter of fact, African advertisers had almost completely pulled out their advertisements before 1928.

62 The *Daily Telegraph* was the greatest exponent of this propaganda. See issues for 1931 and subsequent years.

63 The *Messenger* created a Business Directory in 1921. Ten years later, the *Daily Telegraph* launched its Directory Scheme. The aim in each case was to encourage the African traders to advertise, however tiny such advertisements were.

64 See below (note 66).

65 The yield of the *Daily Times* via the same route in the late twenties and early thirties, fluctuated between £20 and £30 per month.

66 The evidence shows that two daily papers, the *Telegraph* and *Times* could fall into this category. It is of interest to mention that the *Pilot* in its first few years, did not canvass for advertisements.

67 For advertisement rates, see note 58.

68 It would be seen that in the case of the *Pioneer*, the almost 100 per cent increase in the number of foreign advertisements is not fully reflected in the income derived. The reason is that a large number of the fresh advertisements carried by the newspaper was restricted to the twelve-line single-column specification.

69 The *Pioneer*'s two leading advertisers, Elder Dempster and B.B.W.A. disappeared from the page and back pages, the one in June, the other in December 1931. The *Weekly Record* had become, by the end of 1927, a lifeless sheet devoted to patent medicine advertisements.

70 Advertising Houses emerged in the late twenties – a testimony to the increasing development in newspaper economic enterprise. The leading Advertising Houses were D. J. Keymer & Co. Ltd, Buntings Advertising Service; West Africa Publicity Limited.

71 See the Annual Report of the Nigerian Printing and Publishing Company Ltd, for the year 1927/28. *Nigerian Daily Times*, 15 April 1929.

72 See Annual Report above. The management of the newspaper spoke about the need for greater 'nursing' of the advertisements department.

73 Annual Report, *op. cit.*

4 Beginnings of the press offensive 1880–1900

The role of the newspapers during the last two decades of the nineteenth century gives that period a certain character which distinguishes it from the twentieth century. Partly because the press was still in the process of growth and consolidation, prolonged political agitations were few and the tone of political opposition was generally mild. But notwithstanding the incapacities of infancy, the newspapers played a significant role in society. They mounted a vigorous campaign in favour of greater cultural identity and fought hard to protect the independence and sovereignty of indigenous African states. In this chapter, we shall focus on the part which the newspapers played in cultural nationalism and in resistance to imperialism. But before dealing with these questions, we shall briefly sketch the nature of culture and society in Lagos in the nineteenth and early twentieth centuries. This will provide a useful backdrop for the evaluation of the attitudes of the newspapers in politics.

SOCIAL AND CULTURAL SETTING

By 1880, when the Nigerian newspaper press was born, Lagos had already acquired certain metropolitan attributes which were to form the basis of its transformation into the mainspring of national life less than half a century later. The nature of its geographical location, the pattern of its economy and the character of its society ensured abundant resources of wealth and ideas which were inevitably to make it the focus of social and political life in Nigeria.

During the period of about thirty years going back to 1851 when British influence was introduced into the island, its history had been one of gradual physical development, increasing population and spatial distribution and also increasing commercial competition and expansion. Pre-colonial Lagos had been described as 'a very small town occupying a small part of a small island'.[1] In the words of an early newspaper, it was 'an insignificant bogbound islet remarkable for nothing in particular'.[2] Its origins remain a source of controversy between those who hold that it grew out of a war camp founded by a Benin king and those who hold that it was founded by Yoruba-speaking people from Isheri.[3] However, by the middle of the nineteenth century, it had a population of about 20 000. This rose to about 25 000 in 1866, 28 000 in 1871 and 37 000 in 1881. By the end of the century, the population had increased to about 40 000. Like the population, the area of Lagos also underwent considerable growth. From 1·55 square miles in 1891, the island was to grow to 18 square miles twenty years later.

Various improvements were undertaken which had the effect of changing Lagos from a disconnected collection of island settlements divided and surrounded by lagoons and swamps into the nucleus of a modern urban centre. Many swamps were reclaimed before 1900 but it was during the first decade of the present century that the problem began to attract serious attention with the arrival of Governor MacGregor in 1899. By the middle of the present century, more than a thousand acres of swamp had been reclaimed. Road development within the island was not carried out on any systematic and far-sighted basis but early in the history of colonial Lagos two important roads were constructed. In 1861, a wide road was constructed along the southern waterfront which became known as the Marina (formerly called Water Street). Not long afterwards, another street was begun behind the Marina and was named Broad Street. These two streets have remained to this day the main arteries of the central business area of Lagos.

Notwithstanding the paucity of roads in Lagos, there was uninterrupted flow of people from one part of the island to the other and news of events in one part was rapidly disseminated to the other parts. Improvement in the mode of travelling came with the inauguration of train services in 1897. In 1902, a tramway was completed from Lagos Island to the new Railway Terminus at Iddo. Its route ran from the Marina, through Balogun Street, Ereko, Idunmota and to Iddo. Initially there were two trams but these were increased to four in 1910. In 1913, the tramway was abandoned whereupon a leading Lagosian woman, Mrs Obasa, introduced a cheap bus service the following year (the Anfani Bus Service). Lagos began to have modern communication facilities with the introduction of the telephone in 1892. By 1903, the island was already in telegraphic communication with the hinterland as far as Shaki. That year an attempt to establish a pigeon post was abandoned. The underlying assumption in Lagos was that in the network of swamps and lagoons, the telegraph was impossible and there was a need for some means of rapid communication with shipping interests on the coast. Under the inspiration of C. H. Elgee, an English army officer whose hobby was pigeon racing, a pigeon loft was established at Forcados in 1900. But the inadequacy of the accommodation and protection provided for the birds and the scepticism of the British Government about the effectiveness of pigeon communication led to the collapse of the scheme.[4]

The health of the island was, and has continued to be, a matter for serious concern. Poor sanitation, overcrowding and the absence of basic social facilities were blamed for the high incidence of infant and adult mortality. In 1895, it was observed that houses formerly occupied by eight persons were now tenanted by twenty to twenty-five people. Until pipe-borne water was provided in 1916, it was difficult to obtain good water. Many lamented 'the daily travels of maids and boys from one end of the town to another for good water' which was at best 'brackish'.[5] Robert Campbell at one time demonstrated the feasibility of obtaining good water by means of artesian wells sunk to a depth far below the bed of the lagoon but his efforts did not seem to have made a strong impression on the government. In 1891, a call was made for the establishment of a department of Public Health to undertake the provision of good water supply, drainage and sewerage.

The population of Lagos was unevenly distributed in a number of sections or quarters which made up the island community. The most remarkable of these was Old Lagos which was situated in the western third of the island. This was the area occupied by the indigenous people. Their strong attachment to tradition and their anxiety to be left alone and to be excluded from European-inspired programmes of change and development helps to explain why the old city has remained a testimony to the disorder of unplanned growth.

Apart from Old Lagos, there were three important settlements which came into existence as a result of the European contact.

These were inhabited by West African, mostly Sierra Leonian, immigrants (Saro), Brazilian and Cuban immigrants (Aguda or Amaro), and the Europeans. The circumstances surrounding the influx of the Saros and Amaros is a familiar theme in Nigerian history. From a sprinkle of Saro repatriates in the 1840s, the movement to Lagos had gathered momentum in the wake of the British invasion of the island in 1851 and the expulsion of King Kosoko who was no great friend of the immigrants. The Saros occupied the Olowogbowo area in the western extremity of the southern shoreline, and the Amaros established themselves around Campos square. The third group, the Europeans, were located mainly along the Marina. These three settlements were separated from one another as well as from the Old Town by creeks, lagoons and swamps but there were more barriers between the New and Old Lagos than those of physical separation. Indeed, geographical separation diminished with population expansion and land reclamation whereas social distance increased with differential material improvement and social advancement.

The Sierra Leonians felt a strong sense of superiority over the indigenous people who themselves demonstrated their acquiescence in the situation by referring to their new countrymen as black Europeans. The superior air of the Saros derived from their acquaintance in Sierra Leone with the ways of the Western world. Their sense of gratitude to European philanthropy, their great estimation and admiration of European advancement and civilisation and their anxiety to break with their pre-European background – all these predisposed many of them to an initially uncritical appropriation of European culture. In language, religion, dress, names and recreation, they adopted European patterns and established a community which had few social interests in common with the Old Town.

Few things attested the social distance between the old and new Lagos more clearly than religion. Most immigrants professed Christianity which, in accordance with contemporary thinking, was assumed to be superior to African religions as well as to Islam practised in the Old Town. The practitioners of these were looked down upon by the former as heathens and advertisers of superstitions and charms, incapable of any meaningful contribution to the development of the country. 'Neither Heathenism nor Mohammedanism', commented a newspaper, 'is calculated to substantially improve the people and elevate the country.'[6] Christianity was the genesis of educational growth and development which gave a deeper dimension to the cleavage between the indigenes and the immigrants. Acquaintance with Western education, most clearly exemplified by the ability to speak or write the English language, came to be taken as a symbol of greater wisdom and of superiority. Although most immigrants could speak Yoruba, it became fashionable for many of them to seek to acquire an imagined new stature by pretending to be incapable of speaking Yoruba. They claimed to speak only English, and to emphasise their assumed learnedness and superiority, they took great pleasure in the use of lengthy words and Latin phrases.

However, the population of those who spoke English was relatively small throughout the nineteenth century. The census of 1891 listed only about 5 000 speakers out of a total population of *c.* 86 000. In 1897, it was observed that most Lagosians did not understand English in spite of the long historic contact with British influence.[7] This would suggest that the growth in literacy was not considerable in spite of the fact that primary and secondary school education had been introduced and expanded since the 1850s. Among the secondary schools were the C.M.S. Grammar School founded in 1859 and the Female Institution, later the Seminary, established in 1872. Others were the Methodist Boys' High School (1876), Methodist Girls' High School (1879), St Gregory's (1881) and Baptist Academy (1885). Although the establishment of primary and secondary schools helped to expand literacy, the view was expressed in 1882 that there was 'a dense mass of ignorance' in Lagos. It was claimed that 'the number of children at school is so entirely out of proportion to the population and the number of children of school age in the town'.[8]

Although religious and educational cleavages divided the old and new communities, the immigrants themselves were by no means a united group. Indeed, they were severely divided by sub-ethnic differences arising from their conficting loyalties to their different original homes in Yorubaland. On the positive side, the natal connections of the Saro with the Yoruba interior inspired them to advocate and protect the interests of the latter; they became, as one newspaper put it, 'the eyes and ears of the hinterland people'. But where there was no common enemy, basic cleavages became manifest. Conflicts in the Yoruba country were acutely reflected in mutual suspicion and antagonism among the immigrants with important consequences for the social and political history of the island. In 1894, the view was expressed that the 'constant pressure of tribal affinities' constituted a 'besetting and obtrusive affinity' which was responsible for the inability of the people to engage in any enterprise which required organised effort.[9] Politically, the effect of sub-ethnicity could be seen in the prevalence of factiousness in political organisation.

The New Lagos society may have been deeply divided by sub-ethnicity but common characteristics were manifested in occupation as well as in the area of social, cultural and intellectual life. Nineteenth-century Lagos was a trading island. Trading was the popular occupation of immigrants and indigenous people alike. In the words of a newspaper, trade was 'the staple dependence . . . and source of employment to fully nine-tenths of the population'. The census of 1891 gives a trading population of 11 000 which was over thirty per cent of the total population. The commonest feature of trading activity was the shop and it could fairly be said that by the end of the nineteenth century, Lagos had become an island of shopkeepers. So fashionable had shop-owning become by 1900 that a newspaper felt compelled to decry the 'mania which possessed many individuals until they were bankrupt from the effort to maintain a shop along the Marina'. Western habits of entertainment and recreation found eager favour, as did most other aspects of European civilisation. Dinner parties were much cherished and invitations to dinner at Government House received appreciative response. Typical of the select nature of such dinner invitations is the following group of Nigerians who went to dinner at Government House on 11 January 1900 – John Payne Jackson, G. A. Williams, R. B. Blaize, Kitoyi Ajasa, C. J. George, C. Tambaci, Dr Randle, Henry Carr, Bishop Oluwole, Capt. J. P. L. Davies, J. Otonba Payne and Lt C. H. Elgee. Soirées, At Homes, garden parties, concerts, plays, ballroom dancing, debates, lectures and society weddings served the needs of the educated public for entertainment, leisure and intellectual pursuits.

Public debates and lectures were stimulated in the 1880s, principally by the Lagos Mutual Improvement Society founded in July 1879 and led by Robert Campbell and Dr N. T. King. The activities of the society featured group discussions on topical questions and weekly lectures by distinguished personalities. The deaths of Campbell and King, in January and May 1884 respectively, deprived the organisation of its chief pillars but meetings continued to be held until 1890. In 1901, the Lagos Literary

Institute was formed to promote 'mutual improvement in general knowledge'. The Executive Committee included Governor MacGregor as President and Henry Carr as Vice-President, C. J. George, Bishop I. Oluwole, C. A. Sapara Williams, Kitoyi Ajasa and the Rev J. H. Samuel (Adegboyega Edun) who was secretary. Subscription was six shillings per annum. At the inaugural meeting a paper on 'How Lagos is governed' was presented by MacGregor.

A significant product of the intellectual movement was the establishment of public reading rooms. The first was opened by Governor Glover in 1866. More than twenty years later, in 1887, the Memorial Hall built in memory of Glover opened a reading room which was stocked with newspapers and periodicals. Earlier in 1883, Owen Macaulay had established a private reading room to stimulate patronage for his *Eagle and Lagos Critic*. These reading rooms were practically unused by the public who seemed to have preferred the privacy of their own homes. The literary competition which characterised intellectual life in Lagos had apparently lost much of its vigour by the end of the nineteenth century. In 1899, a newspaper lamented the 'entire absence' of any organised efforts for intellectual culture and self-improvement on the part of young men and women who had become devoted to idleness and frivolity:

> the sober joys of intellectual research, literary improvement, profitable debates, the interchange of thought and opinion on current topics and the discussion of questions affecting the welfare of his race and country are unknown to (the youth).[10]

Parties were frequent then as now and provided many people with an excellent opportunity to indulge their habits of extravagance and display. 'On marriage and funeral occasions', commented a newspaper, 'there is the same lavish and showy display, the same struggle to outdo anything that has been done . . . to gain a hollow reputation for exceptional arrangements.'[11] The 'virulent disease' of extravagance was frequently attacked by the newspapers but it apparently proved to be malignant.

The widespread exhibition of luxury and frolic concealed the reality of poverty among a large section of the community. The vast majority of the poor managed to eke out an existence but some did so by resorting to begging. By 1889, the begging trade had become 'an intolerable nuisance' to some observers. As one columnist remarked[12]

The town is simply inundated with begging impostors, mostly from the interior – stout, hale, hearty fellows who, feigning blindness or pretending to suffer from some imaginary malady tramp from street to street and from house to house, chanting some doleful ballad and disturbing the rest and quiet of peaceful citizens who are often compelled to give them a trifle, to be rid of their importunities.

The broad pattern of life in nineteenth-century Lagos, the cleavages between the old and new communities, the acculturation of the Saro to Victorian society, the preoccupation with trade, the adulation of wealth and love of extravagance, the slow rate of literacy expansion – all these remained with little change up to the thirties. There were pressures for radical change in culture and society but this was not to come until a new indigenous educated class had eclipsed the intellectual aristocracy of the pioneer educated elite.

CULTURAL NATIONALISM

The last decade of the nineteenth century witnessed an effusion of cultural nationalism which was inspired primarily by the newspapers. The *Record* and the *Standard* instituted a vigorous campaign of cultural consciousness which sought to stimulate a greater interest in African history, language, dress, names, family life, religion, dance, drama and art forms.

This is not to suggest that there was no movement of cultural expression before the 1890s. Indeed, developments in the 1880s paved the way for what took place in the 1890s. The cultural nationalism of the eighties had its genesis in the spontaneous rediscovery of ethnic and cultural identity on the part of the repatriates as well as in the frustration and disillusionment created in the minds of the Africans by the hypocrisy and racial arrogance of church and colonial administrators. The initial provision of the Education Ordinance of 1882 that the reading and writing of English should be compulsory provoked a strong reaction in the public and the press. The *Lagos Times* in a long editorial denounced the idea as designed to undermine African culture.

We shall not sit tamely to witness the murder, death and burial of one of those important distinguishing national and racial marks that God has given to us in common with other tribes, nations and races, and not protest against it with all the energy that we can command. Such a system as that which we are expected to follow cannot but produce in the minds of the common people eventually the deepest prejudice against their own Native language and social habitudes . . . a prejudice which has extended itself to even Native names and salutations, notwithstanding their rich significance . . . has often shown itself in an affected speaking or a base corrupting of the vernacular, and is evident in the ignoble, unpatriotic and unmeaning preference generally given . . . by schoolmasters to salutations of them from their pupils in English over Yoruba and other salutations, as if we need to learn the commonest act of civility from a foreign people.[13]

In September of that year, the *Lagos Times* considered it 'certainly delightful and refreshing' to notice that some young men were effecting a change in the character of public entertainments by introducing interesting African scenes and performances.[14] In November, R. A. Coker, a distinguished organist, included the melody of a Yoruba song in his composition 'Souvenir de Lagos' which was received with enthusiastic singing in the audience.[15] In 1883, a correspondent to the *Lagos Times*, depressed by the existence of three English language newspapers in the town, called attention to the need for a newspaper in a Nigerian language to help in 'the building up of the Negro race'.[16] By 1885, opposition had developed in the press to the use of pidgin English as the common language of the immigrants. The view was that Yoruba should be spoken. In that year S. A. Allen and D. B. Vincent (Mojola Agbebi) published *Iwe Owe* (Book of Proverbs) and *Iwe Alo* (Book of Riddles). The following year, E. M. Lijadu published a pamphlet on Aribiloso, an Egba 'wit and humorist'. In 1887, M. T. John, a teacher at the C.M.S. Training Institution produced a Yoruba version of the British National Anthem.[17] In that year, the C.M.S. began to publish a local edition of their monthly *Gleaner* which included some Yoruba articles. In 1888, Andrew Thomas founded the *Iwe Irohin Eko*, a bilingual fortnightly. The aim of the newspaper was to promote the development of Yoruba language and literature. In that year, a Yoruba hymn was introduced with the request that Yoruba melodies be utilised with the words. A Yoruba wedding ceremony was also reported.

The cultural nationalism of the eighties was no doubt noteworthy but it was in the nineties that it found a new impetus which was to sustain it up to the first decade of the present century. Some of the factors responsible for this development included the suspensions and dismissals of indigenous church officials on the Niger in 1890, the resignation of Bishop Crowther from the Niger Mission that year and his death in 1891; the increasing subversion and conquest of indigenous African States and the visit of Blyden to Lagos in 1890. Much of the ideological foundation of the cultural movement not only in Nigeria but in West Africa was laid by Blyden whose ideas were an important influence on several cultural nationalists in Nigeria and West Africa.[18] Blyden's cultural nationalism owed its inspiration partly to his acquaintance in the 1870s with Muslim achievement and civilisation in the western Sudan. His famous public address in Lagos in 1890 on 'The Return of the Exiles and The West African Church' is accepted by many historians as the immediate inspiration for the founding of the United Native African Church. Blyden provided tremendous inspiration for John Jackson and George Williams whose cultural nationalism found powerful expression in the *Record* and the *Standard* in the nineties.

The motive of the new wave of newspaper campaign was to compel the 'Europeanized African' or 'Civilized Native' to effect an urgent and critical self-examination in the cultural plane by subjecting his style of life to strong criticism. An editorial in the *Record* entitled 'The emasculation of the Civilized Native' exemplified the temper of the attack.[19]

> To the native mind which is able to emerge from beneath the cloak of blind fatuity with which the civilized native is enveloped, nothing stands out in greater relief than the paralysation and complete emasculation which afflict the native under the spell of his so-called civilized life. Imbued through the course of his training with his conditions of life and surrounding, he is disqualified for fulfilling the first requirement of his existence, namely, adaptation to environment . . . out of accord with the fundamental law of man's existence, the Europeanized native is cut off from the springs of human vitality . . . and presents the anomaly of a monstrous contradiction upon the fixed order of human life . . . in his thoughtless and persistent pursuit of a life which reason and every other faculty of the human senses tell him is fatal to him, the civilized native is exhibiting a lamentable mental incapacity.

In another editorial entitled 'The despair of the Civilized Native', the *Record* asserted that the life of the 'supposedly enlightened native' was 'a medley of sham, pretence and ludicrous travesty cloaked under a sort of respectability which is hollow'. In a further comment, the newspaper asked the question, 'Is the Civilized Native Mad'?[20]

> For although living in his own country and under the aspirations of his own hearth and heath, yet he elects to adopt a life fashion which is not only unsuited to him and incompatible with his environment but positively hurtful to his health and well-being . . . unpalatable as the fact may be there can be no question that in the role which the civilized native plays of the Black European in Africa, he is enacting a farce in which he and his stupidity constitute the comic feature.

The *Standard* summed up the feeling on the issue when it stated in 1898 that 'a black Englishman is an absurdity not only in Europe but also in Africa'.

Besides this kind of generalised condemnation, attention was focused upon some specific aspects of culture which best exemplified the absence of cultural awareness in the society. Among the aspects of culture which attracted propaganda, one of the most discussed was language. By the 1890s, some progress had been made in the fostering of interest and pride in the Yoruba language. During the first few decades of the Colony of Lagos, Yoruba was accorded a very low esteem by the educated Africans. They held the language in contempt and frowned against its use in 'respectable society'. Indeed, it was regarded as uncivilised to speak Yoruba at public meetings and those who did so were embarrassed and humiliated by people leaving their seats in annoyance. Gradually, however, and in response to the cultural revival of the eighties, attitudes began to change, although public support for the *Iwe Irohin Eko* did not seem to have been very wide.

It was, therefore, against a background of general apathy in regard to the use and development of the Yoruba language that the language campaign was launched. In January, 1896, the *Standard* lamented:[21]

> Yorubaland has no literature. Her history and traditions, her wars and troubles, her songs and folklore, her parables, proverbs, axioms, apothegms are collected to this day from the mental storage of elders and dames of sires and grandsires. This misfortune exists also with most West African people . . . considering that we are entering on a new era in the country and are as it were at the childhood of the land it becomes a sacred duty to those who are able and those who are prepared to lose by it to undertake to collect the thoughts, hopes, aspirations, songs, histories of their people together for the use of men.

Considerations of cultural nationalism apart, the *Standard* had other interests in urging the development of indigenous literature.

> A strong and continuous effort at producing a Yoruba literature of every kind and grade so far as circumstances allow will serve in the hands of sincere Christian men as one safeguard against the encroachments of Islam.

The paper stressed that it was not advocating the cessation of teaching or learning the English language. English would probably be spoken and written in Yorubaland for the next three hundred years because it was to some the mother-tongue and to most people the language of business. But it should not be allowed to eclipse the Yoruba language.

> English may be spoken from Verde to Guardafui, from Mediterranean to the Cape but Yoruba will be the language of the home of Yorubaland.

The language campaign gathered so much strength that in 1900 the suggestion was made that all communications in writing from the Abeokuta government to the Lagos government and the compilation of the laws of Egbaland should be in Yoruba. When in 1908, a bilingual mission journal, the *Holy Trinity Church Parochial Magazine* carried advertisements in Yoruba, the event was seen by many cultural nationalists as an achievement of significance. It was an indication of increased self-confidence on the part of the *Standard* that it now shifted its campaign from interest in the language to the quality of expression. In 1908, it criticised those who mixed Yoruba with English in common speech and called for the establishment of a Society for the Preservation of the Yoruba language.[22] Such a body does not appear, however, to have been established.

Another major theme of the cultural campaign was dress. Few themes gave rise to as much detailed comment and vehement language as was exhibited in the dress campaign. In a major outburst in March 1896, the *Standard* denounced the 'Europeanized African' for his indiscriminate adoption of European dress. 'As to dress', the newspaper asserted, 'the Europeanized African is a nondescript, a libel on his country and a blot on civilization . . . a geographical, a physiological and a psychological monstrosity'.[23] The *Standard* conceded that the adoption of European dress was perhaps inevitable at the beginning of missionary intrusion when Africans were in the 'house of bondage' and were generally 'untaught, unconverted, unthinking, low and weak'. The Christian missionaries 'were not Africans and had no African dress; they were Europeans and they gave to their converts European attire'. If they had treated the early converts differently, they might have been accused of discrimination. However, the times had changed except that the educated African had chosen the path of reaction.

> The failure to institute a reform in such a matter as dress or of improving and adapting existing patterns is a tacit admission that the Europeanised African left to himself can do nothing of or for himself. It further implies that the 'philistines' of slavery are yet upon him. He is still wishful of and willing to abide by the whims and caprices, the weather-cock turnings and the fasion gee-gaws of his former master.

The newspaper submitted that most cultural phenomena were a function of geographical location and that the issue whether a particular cultural system was superior or inferior to another did not arise.

> In the world around and above us, every beast has its skin and every fowl its feathers. The beneficent creator covered the back of the sheep with wool in the wintry clime and deprived it of wool in the tropics. He plants Africa with palms and coconuts and Europe with oats and myrtle trees. Every creature for its habitat and every costume for its clime.

Some European missionaries on the Niger had tried in the early nineties to identify themselves with their host environment by living and dressing like Africans but rather than encourage them or learn a lesson from them, the educated Africans only scoffed and jeered. 'We should be ashamed of ourselves', the newspaper asserted, 'ashamed of our incapableness, our unreadiness and often times our unreasonableness.'

The question of African dress was often linked with that of African names in the campaign for the preservation of African customs. 'Like to dress', observed the *Standard* in 1896, 'most names of the Europeanized African are importations, being originally names of slave owners, of benefactors, of missionaries and teachers'.[24] The situation in which educated and Christian Africans abandoned or ignored African names during birth and baptism ceremonies could no longer be approved of as this had the effect of perpetuating a historical tragedy which responsible and imaginative Africans did their best to efface.

The crusade in support of the adoption of African dress and

names revealed a lack of unanimity in the ranks of the newspapers. The *Lagos Echo* did not share the cultural enthusiasm of its contemporaries whom it rebuked for making unnecessary noise about cultural revival: 'we feel inclined to reprobate this new development as a mere fad, productive of no good and born of a spirit of self-conceit and overweening confidence'.[25] The argument advanced by the newspaper was that it was 'incongruous' for professing Christians to bear African names many of which were of 'heathen origin' and also that the Yoruba had no indigenous dress ('we shall be immensely obliged to anyone who will tell us of any costume indigenous to Yorubaland that can be dignified by the name of dress'). These misrepresentations were a negative approach to the issue and were out of tune with the progressive outlook of the *Echo*. It is not clear why the newspaper took this reactionary stand, but it would not be entirely surprising in the circumstances of the editorial instability which it suffered during its brief existence.

There were other indigenous institutions and customs which fascinated the leading newspapermen. One was polygamy. The newspapers may not have dwelt on the topic as repeatedly as its controversial nature would suggest but it enjoyed much recommendation particularly in the *Record*. Initially, in 1894, the newspaper expressed strong opposition to polygamy which it described as 'the outcome of a state of ignorance and depravity'. Three years later, it reversed its opinion. 'We . . . range ourselves with those . . . who distinctly deny that monogamy is a Divine institution enjoined upon mankind without reference to circumstances.' After another ten years, the *Record* had become a fervent advocate of polygamy. It is not clear what brought about the change but the inconsistency achieved enough attention to provoke a reaction from Henry Carr who in a letter to the *Standard* in 1908 took John Jackson to task for 'denouncing today with vehemence what he cordially recommended yesterday'.[26]

Secret societies became a topical issue in 1898 when the *Sierra Leone Times* painted an ugly picture of the Poro Society in Sierra Leone describing it as a 'degrading and superstitious organisation of blood thirsty cowards'. The *Standard* disagreed with the views of its Freetown contemporary which it described as 'the sentiments of a stranger and sojourner'. It pointed out that secret societies had existed in Africa from earliest times and that they were 'institutions for establishing general understanding and unity of feeling among people'. They 'inculcate the duties of reciprocity, the love of fatherland, stimulate national aspirations and delineate the rules of society'. This was why in many parts of West Africa, it was argued, European missionaries had initiated themselves into the mysteries of the secret societies.[27] Interest was also aroused in indigenous plays which should embody recitals of incidents in the life of the people. Such plays, the *Record* remarked, would 'enhance our own self respect and elevate and give tone to native sentiment'.[28]

Attention was focused on the need for a history of the Yoruba people. In 1896, the *Standard* announced with a sense of jubilation that a 'History of Yorubaland' was 'in manuscript and near publication'.[29] In 1905, the newspaper began to serialise a work by 'Yoruba Historian' entitled 'General History of the Yoruba Country'.

The newspapers blamed the failure of the African to possess cultural identity on the excesses of the European agencies who, according to the *Record*, tended 'to force the civilization of Europe upon the African without any regard to its adaptability or any concern as to its ultimate effect'. To the extent that European civilisation had been imposed, it was in the opinion of the *Record* 'an accretion, not a growth . . . an incrustation not a development'.[30] The *Record* saw European civilisation as a dangerous influence in Africa – physically, the results were highly injurious if not absolutely fatal; socially, the life of the African was 'a travesty without any settled force to sustain it and guide it'. The *Record* was of the view that European civilisation had severely undermined the foundations of the African social system with serious consequences for the stability of family life. 'The introduction of the European mode of life . . . has availed to weaken and nullify parental control as the chief governing factor and relegated the social system of the native to the chaos of utter confusion and disorder, bereft of all governance and guidance and a prey to anarchy'.[31]

In blaming European agencies for frustrating African cultural expression and development, the newspapers evinced the greatest antipathy against the Christian missionaries. They reflected and intensified contemporary opposition to what was regarded as the denationalising aspects of Christian influence. In numerous editorials, they called attention to the cultural implications of mission school education .The supply of European garments to the schoolchildren was expected to effect 'a complete change of disposition, habits, customs and idiosyncrasies of race'. As the *Standard* put it, 'the native child is taught to look down upon and despise the customs of his country; all race pride is destroyed; the very books from which he learns in school teach that the race is an inferior and degraded one in the family of nations'.[32] The *Record* took a wider view of the matter. 'The neophyte convert is no convert unless he is arrayed in European habiliments, and assumes European manners; but the chief mischief is wrought in the instituting into the mind of the convert the idea that all the customs of his people are degraded and abhorrent'.[33]

The alleged disadvantages and inadequacies of Christianity were underlined by frequent comparisons with Islam. The view that Islam was a more acceptable and powerful factor in shaping the future of West Africa was strong in the *Record*. In a comparison of the Muslim and Christian African, the newspaper stated:

> While the Moslem African developed into a mosque-creating, self-reliant propagandist, the Christian Africans blossom into 'House' builders and apron-string saints. Islam has produced munificent Africans, liberal, generous, public-spirited men . . . Christianity has produced but money grabbers, close-fisted, grovelling, sneaking men and usurers.[34]

There can be no doubt that in the period between about 1896 and 1910, the consciousness of African culture found vigorous expression in the press. The leading newspapers not only gave a piquant focus to existing currents of cultural thought but also provided a considerable intellectual stimulus which gave the campaign a unique character. Whether the cultural movement brought about any outstanding institutional changes is another matter. Immediate practical accomplishments were quite modest and probably related only to the greater development of the Yoruba language through its use in advertisements. The major preachers of the cultural sermon failed to provide a practical demonstration of their sincerity. Neither John Jackson nor George Williams discarded their European names and dress or assumed a new style of life which accorded more with African expectations.

THE PRESS AND THE EUROPEAN CONQUEST

Coeval with the high tide of the cultural movement in the nineteenth century was the movement of intellectual resistance to

European penetration and domination. The cultural and anti-imperial movements interracted, providing each other with inspiration and stimulus and together contributing to heighten the tone of criticism and propaganda. In considering the role of the newspapers in the struggle against European imperialism, attention must be drawn to certain limitations of the social background of the educated elite and the restrictions of their geographic location. As has been pointed out, the journalists and their supporters were mostly Saros, for whom Yorubaland, being their original homeland and forming the hinterland of Lagos, had a special interest. Difficulties in Yorubaland aroused their concern and sympathy sometimes in directions which were more emotional than rational. More significantly, the critical importance of the Yoruba hinterland for the economic achievement and survival of the educated elite was a major influence in their reactions to issues of foreign policy. Trade was the paramount occupation and its politics bred absurd alliances. These considerations provide the key to certain significant inconsistencies in the attitudes of the newspapers to European imperial invasion. For although the general attitude of the newspapers to European intrusion was that of vigorous resistance, of resolute endeavour to safeguard the independence and sovereignty of indigenous African states, the British occupation of Yorubaland enjoyed the enthusiastic support of public opinion in Lagos. In contradistinction to their usual verbal warfare against the European intruders, the newspapers were vociferous in demanding British interference in the internal affairs of the Yoruba states. They mounted strong propaganda in favour of British expansionist policy in the Lagos hinterland even though, at the time, they continued to criticise and condemn the imperialistic policies of Britain and other European powers in areas outside Yorubaland.

The events that were to lead to the British occupation of Yorubaland happened to have begun to unfold on the eve of the emergence of indigenous newspapers. There could not have a better ready-made issue for comment. The Sixteen Years' War began in 1877 when the Egba and Ijebu declared war against Ibadan and thus opened a new and critical chapter in the belligerent relations between various Yoruba states since the collapse of the Old Oyo empire. In 1878, the Ekiti and Ijesha entered the war against Ibadan. Ilorin and Ife soon followed suit the following year and by the end of that decade, Ibadan was engaged in war against a wide coalition. This is not the place to examine the background and diplomacy of this conflict but rather to note that before the arrival of African-conducted newspapers, it was the *African Times* which provided the forum for the sub-ethnic disagreements and rivalries in Lagos. Some partisans took more practical steps by raising contingents whom they sent 'home' to act as 'advisers' and sources of encouragement to their people. Others organised the flow of ammunition from Lagos. However, although the educated elite unhesitatingly strained every nerve in defence of their local homelands, in the process exacerbating divisions in their own ranks, they were nevertheless not opposed to British interference in the affairs of their people. They shared common ground in the belief that British intervention would result in every advantage for all concerned – the desire of many war-weary Yoruba rulers to arbitrate the conflict would be satisfied and peace would descend on the ravaged country with hopeful consequences for the revival of trade; also, British prestige and influence in Yorubaland would increase and would be a factor for permanent peace as well as create incentives for the greater promotion of Christianity and Western civilisation in Yorubaland. Themselves products of the missionary movement upon whose arguments of the correlations between Western civilisation and Christianity rested the foundations of their outlook and aspirations, the educated elite saw Christianity as the essential preliminary to the building in West Africa of a nation whose society would be modelled on that of the Western world. The view has been expressed that Christianity was also seen by some as a solution for the problem of disunity in Lagos and in the Yoruba country. It was believed by James Johnson and others that by encouraging a common consciousness, derived from the missionary teaching of the brotherhood of all men before God, narrow and sectional loyalties would be reduced and a closer sense of nationality would emerge.[35]

Humanitarian considerations aside, economic factors were of decisive importance in influencing the attitude of the educated Africans. The desire to seek opportunities of trade had been a major factor in their return to Lagos and for them, as well as for most of the Europeans and the indigenes of Lagos, trade was 'the premier and dernier resort'. It has been estimated that in 1881 about fifty-seven per cent of the population of Lagos were engaged in trade.[36] The bulk of this trade was carried on with the Yoruba interior and its fortunes depended upon conditions there. Indeed, conditions in the interior were virtually a barometer by which the state of the economy of Lagos was measured. Interruptions or dislocations of Lagos trade reduced government revenue, generally weakened large commercial houses and ruined the 'petty-traders' to which class the vast majority of the Saro population belonged. It is not surprising that what Governor Moloney termed the 'Interior Question' loomed so large in British policy in Lagos.

For many years before and after the establishment of British presence in Lagos, the trade of the island was intermittently interrupted as a result of wars and rumours of war in the interior and also as a result of the interdiction of trade by the Egba and the Ijebu in reaction to British provocation in Lagos. In the period before 1877, the disruption in trade had ruined many small Saro as well as indigenous Lagosian traders and not a few of the more important European and Saro merchants. The method by which the Lagos government sought to deal with the problem varied between non-interference, which was for a long time the official British policy, and interference spiced with occasional armed demonstration and invasion. The Saros, in the postures they assumed, present a picture of inconsistency born out of conflicting loyalties.[37] As traders, they were concerned, like their European competitors, to protect their trading stations and contacts in Yorubaland and were therefore not slow to demand British intervention as occasion warranted. Opposition to intervention stemmed from those who had little confidence in the way policy was applied and those for whom opposition was politically convenient. For in the rivalry between the different sub-ethnic Saro groups, some of the groups showed great concern to safeguard only the interests and the sovereignty of states with which they were connected. But whatever was the real strength of the enemies of intervention before 1877, it was undermined by the general hardship which the outbreak of the Sixteen Years' War brought to the people of Lagos. In the 1880s and 1890s, trade was in the doldrums and depression set in.[38] Instability, uncertainty and anxiety in economic activity reached a new peak, and the position was not relieved by a stalemate in the fighting. It seemed obvious to the commercial community as well as to the government that for Lagos to survive, the hostilities in the interior must be terminated.

Saro traders, big and small, saw their economic prospects bound up with those of the Lagos colony as a whole but there was a significant reason why the lack of peace in the Yoruba country worried the Saros most. Many of them, particularly the well-educated ones, out of considerations of racial pride and nationalist feeling, were inclined to demonstrate that the only difference between them and Europeans was the colour of the skin. They sought, among other things, to show that they were the equal of any white man in business acumen and organisation. They, therefore, rejected the idea of working under European direction and strove to succeed not only on their own but in direct competition with the European traders. However, unlike the European traders, the Saros had a limited supply of capital and were no match for their European competitors, particularly in critical periods. This was appreciated by those who up to the middle 1880s entered the trade between Lagos and the River Niger. They were eliminated and commercially crushed and some of them had to attempt to earn their livelihood by founding newspapers. In the trade between Lagos and Yorubaland, the Saros were at an advantage over their European competitors in that being 'sons of the soil', they profitably exploited their contacts and connections to strengthen their position as middlemen. They thus had a good chance of at least holding their own against the European traders. For this class of Saros, therefore, to tolerate general insecurity and hostility in the Yoruba interior was to perpetuate European economic dominance in Lagos.

For the newspapermen, it must be emphasised, the depressing economic situation in the 1880s and after was particularly burdensome and economic considerations must have outweighed ethnicist and patriotic feelings among newspapermen, like R. B. Blaize and perhaps a few others, who had noteworthy connections with the Yoruba interior. All the newspapermen, at least up to the end of the nineteenth century, were traders, their trading activity varying from the large establishments of Blaize and J. S. Leigh, to the commercial agencies of John Jackson.[39] They therefore shared the anxieties of the commercial community. In addition, however, the conflict threatened not only the advertisement patronage which kept the newspapers alive but also the possible expansion of the newspaper market into the interior of Yorubaland. The newspaper circulation in Lagos, which in the 1890s fluctuated between 300 and 500 a week at threepence per copy, cried for expansion into the hinterland but the roads inland were no better than forest paths and hostilities there added the problem of insecurity to that of poor communications. Humanitarian considerations and economic self-interest were thus the factors which provoked the educated elite to embark on an unusual pro-British crusade. The factors destroyed the capacity of the educated elite to perceive that they were unwittingly encouraging the supercession of indigenous authority and the enthronement of British sovereignty in Yorubaland. Time was to elapse before the scales were to fall from their eyes to reveal to them, in retrospect, the naivety of their imagination that Britain's role in Yorubaland could be that of a disinterested arbitrator.

In the three issues of the *Lagos Times* before the year ran out, the newspaper gave its full support to advocates of positive executive action.[40] In 1881, it continued to emphasise that the British policy of non-intervention was 'altogether ruinous and suicidal'. From the nature of the matter, it frequently argued, the Lagos government could not, without inflicting untold miseries upon the colony, refuse to 'inter-meddle' in the politics of the interior.[41] The same note was struck the following year by the *Observer* when it appeared. It deprecated the 'impunity with which every petty ruler' could disturb the peace of Lagos and called on the government to relax its 'deplorable high tension of indifference'.[42] In 1884, the *Observer* assured the government that the 'brethren on the mainland' would readily welcome the intervention of a foreign power.[43] When the intervention of Governor Moloney in 1886 resulted in the suspension of hostilities, which proved to be only temporary, the *Observer* congratulated the Governor most enthusiastically, rejoicing at the prospect of delivery from the 'prolonged and dreadful carnage'.[44] The resumption of hostilities and other bellicose developments decided the British Government to establish a garrison at Ilaro in Egba territory. In reaction, the Egba interdicted trade and their Ijebu allies closed their roads. The attitude of these Yoruba governments was condemned by the *Weekly Times* which, romanticising the administration of John Glover in the 1860s, recalled the 'palmy past' of the colony when, as the newspaper put it, the government possessed sufficient influence with the interior peoples to have its behests attended to and its wishes complied with. A policy of 'non-intervention and apathy' had cost the colony that influence and it was now necessary to assert it forcibly.[45] When, the following year, Ilaro and Ado were annexed to Lagos, the *Weekly Record* saw the action as marking a turning point in British policy. The annexation was 'highly politic and satisfactory' evincing 'a determination to endeavour to promote the interest and welfare of the colony by adopting more tactile and effectual methods in dealing with the surrounding native tribes'. While hoping that the action was an indication of the vigour with which the government's hinterland policy would be pursued, the newspaper remarked that while there would be those who would frown at the action as an infringement of the rights of African chiefs, the 'majority of intelligent natives' would regard it as 'an imperative initiatory step' towards the future well-being of Yorubaland. [46]

The demand by Nigerian newspapers for British intervention in Yorubaland reached a new intensity with the arrival of Governor G. T. Carter in September 1891. Carter believed that the Egba and the Ijebu were the major obstacles to peace and that they must therefore be broken. It may fairly be said that it was the joint vehemence of the press and the Governor that produced a military solution to the 'Interior Question'. Only the *Weekly Record* was existing at the time and its militancy was comparable with Carter's aggression. The Governor's pinpricks against the Egba and the Ijebu were lauded by the newspaper which hailed Carter's 'determination and firmness of purpose'. Regarding the apology demanded from the Ijebu people for an alleged insult to Acting Governor Denton whose 'gifts' were rejected by the Awujale in April 1891, the *Record* blamed what happened on 'pernicious influences in the interior' which must be removed 'in a determined and effectual effort'. However much it might deprecate a resort to violence to achieve this end, the newspaper could not but confess to 'a feeling of relief' in finding the government pledged to a definite and determined policy. [47] And when in January 1892 an Ijebu deputation held a peace meeting with Carter in Lagos, the editor of the *Record* was officially invited to attend. [48]

During the next three months, the *Record* constituted itself the assessor of Egba and Ijebu policy. So keen was it on a showdown that when in March a rumour spread that a contingent of Indian troops was *en route* for Lagos, it commented, their 'presence would impress the interior peoples that resistance would be futile'. [49] The *Record*'s interest in armed intervention outran the wishes of a section of its readers some of whom wrote to criticise it. Opposite views were also expressed in the Legislative Council where the two African members, C. J. George and Rev. James Johnson, warned against a resort to violence. [50] The *Record*, however, thought little of such 'narrow conservatism'. [51]

Convinced that the opening and maintenance of interior routes will confer a great and lasting benefit upon the country at large, we cannot permit our sentiments of patriotism to impair our judgements or deaden our instincts of right and reason; we are therefore bound to give our adhesion and support to measures calculated to produce the greatest good, or to promote the interest of the largest majority. And we feel confident that in this determination we have the endorsement and sympathy of all right-minded intelligent natives.

In the three months that followed, the *Record* ceaselessly denounced the Egba and Ijebu and happily announced that it was only a question of time before they became an integral part of Lagos. The warmongering propaganda of the *Record* certainly played a key role in the events of 1892. Its uninstigated belligerence, which had a large measure of public support evidenced by a rise in the circulation of the newspaper,[52] must have made a strong impression on the mind of Carter and convinced him that his policy had the support of at least a majority of the thinking public and perhaps also of the general population whose economic interests in this case coincided with those of the educated elite. The interpretation must have contributed to accentuate 'punitive' feelings on the part of the Lagos government and to have driven it to a more uncompromising position. In May, the Lagos government found cause to launch the so-called Ijebu Expedition. John Jackson accompanied the Lagos army as Special Correspondent and sent back graphic reports of the 'sharp and decisive' operations of the troops.[53]

Jackson's involvement in the Anglo-Ijebu war made such a favourable impression on Carter that he unhesitatingly but unsuccessfully urged the British Government to grant the journalist a military medal.[54] Indeed, John Jackson's role war was in the the genesis of a lifelong friendship between him and Carter. The Governor sought and respected the editor's advice and, by way of assistance, paid him from public funds an annual subsidy of about £150 ostensibly for advertising space. All this assistance and friendship was not exactly calculated to enhance the independence of the *Record*. Indeed, Jackson became over-appreciative of Carter' work and put the *Record* in the awkward and ultimately impossible position of being at one and the same time the mouthpiece of the people and an ally of the government.

To return to the Anglo-Ijebu war, the *Record*, exuding a new self-confidence born out of a sense of victory and of power, now directed a fusillade of words against the Egba people. It mounted a campaign of denunciation aimed at provoking another war. Commenting on the failure in July of a diplomatic mission to Abeokuta, the newspaper asserted that:

> It is impossible that the progress of development and civilization in Africa should be retarded by the ignorant caprice of native chiefs and all opposition made by them to such progress, only tends to diminish the chances of their rights being recognized or their independence maintained.[55]

During the next few months, the *Record* regularly invoked the spectre of the fate of 'Jebu' to terrorise the Egba and, indeed, any other Yoruba state whose policy it considered unfriendly to Lagos: for example, the people of Ijebu-Remo whom it warned to demonstrate their 'friendly neutrality' by opening their markets to uninterrupted trade. The fury of the newspaper's intimidation must have helped to drive the Egba to capitulate and avoid violence. For thanks to pro-Egba pressure in and outside Lagos, it was possible to resolve Anglo-Egba differences without adopting the extreme course of going to war. Carter's celebrated 'diplomatic' mission of 1893 in which he brought the Yoruba wars to an end and established treaty relations with Yoruba rulers brought to the *Record* the delight and satisfaction of having played a leading role in the triumph of a cause.[56]

Carter's return to Lagos from the hinterland was a remarkable event. A crowd estimated at 3 000 welcomed him to the island in what the *Record* described as 'inexpressible ecstasy and enthusiasm'.[57] Every section of the community was said to have 'united with one genuine rapturous accord to tender their hearty greetings and congratulations'.[58] On 17 April, the Chamber of Commerce organised a banquet to congratulate the Governor on his 'tranquillization of the interior'. 116 guests attended. An address was presented by 'merchants, traders and residents of Lagos' in which they expressed their 'high appreciation' at the 'unprecedented success' which had distinguished the Governor's administration. They lauded Carter's 'administrative experience . . . coupled with diplomatic tact and judgement' in dealing with Nigerian questions. Among the 52 signatories were C. J. George, J. W. Cole, D. C. Taiwo, J. P. Jackson, J. A. Savage and S. H. Pearse.[59]

From the foregoing, it seems obvious that the paramount factor which determined the attitude of the Nigerian newspaper press to the British invasion of Yorubaland was economic. The extent to which considerations of trade were crucial is amply attested by the fact that where the commercial interests of the educated elite were not directly involved, the newspapers voiced strong opposition in defence of the sovereignty of African states and the preservation of the African race.

The Nigerian press was strongly opposed to the Berlin West African Conference and stigmatised European staking of claims to African territory as 'high-handed robbery'. At a public debate in February 1885, the motion that 'the present efforts of European countries to acquire and to increase their possessions . . . and to develop their commercial interests therein, are calculated to be an advantage to Africa and the African race generally' was overwhelmingly rejected.[60] Between 1886 and 1890, the Nigerian newspaper press waged a relentless war against the Royal Niger Company and company rule generally. Supported by influential British opponents of the company, the press strenuously campaigned against the extension of its influence to the Oil Rivers and for the revocation of its Charter which was effected in 1899.[61]

French aggression in Dahomey in 1892 was denounced at the same time as British aggression in Yorubaland was being ardently supported. The *Record* fulminated against the 'impatience and impetuousity' of the French character contrasting the 'irksome and intolerable' nature of the French colonial system with that of the British which was 'more appreciable and palatable'. The newspaper denounced French designs on Dahomey which it believed were motivated by the quest for the accumulated wealth of the Dahomeyan kings.[62] So personally involved was J. P. Jackson in the Dahomeyan resistance that in March 1893, he drew up a catalogue of French atrocities in Dahomey which he submitted to world opinion on behalf of King Gbehanzin Ayiyijere Bowele. In October, he accepted Gbehanzin's invitation to accompany a Dahomeyan diplomatic mission to France to seek the French President's intervention in the Franco-Dahomeyan war.[63]

The role of the *Record* in the Dahomeyan resistance was comparable with its stand in Samori Ture's confrontation of the French. Samori (or Samadu), a distinguished Mandingo chief, was drawn into war with the French in 1887, defeated eleven years later and deported to what is now Congo Brazzaville where he died in 1900. The *Record* thought that given the opportunity, Samori 'would have been a useful and powerful instrument in the work of tribal consolidation'.[64] As a token of esteem for Samori, Jackson named his printing press 'Samadu Press' and his premises on the Marina 'Samadu quarters'.

What about the extension of British supremacy in parts of Nigeria other than Yorubaland? The earliest manifestation of newspaper opposition to European activity considered to be disruptive of established African authority was concerned with the banishment of King Jaja of Opobo. Deported to the West Indies in 1887 for his stubbornness in defending his sovereignty and commercial interests against the encroachments of a British commercial faction, Jaja was hailed by Nigerian newspapers as epitomising the resentment of Africans to European intrusion. Throughout 1887 and 1888, 'Jaja's scandalous episode' constituted a regular editorial topic.

Similar censures were published in 1894 over the British war against Nana Olomu, Governor of the Benin River. Like Jaja, Nana experienced military defeat, trial and deportation (to the Gold Coast) for offering resistance to the intruding British power. The *Record*, which only the previous year was jubilant over Carter's 'tranquilization' of Yorubaland, deplored the war. When news of the Ebrohimi war reached Lagos, the *Record* made a typical comment:

> To the African anxious for the preservation of his race, there is something despairingly distressing in the spectacle of Native chiefs and tribes being hunted down and made fugitives throughout Africa by civilized nations armed with the murderous weapons of modern warfare.[65]

Nana surrendered to the British in Lagos, where his cause became a public issue as a result of John Jackson's intervention. He had an extensive interview with Nana which he published and commented upon. Nana's account of events moved John Jackson deeply and in an editorial, he attacked British newspapers for their distorted versions of the causes of the Ebrohimi war and sought to arouse public sympathy for Nana and to influence the Lagos government in his favour. He was powerless to prevent Nana's trial and deportation by the Niger Coast Protectorate government but by keeping the issue alive and by providing strong newspaper backing for the campaign in Nigeria and Britain for Nana's release,

John Jackson played an important role in securing the return of the Itsekiri leader from exile in 1906.

The circumstances which led to the sack of Benin in 1897 did not escape the censure of the Nigerian press. The *Record*, on 16 January, deplored the tragedy of Acting Consul-General Phillips of the Niger Coast Protectorate but blamed him for having displayed much 'indiscretion, rashness . . . ill-advised imperiousness or recklessness'. It claimed that Phillips' action was indicative of the contempt and disregard in which the British official held the indigenous African ruler and concluded:

> The African being more sincere in his attachment regards this attitude of the foreigner a downright sacrilege and does his best to resent it. And taking into consideration the many formalities exacted in civilized countries in connection with Royalty and the importance which is attached to them, the African is hardly to be blamed for any excesses he may commit in resenting an outrage upon what he regards as his most sacred traditions.

In a second editorial on 23 January, the *Record* scolded those who advocated the 'smash up' of Benin. Such suggestions were 'wild-brained' and a policy of retaliation detracted from the Christian principles which were supposed 'to actuate and influence civilized Governments'.

The *Standard* withheld its judgment until the British sack of Benin and then joined the *Record* in denouncing the 'avaricious whiteman' and calling the punitive expedition a 'national blunder and (an) agregious robbery'.[66] Then quite suddenly a most dramatic thing happened. The *Standard* made no further comment and the *Record* stopped publishing for two weeks. When the *Record* returned to the streets, it had executed a dramatic *volte-face*. Without any explanation or the merest hint of its reasons, it began to praise the British attack on Benin which immediately before its temporary suspension it had condemned in the strongest terms. It described the sack of Benin as 'just retribution for the dreadful act of slaughter perpetrated by that people'.[67]

> The attack upon and murder of the peaceful mission, was a premeditated and carefully planned measure and which was carried out with unrelenting savage ferocity upon white officials and the native carriers. The narrative (written by 'one of the few survivors of the dreadful disaster') can but awaken a feeling of intensified horror at the ghastly massacre in cold blood of hundreds of unarmed men on a mission of peace. . . .

For the next few months, Benin became the favourite spot on which the *Record* and foreign newspapers focused their attention. The former reproduced with enthusiasm comments and features from a number of imaginative, highly prejudiced and sensation-mongering British newspapers (chief among which was the *Times Weekly Edition*) which delighted in pouring ridicule on African institutions and depicting Oba Ovonranwen as a 'savage'.[68]

What caused this dramatic reversal? What could have caused Williams's reticence in the *Standard* and driven Jackson to humiliate himself before the Nigerian public? The single editorial in the *Standard* after Benin fell was severe and exhaustive which perhaps made any further comment on the matter unnecessary. The more puzzling thing is the *Record*'s change of camp.

Two possible explanations immediately come to mind. First, Jackson might have accompanied the expedition and, afforded the opportunity to carry out his own investigations, changed his attitude on the basis of his findings. But this does not explain the two-week suspension of the newspaper. He usually had people to act for him when he was away on such missions. In any case, it would have been obvious from the *Record* that it had a temporary 'special correspondent' at Benin. Secondly, the Samadu Press might have broken down and by the time printing resumed, Jackson had reappraised the whole situation and turned anti-Benin. The objection here is that Jackson would have apologised for the break in publication and given some hint why he changed camp.

It is evidently difficult to provide a completely satisfactory explanation for what happened but it seems fairly obvious that Jackson had come under tremendous pressure most probably from the entire European community in Lagos. He derived his major source of revenue from advertisements inserted by the European firms and it does seem from oral accounts that the European merchants, irritated by his apparent approval of what they must have considered to be inexcusable crime, threatened to withdraw their patronage unless he changed his tune. Jackson, unprepared to lose his advertisement patronage and subsidy – that would have meant the collapse of his enterprise – but anxious to protect his editorial independence, presumably had to suspend publication while he reappraised the whole situation. It must have been a difficult decision for Jackson to make and whether the most honourable way out would have been to accept the challenge of the

European commercial patrons and bear the painful consequences will remain an open question.

Notwithstanding the aberration of the Benin about-face, the *Record*, in the nine years that followed, joined its contemporaries in mounting vigorous opposition against the expansion of British influence in Nigeria. Most of the wars which led to the establishment of British rule in the former Northern Nigeria were wholly resented and given bad publicity. The view was repeatedly expressed that the expeditions were inspired by considerations of self-aggrandizement. 'The unhappy policy' observed the *Record*, 'which forms a feature of British rule and makes it necessary for expeditions to be undertaken in order to give a chance to the military element to do something and earn cheap glory has found sad verification in the case of Northern Nigeria.'[69] Said the *Standard*, 'the opportunities those expeditions offer of achieving cheap military fame and preferments are sometimes too great to be resisted'.[70] The wars against Nupe and Ilorin in 1897 were decried and when rumours reached Lagos early in 1903 of a projected expedition against Kano and Sokoto, the newspapers expressed strong disapproval. 'This ancient and famous kingdom,' the *Standard* lamented, 'this land of peace and plenty . . . should now incur the fate of the destruction and desolation inseparable from military expeditions.'[71] An article in the *Manchester Guardian* critical of British policy towards Sokoto was reproduced in this newspaper. It is not surprising that when the Satiru Rebellion broke out in February 1906 posing a major threat to the survival of British ascendancy in 'Northern Nigeria', the event was applauded by the press.[72]

The newspapers also concerned themselves with similar developments in the southern parts of the country. When towards the end of 1901 preparations was being made for the Arochuku Expedition in Igboland, the *Record* remonstrated against what it called the 'mission of war and bloodshed'.[73] By the end of 1905, the persistency of warfare had forced the newspaper to the conclusion that the British administration of the country had become 'a system of violence and war'.[74]

The theme of resistance to the imposition of alien rule has always emphasised the incidence of military confrontation but, as this survey indicates, the intellectual leadership of the movement of resistance cannot be ignored. The moral assistance provided for victims of alien penetration and conquest, the involvement of the newspapers in anti-imperialism propaganda, the influence of the opposition press on liberal opinion in Britain regarding British imperial policy in Nigeria: all these are difficult to evaluate with any precision but there can be no doubt that the newspaper press was an important instrument of resistance to foreign domination. No doubt, there were inconsistencies in the attitudes of the newspapermen but these were not entirely abnormal in the circumstances prevailing at the time. Absurdities of alliances and associations were hardly avoidable in the atmosphere of unsettled ideological perception and myopic economic ambitions which characterised the attitude of the educated Nigerians in the last two decades of the nineteenth century. By 1900, however, the situation had changed considerably with important consequences for the tone and outlook of the newspapers. In the next chapter, we shall examine the background and essence of this development.

Notes

1 Akin L. Mabogunje, *Urbanization in Nigeria*, London, 1968, p. 241.
2 *Lagos Standard*, 5 December 1902.
3 See J. U. Egharevba, *A Short History of Benin*, Ibadan University Press, 1968; J. B. O. Losi, *A History of Lagos*, Lagos, 1967; J. B. Wood, *Historical Notices of Lagos, West Africa*, Lagos, 1878.
4 C.O. 147/142, MacGregor to Chamberlain, 5 May 1899; C.O. 147/145; 147/156, C.O. 147/166, MacGregor to Chamberlain, 4 December 1899, 11 January 1901, 14 July 1903.
5 See *Lagos Standard*, 29 May 1895.
6 *Lagos Times*, 12 July 1882.
7 *Lagos Weekly Record*, 6 December 1897.
8 *Lagos Times*, 11 January 1882.
9 *Weekly Record*, 5 May 1894.
10 *Lagos Standard*, 11 January 1899. Also 25 January, 22 February 1899; 31 August, 1904; 1 February 1905.
11 *Lagos Standard*, 16 June 1909, 1 September 1909; 31 March 1900; 6 July 1904.
12 Janus, 'Lagosian On Dits', *Lagos Standard*, 11 January 1899.
13 12 July 1882.
14 13 September 1882.
15 *Lagos Times*, 8 November 1882.
16 A Native to *Lagos Times*, 22 August 1883.
17 C.O. 147/60, Moloney to Holland Bart, 31 May 1887.
18 For a scholarly study of Blyden, see Hollis Lynch, *Edward Wilmot Blyden, 1832–1912*, London, 1907.

19 16 May 1909.
20 16 May 1908. Also 25 April 1908.
21 22 January 1896.
22 1 July 1908.
23 11 March 1896; 28 August 1907.
24 18 March, 25 March 1896.
25 28 March 1896.
26 Henry Carr to *Lagos Standard*, 22 July 1908.
27 See *Lagos Standard*, 2 August 1898.
28 14 November 1903.
29 26 February 1896.
31 23 April 1904; 27 August 1904.
30 21 May 1908.
32 31 July 1901.
33 27 July 1900.
34 26 August, 28 October 1893; 26 November 1904.
35 See E. A. Ayandele, 'An Assessment of James Johnson and his place in Nigerian History, 1874–1917', Part I (1874–1890). *JHSN*, ii, 4, 1963, pp. 486–517.
36 S. H. Brown, 'A History of the People of Lagos 1852–1886', unpublished Ph.D. thesis, June, 1964, p. 87.
37 A standard work on this subject is S. O. Biobaku, *The Egba and their neighbours, 1842–72*, Oxford, 1957.
38 C. W. Newbury, *The Western Slave Coast and its rulers*, Oxford, 1961, p. 94; *Lagos Observer*, 15, 22 May 1886.
39 The agency system was established on the coast in the 1820s by which British firms in the United Kingdom sent goods on credit to West African representatives in exchange for shipment of palm oil.
40 24 November, 8 December 1880.
41 See 27 April 1881; also 6 January, 3 February, 14 April, 25 May, 23 November 1881.
42 2, 16 March 1882.
43 28 February, 24 April, 25 September 1884.
44 17 April, 1 May, 15 & 22 May, 5 June 1886.
45 See, for example, 17 May 1890.
46 29 August 1891.
47 7 November, 19 December 1891. Also 16, 23 January 1892.
48 For an account of the meeting, see *Lagos Weekly Record* 23, 30 January 1892.
49 19 March 1892.
50 *Legislative Council minutes*, 19 April 1892. See also 27 November 1891; 18 June 1892.
51 5 March 1892. Also 12, 19, 26 March; 9, 16 April; 7, 14 May 1892; 29 April 1893.
52 Various correspondents remarked upon the increased popularity of the *Record*. See, for example, issue of 16 April 1892.
53 It has been claimed that Ijebu-Ode would have been set on fire but for Jackson's presence of mind. He reportedly detected the white flag which the Ijebu people hoisted in surrender and swiftly contacted the

British commander who ordered his men to cease fire. See 'Kekere Ilu', *Eko Akete*, 1 August 1925.

54 C.O. 147/86, Carter to Ripon, 21 December 1892.

55 9 July 1892. The *Record* would stick to this opinion long after the enthusiasm over British interference had cooled:

> Millions of people spread over a vast extent of fertile country, speaking the same language or at least understanding each other, have dissipated their national life in a multitude of little munici- palities with rulers that do not rule, each trying to establish a separate influence for itself, impatient of subjection, constantly fighting for precedence and ascendancy and raising insurmountable obstacles in the way of their own progress. It should be considered an inestimable blessing that a great foreign power has come in to aid them to settle their differences, to allay their jealousies and point out at least the possibility of consolidating the scattered elements of what might be a great nation.

56 14 January, 28 January 1892; 4 March, 18 March, 25 March 1893.

57 5 April 1893.

58 *Lagos Weekly Record*, 22 April 1893.

59 C.O. 147/89, Denton to Ripon, 19 April 1893 (Enclosure I).

60 *Lagos Observer*, 19 February 1885; 16 April 1885, *Eagle and Lagos Critic*, 31 January 1885.

61 *Lagos Observer*, 19 February 1887; 21 May, 4 June 1887; 11 and 12 January; 22 March 1890.

62 12 November 1892. Also 12 September 1891; 27 August 1892.

63 *Manchester Guardian*, 3 November 1892, reprinted in *Lagos Weekly Record*, 2 December 1893. The envoys left Lagos in October 1893 and arrived in France on 20 December.

64 28 July 1900.

65 6 October 1894.

66 24 February 1897.

67 27 February 1897.

68 See, for example, 'The Benin Massacre, An Account of Benin and its King', *Times Weekly Edition* (n.d.), reprinted *Weekly Record*, 20 March 1897.

69 12 September 1903.

70 5 June 1901; 20 November 1901; 4 February 1903.

71 4 February 1903. *Lagos Weekly Record*, 21 February 1903.

72 *Lagos Weekly Record*, 3 March 1906.

73 9 November 1901.

74 10 December 1905.

5 A new ferocity and unanimity of opposition

From 1900, a new ferocity entered into the involvement of the newspaper press in Nigerian politics. Various government policies, at least during the previous decade, had attracted censorious reactions but these were muted rumblings compared with the torrent of agitation which threatened to overwhelm the governments from that of Governor MacGregor onwards until other instruments of high pressure agitation began to emerge from the third decade of the century. It was as if political activity in the nineties had perpetuated the moderate and respectable tone of the eighties and the placid mood had suddenly given way to an eruption of scathing attacks. Although there were important controversies in the late nineties, controversies whose tone the *Indianapolis Freeman* thought was 'pitched high enough for imitation' in the United States,[1] the new temper of uncompromising opposition and prolonged agitation gives a different dimension to the controversies which began from the first decade of the present century.

A number of considerations help to explain the increased hostility of the newspapers. In the first place, the cultural and anti-imperial emphasis of the 1890s had resolved itself into more practical political agitation by the end of the century. In mounting propaganda against cultural enslavement and imperial conquest, the newspapers intensified the spirit of criticism and unrest in the society. Secondly, the new critical temper can be seen as a positive expression of the sense of frustration experienced by the educated Nigerians in their relationship with the colonial government. After the British occupation of Yorubaland, every action of the government began to increase the disappointment and indignation of those who had sought British 'pacification' but who were gradually grasping the significance of the British intervention and regretting their interventionist zeal. These had begun to see themsleves as 'the dupes of an easily accommodated administration'

132

which by a master stroke had taken over Yorubaland. The awakening anti-British mood was not soothed by the social and economic
results of British invasion. The economic arguments which under-
lay the movement of 'tranquillization' were not justified by results.
According to the *Standard*, 'the idea which was a potent factor in
bringing about the Ijebu war, of a country beyond, exceeding rich
in natural products, has long ago been exploded by actual experience and more accurate knowledge'.[2] The 'smash–up' of Ijebu-
Ode was followed by what was described as a 'deadlock on trade'
and the government was constrained in 1889 to set up a five-man
commission, including R. B. Blaize, to study and report on the
situation. Furthermore, although the British presence was advertised as a guarantee of peace and order in Yorubaland, a new
horror emerged in the authoritarian activities of the District and
Travelling Commissioners, most of whom were military men, who
were stationed in Yorubaland as administrators. A newspaper
remarked that 'nothing but dissatisfaction, disruption and disorganisation' followed in their train.[3]

If the British commissioners flogged the people with whips, the
soldiers under them flogged them with scorpions. The soldiers,
who were mostly Hausa-speaking, allegedly plundered, looted and
raped. The *Standard* in 1895 reported the situation:[4]

> From time to time reports have been borne to this colony testifying
> that they have ceased to keep the peace, that on the contrary they have
> turned themselves loose upon the people filling up the role vacated by
> kidnappers and rioters . . . marauders and freebooters. From Ijebu to
> the further interior there is one painful cry echoing from town to
> town, from city to city of the evil deeds of the Lagos constabulary.
> Goods have been seized from traders, maidens have been assaulted,
> youths have been plundered, men have been brow-beaten, women
> have been robbed . . . fresh dread, doubt and unrest prevail in the
> country.

The bitterness which the activities of the soldiers provoked in
Lagos and Yorubaland reached its highest point when the Awujale
of Ijebu-Ode in 1896 had to seek asylum from them in Lagos. A
wave of dissatisfaction swept through the land and spurred the
Lagos government to intervene, albeit without much success. The
soldiers were eventually replaced with policemen, but they were
also accused of 'blackmailing, looting, terrorism and unbridled
license'.[5]

Government interpreters in Yorubaland increased popular aversion to the British presence. Like the court-clerks in the Warrant Chief System of the former Eastern Nigeria early in this century, the interpreters arrogated much power to themselves and ordered arrests purporting to have been ordered by the British administrators. The interpreters were often responsible for misunderstandings and consequent conflicts between the British officials and the indigenous authorities.

Finally, and most importantly, Britain, with a new self-confidence gained from her sense of conquest, was quick to underline the reality of her power in Yorubaland. In 1895 at Ibadan, she hoisted the Union Jack and proceeded to grant to a European firm based in Accra (Messrs F. & A. Swanzy) a monopoly for the collection of rubber in the district. That same year, to the further astonishment of the people of Lagos, the palace of the Alafin of Oyo was bombarded and partially burnt on the orders of Captain R. C. Bower, the Resident at Ibadan. These and similar incidents aroused widespread anxiety about the constitutional position of the British hinterland government and what was enthusiastically hailed as 'a master piece of diplomacy' increasingly became a source of profound distrust. The educated elite and their newspapers now began a long but belated struggle to arrest total British occupation and control by fighting doggedly in the interest of the indigenous states whose sovereignty they had helped to undermine and destroy.

The third explanation of the new fervour of press opposition was the decisive re-entry of John Jackson into opposition politics. This issue is of fundamental importance to an understanding of the role of the *Record* in politics and it is necessary that it be gone into in some detail. We referred in Chapter 2 to the lasting friendship between Governor Carter and John Jackson. As was indicated, the editor's collaboration with the Governor resulted in a rather curious ambivalence. In such issues as European imperialism (outside Yorubaland) and cultural nationalism, John Jackson displayed his characteristic vigour and brilliance; but in local political questions, he tended to proceed to the uninspiring defence of the government or at best offered a mild criticism. For example, he failed to join the widespread criticism of the excesses of the occupation soldiers in Yorubaland, preferring to make apologies for their misbehaviour and to advise their victims to bear their afflictions 'philosophically'. Although he protested against the bombardment of Oyo in 1895, unlike George Alfred Williams, he seemed over-anxious to express his regrets when investigations apparently cleared the government of blame. Three years later, in the post-Carter period, he would accuse the *Sierra Leone Weekly News* of 'transcending the bounds of legitimate criticism' for referring to Governor MacCallum as an utterly inexperienced officer'. Not that John Jackson's support for Carter was total or indiscriminatory; indeed, over a number of domestic issues, he spoke his own mind. For instance, in the agitation against the proposal to introduce electricity rates in 1896, his leadership of the movement made a strong impression on Acting Governor Denton.[6] But the fact remained that between 1891 and 1896, the *Record* assumed the character more of an ally of the government than in a vehicle of popular opinion.

Those opposed to John Jackson's policy accused him of 'pandering to officialism . . . at the expense of the public weal', but it is noteworthy that these same people also conceded that his views on matters of public interest 'carried great weight in official circles'.[7] What sort of weight his views carried and in what direction are difficult to ascertain but it was generally known that Governor Carter regularly sought Jackson's advice and had much admiration for his candour and capability. It is notable that John Jackson succeeded in creating for himself a position of privilege and influence under Carter's administration while at the same time he continued to enjoy a large measure of public support. The circulation of the *Record* continued to grow, although its rate was not as rapid as that of the *Standard* after it was launched in 1894.[8] Nonetheless, the fact remains that many important Nigerians spoke with concealed envy about John Jackson's favoured status and did not hesitate to employ his good offices to advance their own interests.

Jackson's collaboration with Carter enabled him simultaneously to advance his campaign of cultural nationalism without equivocation and to remain basically faithful to his anti-imperialist position, which by implication subverted the very basis of the Lagos government. He would from time to time disagree vehemently with the government to the astonishment of his critics who wished to see more of such 'departures'.

The kind of relationship that developed between Governor Carter and John Jackson was rather unusual and it is essential that the circumstances be fully appreciated. In Jackson's capacity as adviser, he seems to have become involved in the mechanics of government so much so that he came increasingly to see problems from a more practical and sympathetic perspective, to appreciate the Governor's receptivity to African advice and to be drawn closer into the Carter/Blyden orbit. Blyden and Carter had become acquainted in the 1880s and grew to be great friends. It was at the Governor's instance that Blyden was appointed Agent for Native Affairs in Lagos in March 1896.[9] Carter adopted many of Blyden's ideas; for example, on Islam, polygamy and the need for a West African University.[10] When Carter was forced to retire prematurely in October 1896 on account of ill-health, Blyden expressed misgivings about his continued stay in Lagos.[11] He eventually resigned at the end of 1897. It is possible that the administration of Lagos for most of 1896 was a triumvirate of Carter, Blyden and Jackson. Indeed, it might well be that Jackson's admiration of Blyden and Blyden's estimation of Carter provide the key to the genesis as well as the essence of the Carter–Jackson friendship.

After Governor Carter's departure, an unmistakable note of change emerged in the *Record*. The possibly lingering mediating effect of governmental experience and the need to safeguard the subsidy came to weigh much less than the impact of Carter's absence, the growth of rival newspapers, especially the *Standard*, and perhaps John Jackson's sense of humiliation in the 1897 drama. Jackson's policy in the nineteenth and early twentieth centuries can be said to have undergone an evolution – from partial collaboration in the Carter era, to a more positive realignment in the late 1890s and fervent and total opposition from 1900. The realignment was reflected in various anti-government actions, including his strong criticism of the government's decision to site the coast-end terminus of the proposed railway at Iddo, rather than in the Lagos Island as demanded by Lagos merchants; his denunciation of the mishandling of the insurrection scare of the same year which led the European population, acting on the advice of Governor McCallum, to take precautions for their defence against a supposedly rebellious African populace, and his vehement opposition to the attempt in 1899 to codify and amplify the existing criminal laws in a bid to increase the coercive powers of the government.[12] Governor McCallum apparently rode out the newspaper storm, but his successor, William MacGregor, was less accommodating. Probably seeking to re-enact the drama of

Jackson's rout of 1897, he decided to discontinue the advertisement subsidy arrangement. Jackson would naturally have anticipated this punitive action in the light of his increasing dissociation from government and his response was to take up the
gauntlet and intensify the nationalist struggle. Jackson's new path
of journalism was followed by George Williams and the joint
vehemence of their two newspapers defined the tone of political
activity for a long time.

JURISDICTIONAL DISPUTES

Against the backdrop of the rising tide of press antagonism, a
crisis developed over the constitutional status of the Yoruba
Kingdoms. The treaties and agreements made between the British
Crown and the chiefs of Yorubaland in the 1880s and 1890s
defined the limit of British power and authority in the Lagos
Protectorate. Many of these treaties recognised the independence
of the contracting kingdoms with the result that when the colonial
government sought to expand its authority and jurisdiction further,
it found that it had to contend with constitutional difficulties
identified and agitated by the educated Nigerians. Its decision in
1901 to assume the power to regulate the cutting of timber and the
collection of rubber in the Lagos Protectorate and also to regulate
local government in the area provoked an antipathy and resistance
the like of which had not been seen before in the Nigerian newspaper press. Officials of the Colonial Office were later to remark
upon 'the violent language' of the opposition press and to acknow-
ledge the vehemence of its campaign.[13]

The instrument by which the Lagos government sought to
extend its authority in Yorubaland was the Order-in-Council of
24 July 1901 which was to come into operation on 27 August 1901.
Reaction was calm. The *Record* commented:

> Concern has naturally been awakened as to the extent and nature of
> the jurisdiction sought to be exercised under the Order in question
> and which if so exercised must avail in a more or less degree to affect
> the present status of the governments of the Native States of the
> Hinterland and the authority of the ruling chiefs. . . . At any event we
> hardly think that there is any ground for the supposition that the
> authorities contemplate any wholesale incorporation of the hinterland
> area as part of the colony.[14]

What the attitude of the *Record* would be in the unfolding crisis had been clearly indicated in the advice which the newspaper offered to MacGregor six days after he arrived in Lagos on 14 May 1899. 'What is to be guarded against', the *Record* emphasised, 'is the impairment of native authority and the overthrow of existing institutions which can only lead to disorganisation and political and social anarchy.' It is therefore not surprising that the initial attitude of restraint soon disappeared after Governor MacGregor introduced the Forestry Bill in the Legislative Council on 2 September. The aim of the Bill was to conserve timber, rubber and other forest produce by prohibiting such dealings without a licence or concession.[15] A similar measure, introduced in 1897 under Governor MacCallum, had been abandoned after the first reading in response to hostile public opinion. The 1901 measure was a resuscitation and an elaboration of the earlier proposal in addition to raising keener constitutional issues. The first reading of the Bill in the Legislative Council provoked strong opposition from the Nigerian unofficial members.

However, it was the newspaper press that turned the initial skirmishes into a full battle. With great intensity of feeling, the newspapers flayed the government and inspired prolonged public agitation. On 7 September, the *Record* challenged the constitutional right of the Legislative Council to legislate for the Yoruba states for, it was contended, they had never by treaty or otherwise conferred such rights upon the British Crown. The exercise was 'a new and alarming extension of power' and should be resisted. Editorial comments on 14 and 21 September stressed the same theme. Meanwhile the *Standard* had on 11 September stated that all West African people were bound to meet the proposed legislation with 'downright aversion and opposition'. It was a 'hasty, ill-considered legislation framed in arbitrary disregard of solemn treaty obligation'.

On 14 September, a mass meeting of what an official of the Colonial Office described as 'the Chiefs of the town and neighbourhood and over 5000 inhabitants',[16] was held in Balogun Square. The Bill was attacked in the strongest terms and a petition was drawn up by John Jackson which carried 800 signatures. C. J. George presented the petition to the Legislative Council on 24 September, whereupon it was remitted to a Select Committee consisting of two official and two unofficial members, one of whom was a Nigerian.

Meanwhile the Balogun Square rally had been followed by more editorial attack. On 18 September, the *Standard* drew attention to 'the high pitch to which public feeling had been wrought in the community' and a week later was to call for 'cool, cautious and deliberate procedure' in the administration. On 21 September, the *Record* demanded an immediate withdrawal of the Bill. It has been claimed that some of the objections raised against the Bill were met before it was sent to London for allowance on 2 October.[17] However, there was no relaxation of the agitation.

The mood of belligerence persisted and it was an indication of the great surprise and puzzlement generated by the Bill that the *Standard* refused to believe that MacGregor could have been the author. It was 'Downing Street Dictation'. MacGregor was 'too good' to father such a measure: he had identified himself as no other governor since John Glover had done with the Nigerian people; he had gone out of his way to promote cordial relations with indigenous authorities; his speeches at important Nigerian functions had been 'models of statesmanship'. No man with such a record should have introduced the Forestry Bill upon his own initiative. 'The transition is too abrupt, the contradiction too manifest.'[18]

Accounts in the Nigerian press generated sympathetic pressures in the Colonial Office[19] and inspired the Aborigines' Protection Society and the Manchester and Liverpool Chambers of Commerce to oppose MacGregor with the same verve as they opposed Ralph Moor who had also promulgated a Forestry Proclamation for the Protectorate of Southern Nigeria which came into force without manifest public opposition on 11 December 1901. The Colonial Office, much impressed by the strength of the newspaper and humanitarian opposition, impressed upon MacGregor the need to take this into account in meeting some of the important objections raised against the proposed legislation. The Governor was anxious to play down the newspaper opposition and in his reply informed the Colonial Office that he did not deem it necessary to attach any serious importance to the 'utterances' of the newspaper press because it condemned 'practically everything' done by his government. He acknowledged the *Record* as 'the leading newspaper' but falsely and contemptuously dismissed John Jackson as 'a foreigner, a Krooman whose knowledge of forestry, of land tenure, or of the Lagos interior in any form is naturally extremely superficial'.[20] He accused John Jackson of blackmail, alleging that he was offering a relaxation of opposition in exchange for the restoration of his subsidy of £120–£150 discontinued in 1900.[21] MacGregor's conclusion was that 'were the local press to carry weight in matters of administration, government without the concession of special favours to the editors would become an exceedingly difficult task'.

MacGregor's efforts to throw discredit on John Jackson and the Lagos press generally seem to have had some success. A Colonial Office official minuted: 'Opposition of the local press is not only insincere but founded on personal and most improper motives'.[22] There was really no logical basis for this view because it was John Jackson's vigorous opposition to the government which led MacGregor to cut off the subsidy in the first place. The opposition was sincere and founded on patriotic motives and only became more vigorous in reaction to the Governor's supposedly punitive measure. However, whatever weight the official's misinformed opinion carried, MacGregor's compromise proposals apparently won the support of the British Government. On its part the Colonial Office had abandoned its former insistence on uniformity of legislation in the Protectorate of Southern Nigeria and Lagos and thus given MacGregor a freer hand to amend the Bill along the lines he much preferred.[23] On 17 February 1902, the amended Bill which now allowed the local authorities to play a more positive role in the determination of forestry regulations was re-introduced in the Legislative Council. Those who had already dreamt of victory saw the reopening of the question with a feeling of extreme regret and disappointment.[24] In a final protest effort, a mass meeting was held on 20 May 1902 at which a delegation was appointed to wait on the Governor. Twelve leaders, including John Jackson, Dr Randle and Herbert Macaulay, met MacGregor on 21 and 22 May and demanded that the Bill be withdrawn but it was passed into law on 23 May 1902.[26]

The storm of controversy which characterised the years 1901–2 owed its fury to the fact that another jurisdictional dispute had been precipitated coevally with that of the Forestry Bill. In September 1901, MacGregor had also introduced into the Legislative Council the Native Councils Bill which sought to regulate local government in the Lagos Protectorate. The draft legislation provided for the establishment of a Central Native Council for the Colony of Lagos, Provincial and District Councils and Town and Village Councils. There was little that was revolutionary in the

provisions of the Bill, based as they were on MacGregor's predecessor MacCallum's administrative arrangements in Lagos and
Yorubaland. Between 1897 and 1898 Local Councils had been
established in a number of towns in Yorubaland and in 1897 the
Native Advisory Board had been inaugurated for the Colony of
Lagos. Notwithstanding the familiar background to the Native
Councils Bill, the educated Africans felt bewildered by the
'unprecedented revolution' in governmental legislation. The title
of a *Standard*'s comment, 'Troublous Times' effectively captured
the mood of the period. But in spite of strong opposition by the
press, the Nigerian members in the Legislative Council, the
Aborigines' Protection Society and the Manchester Chamber of
Commerce, the Native Councils Ordinance was passed with
minimal change in late October, 1901. 'The Native Councils Bill',
the *Record* had conceded afterwards, 'has been enacted into law . . .
and the principle against which we have contended so strongly,
namely, the right of the local Legislative Council to legislate for
the Hinterland Countries had been established.'

The enactment of the Native Councils Ordinance removed some
of the force from the jurisdictional arguments in the forestry
agitation but this did not reduce intensity of the public outcry. As
we have seen, the agitation continued up to 20 May 1902 when
the law was passed and even some time after. For the newspapers,
the Forestry Ordinance marked MacGregor's final failure as an
administrator. On his arrival in May 1899, he had been described
as 'an enlightened and sagacious administrator'.[27] By the middle of
the following year the 'hopes and expectations' inspired by his
appointment had been 'sadly disappointed'. His policy of 'indifference and drift' showed that he did not have 'an intelligent
and comprehensive conception' of government.[28] At the end of
May 1902, public and departmental administration was seen to be
in 'lamentable disarray' with the government degenerating into a
'vicious and impotent system of arbitrary rule'.[29]

'AUTONOMY' PRESERVED?

It was inevitable that the aftermath of the jurisdictional agitation
would be a keener scrutiny of government policy in Yorubaland.
Rumour had spread in November 1901 that plans were on foot
to introduce legislation to muzzle the press and this had been

confirmed in April 1902[30] but this made no difference to the temper of the newspapers. Like bloodhounds sniffing for clues, they exposed every proposal or decision of government concerning Yorubaland to the most thorough examination. They apparently were itching for another fight which soon ensued over inland tolls. The irony of the situation at this time, however, was that the press and the Governor were in one camp against European traders and the Colonial Office.

Tolls were duties paid on goods passing through the Yoruba Kingdoms and they affected both the caravan trade with the northern parts of Nigeria and the internal trade within Lagos Colony and Protectorate.[31] Both European and African traders paid tolls but whereas the former wanted them abolished, the latter wanted them permanently retained. For various reasons, MacGregor was opposed to the abolition of tolls but he thought he could satisfy the European merchants by introducing some method into the process of toll collection and providing a printed tariff of charges. The tolls at Abeokuta were acceptable to the Europeans, but not those at Ibadan. To them, the 'innovation' of regulating Ibadan tolls was a direct interference with free trade and a violation of nineteenth-century treaty rights. In precipitating the great controversy, the European merchants had the backing of the Manchester and Liverpool Chambers of Commerce whose presentments made a favourable impression on the Colonial Secretary.[32] The battle of the indigenous authorities was fought by the Governor, the Nigerian members of the Legislative Council and most heatedly, by the press.

From about the middle of June 1903 and for the next seven weeks, the toll controversy dominated newspaper activity. The *Record* focused on no other issue between 20 June and 1 August. Seven times in seven weeks, the newspaper launched attacks against opponents of the toll system and carried reports of pro-toll rallies and demonstrations at Ibadan and Abeokuta. It repeatedly warned of the various implications of toll abolition – the invasion of the rights and liberties of the people which it would connote, the undermining of the autonomy of the indigenous states and the subversion of the traditional economic system. What the merchants demanded was that 'the treaty undertakings with the Native States should be cast to the winds and interference in the internal administration of the native government, which His Majesty's Government had solemnly promised would be strictly avoided on its part, carried to the extent of depriving the people of the right of collecting a revenue and reducing them to the position of dependent beggars'. On the idea of annual subsidies to be paid to local authorities in lieu of toll revenue, the *Record* insisted that this had no merit whatsoever.

> A stipend or subsidy to a native chief or government can never be invested with the public character and purpose that pertain to revenue collected by a government and which is a contribution by the people towards the support of the government with which their interests are identified and by virtue of which they acquire a right to a voice in the management of its affairs.[33]

Many of these points were also made by the *Standard* which resented any 'elimination of the quasi-autonomy' enjoyed by the Yoruba states.[34]

In addition to the campaign of the newspapers, pressure was exerted on MacGregor from various sources. Petitions poured into Government House from the Alake of Abeokuta, the trading community of the town as well as the principal chiefs. James Johnson waded in with a protest letter in which he charged that the dislike of the European merchants was not to toll paying as such but to toll paying to 'a Native and an African Government'. He added, 'offering a subsidy to Abeokuta in lieu of toll collecting will be regarded as inviting it to surrender its independence'.[35]

At the height of all this agitation MacGregor wrote a lengthy and scholarly memorandum on tolls to the Colonial Secretary setting out the basis for his position in the matter and drawing attention to arrangements of compromise. Through persuasion, the Abeokuta and Ibadan authorities had agreed to publish annual estimates of revenue and expenditure and reports by trained auditors. Ibadan had also agreed to submit its estimates for the Secretary of States' approval. Existing regulated tolls would also not be increased without the sanction of the Secretary of State. MacGregor's recommendations and arguments, which impressed a Colonial Office official as 'good and statesmanlike' attracted a lengthy and appreciative reply from Chamberlain.[36] The concessions were significant but the indigenous authorities had won the battle. MacGregor's personal opinion in the matter was of paramount importance, but the press campaign must have confirmed him in the reasonableness of his position and enabled him to withstand powerful pressure from the European merchants in Nigeria and Britain as well as from the Colonial Office. Therefore the press might justly claim that it had succeeded in establishing 'the principle of upholding, strengthening and consolidating of native authority'.[37]

MacGregor's role in the toll crisis restored him to the favour of the Nigerian press albeit for a brief period. In the remarkable and numerous clashes between certain foreign newspapers, for example *West Africa* and the *West African Mail*, and the Nigerian press over the latter's attitude to MacGregor, the accusation of prejudice had been made by one party and rejected by the other. Perhaps in retrospect, the accusation was justified but the fact is that campaigns of propaganda provide little room for objectivity. Responses are determined by present realities and that is why the *Record*, in its reflection on the tolls agitation was able to state that MacGregor's 'uncompromising attitude in the defence of native rights' would earn for him 'the undying gratitude of the people of the Yoruba country'.[38] How deep this eulogy went in the minds of the newspapermen, only the future could have told, but MacGregor left Nigeria shortly afterwards.

REASSERTION OF NATIONALIST COMMITMENT

Governor Walter Egerton arrived in Lagos on 26 September to the enthusiastic welcome of 'great crowds'. But below the hospitable surface was a cauldron of anxiety and vigilance in press and public. Within six months, complaints were being made about the Governor's 'impetuosity of youth' and his 'desire to acquire fame quickly'. By the end of his first year, it was asserted that his administration was anything but 'successful and propitious'. He could not be depended upon 'to ensure the permanent peace, prosperity and progress' of Lagos and Yorubaland. In 1907, everyone in Lagos was reported to be holding him in 'a disesteem involving unqualified disrepute for his name'.

To the public mind, the touchstone of Egerton's performance was the finding of an effective solution to the prolonged administrative confusion, in parts of Yorubaland, especially at Ilesha. Since the introduction of MacGregor's conciliar system, the history of local government in Ilesha had been a sad story of endless contest and conflict between the Ilesha leaders and the British representatives. Relations between Owa Ajimoko and District Commissioner Reeve-Tacker were as bad as those between

Owa Ataiyero and District Commissioner Ambrose.[39] The troubles at Ilesha actually began during the regime of MacGregor but they became worse under Egerton. Hopes that the latter would control what the newspapers called his 'inexperienced and indiscreet officers' were utterly disappointed when in March 1905 he forced Owa Ataiyero to undertake a tour of self-education to Benin City. The Governor's previous indiscretions could be tolerated but not this 'temporary deportation' of an indigenous ruler. 'Egerton's action', asserted the *Record*, 'disclosed a policy aimed at banishing peace from her favourable haunts and precipitating an undesirable state of affairs.' His 'impetuosity of youth' was bound to receive a 'rude shock'.[40]

In addition to the press campaign, representations were made by the Aborigines' Protection Society to the Colonial and British authorities in London and in Lagos, a petition drafted by John Jackson and endorsed by about 4 500 signatories was sent to the British Government in protest against the 'weakening of native rule and authority' in Yorubaland. The appointment of District Commissioner F. C. Palmer the following year would usher in a new period of co-operation at Ilesha but although this development was to gratify the newspapers, it did not assuage their impassioned scrutiny of administrative measures generally. Indeed, the bellicose enthusiasm of the press had begun to be more keenly fed by new grievances and aspirations which would form the basis of later agitations. The lack of representation was becoming an important target and what many saw as a depressing outlook for virile and discerning administration now helped to heighten the sense of frustration and antagonism. By the middle of 1905, the movement of caustic opposition had hardened so much so that the *Record* felt constrained to reassert its sense of commitment to the nationalist cause.[411]

Under the new order of things introduced into West Africa, two points of view have evolved; the European point of view, and the Native point of view. The European point of view is not only given emphasis and widely by both pen and voice; but finds expression also in the direction, aim and purpose of civilised life in West Africa vociferously. On the other hand, the Native point of view is seldom voiced and is on the whole accorded but scant recognition. Our aim is to give greater prominence to the Native point of view, feeling confident that no solid progress can be made in any direction without there being a thorough comprehension on both sides of the views held by each, and a united effort to bring these into reconciliation where they happen to clash or differ. In fulfilling our role as the exponent of the native point of view, we are not infrequently led to take up a position which is directly opposed to and in antagonism with the prevailing view held by the European. This must in the nature of the circumstances happen if we are true to our trust; but it does not imply *animus* nor is it right or reasonable to impute *animus* in the case of the exposition of view which is known to come into sharp and accentuated contrast at many points with the cherished view of the European.

At this time, Governor Egerton had hardly spent a year in Lagos and the tone of the opposition press must have proved so unsettling that the Europeans deemed it necessary to demonstrate their support for the government. At a meeting of the all-European Lagos Chamber of Commerce on 16 June 1905, a resolution was adopted which expressed disapproval of the tone of the press and its confidence in the government:[42]

> That this meeting strongly deprecates the tone adopted . . . by the Native Press of Lagos, particularly with regard to matters concerning the Government of the Colony and European government officials. That this meeting expresses its complete confidence in and approval of the progressive policy of the government. . . .

The press countered with a seathing attack on the Chamber of Commerce whose resolution was dismissed as 'wild and ill-conceived'.[43]

As has been indicated, the newspapermen usually went beyond mere words in their efforts to ensure the redress of grievances. They were key members of deputations which waited on the government on various issues and many times were mandated by aggrieved sections of the public to negotiate on their behalf or to prosecute their cause to conclusion. A case in point was the Forest concession dispute at Ijebu-Ode in 1907. By an agreement dated 5 October 1906, the *Awujale* and Chiefs had granted to Robert Brown, a British businessman, a concession to prospect for a suitable area of the forest in which to cut timber. Brown was given six months, at the end of which time a further agreement was to be entered into to delimit the area within which actual cutting of timber was to be undertaken. Brown subsequently claimed exclusive rights to fell timber in the area and began to interfere with local licensed cutters. He ran into difficulties which led the Ijebu leaders to repudiate the agreement and to seek the intervention of the Lagos government. The claims and counter-claims became a source of public debate and controversy in which the *Record* played a central role. In numerous articles in May and June 1907, the newspaper flayed Robert Brown for having 'exceeded and violated the conditions of his agreement' and attacked the government for its apparent lethargy in settling the problem.

John Jackson became an adviser to the Ijebu people and drew up a petition which he forwarded on their behalf to the Colonial Office. He also forwarded a copy of the petition to the editor of the *West African Mail* soliciting that newspaper's assistance. At a stage in the dispute, the government felt compelled to counter in the Colonial Office the hostile propaganda of the *Record*. 'It is well-known', it was asserted, 'that this newspaper is notorious for the virulence and malice of its misstatements against all government officials from the Governor downwards.'[44]

In August, Thomas Horatio Jackson, representing his father, took the matter to London where he caused it to be raised in the British Parliament. In addition, he secured the sevices of a London solicitor, Mr Crooks, and accompanied a deputation which met the Under-Secretary of State, Lord Elgin. The latter made the suggestion that the Ijebu chiefs should consider the possibility of taking the case before the courts to try to obtain an injunction to prevent Brown from cutting timber. 'It is for the courts', he said, 'to examine the validity of rights.'[45] Actually, the Colonial Office had little faith in the validity of Brown's claims and in any case, the publicity and controversy over the issue did not reveal a satisfactory state of affairs in the method of supervising grants of concession to Europeans. It is not surprising that the Lagos government eventually intervened to halt Brown's activities and thus to admit the victory of John Jackson and of the Nigerian press.

TAXATION AND REPRESENTATION

In Nigerian press history before the outbreak of the First World War, the period 1908–10 posed the severest challenge to the nationalist newspapers. The introduction of a succession of measures which touched upon the principles of taxation and representation provoked a fierce burst of embittered opposition which had no precedent whatsoever. The scheme of 1908 to supply pipe-borne water and to levy a water rate had yet to win the approval of an angry public when decisions were taken in 1909 to launch at the beginning of the following year a non-elective municipal council with powers to impose taxation. Public excitement and rage attained quasi-revolutionary heights. And as furious barrages multiplied in a seemingly endless chain of crisis, Governor Egerton groped for shelter under a muzzling seditious law.

The principle of representation formed a constant theme in nationalist politics from the early days of colonial rule. The theory and practice of that rule made no allowance for democratic African participation. Under the Crown Colony System that operated at the time, the direction of policy was in the hands of the governor alone, subject to the supervision and control of the Secretary of State in London. An Executive Council from which Africans were excluded until the fourth decade of this century, had only an advisory role and the Legislative Council, subordinate to the Executive Council, admitted only nominated African membership from 1862 to 1874 and from 1886 until the introduction of the 1922 Constitution. A third source from which the governor received advice – the Heads of Departments and other senior officials – was almost exclusively European. Starting from the 1880s, the inadequacies of the system began to constitute a persistent strand in African thought. In the agitation for separation from the Gold Coast into which Lagos was incorporated in 1874, the issue of representation attracted much remark. In 1881, the *Lagos Times* lamented: 'No Council, No House of Assembly exists on which the people sit as their own representatives'.[46] Two years later, the newspaper moaned that 'a people who had governed themselves . . . were compelled to be mere spectators of what the government does'.[47] After Lagos was separated from the Gold Coast in 1886, the *Observer* called for the establishment of a legislature composed of men whose 'unofficialism' would permit them to 'denounce openly and fearlessly acts of misrule, abuse of power, official terrorism and nameless annoyances'. It declared.[48]

> In the name of the whole of Lagos Community, we ask . . . how long will we tamely submit to taxation without representation . . . there should arise from Lagos one general cry for political freedom loud enough to reach the ears of Downing Street, if not louder still, to penetrate the Houses of Parliament.

With the establishment of the *Lagos Weekly Record* and the *Standard* in the nineties, the focus on the lack of representation became much sharper. The career of James Johnson in the Legislative Council from 1896 until he was removed in 1894 demonstrated that a nominated African member could be an effective representative – the same would apply to C. Sapara Williams, appointed in 1901 – but it was significant that the African members appeared to the *Record* in 1897 only as apathetic and over-moderate persons 'within the plain of mere interrogatives'.[49] It was in that year that the *Record* called attention to the 'most unenviable position' of the British West African Colonies the worst feature of which was that the people themselves had little or no voice at all in the administration of their affairs.[50] This view was to be further emphasised a few years later when the newspapers repeatedly remarked that in a Crown Colony environment where the system of government was such as 'to reduce citizenship to a nullity' and to place the Africans on the footing of aliens and strangers in their own land while the wealth and resources of their country were exploited for the benefit of a favoured and limited class who were mere birds of passage, the role of the African was that of 'a voiceless, powerless and impotent creature'.[51]

As Nigeria entered the twentieth century, the issue of representation began to acquire a greater urgency. Among the new influences were the constitutional agitation of 1901–2 which raised in the minds of some educated Nigerians the issue of their own constitutional or political status, the intensification of the cultural campaign, the triumph of Japanese nationalism reflected in Japan's defeat of Russia in 1904–5 which convinced the educated Nigerians that the black man had a future and that given the opportunity, he could contribute to build a nation-state which would be respected by the whole world; and, in addition, the increasing incidence of social and institutional discrimination which called for serious check. From the 1890s, the policy of allowing Nigerians to fill posts of responsibility began to be abandoned[52] and with the arrival of Egerton, racial discrimination and segregation became the basis of appointments and domicile. It was in more practical response to all this challenge that the Lagos Aborigines' Protection Society was founded in 1905 to serve as 'a corrective against the imperfections of the Crown Colony System'. Prince Eshugbayi was President, and C. Sapara Williams one of the vice-presidents; Samuel H. Pearse was Secretary and George Alfred Williams auditor. The unofficial members of the Executive Committee included Herbert Macaulay.[53] By 1908, notwithstanding the early collapse of the Aborigines' Protection Society, the issue of representation had clearly emerged as the most sensitive problem of the time.

From the foregoing, it is possible to appreciate the climate of Nigerian opinion in which the controversial measures of 1908–10 were introduced. Some educated Nigerians, like James Bright Davies, did unreservedly support taxation and were courageous enough to say so in public but they were in an extreme minority. Most people rejected taxation and for various reasons. Many, like John Jackson, opposed taxation unless provision was made for elective representation. When proposals were introduced in 1890 for an elected municipal government, John Jackson had supported taxation because the municipality was to be elective. So also had James Johnson, J. S. Leigh, R. B. Blaize, and C. SaparaWilliams.[54] To the Jacksonian school of thought, an elective franchise was the only basis on which taxation could be founded. However, there were others who opposed taxation either from force of nationalist habit or from age-old aversion to rates and taxes imposed by the government. It was for this reason, as will be seen later, that the idea of a municipal government was publicly opposed in 1889, 1890 and 1899 and the Electric Light Scheme ran into trouble in 1895.

The Water Supply Scheme supplied the initial jolt. An official analysis of Lagos wells carried out in 1907 showed, what was common knowledge, that the supply of water was insufficient and poor in quality. The analysis attributed the prevalence of dysentery in the community to the poor quality of water. The need for good drinking water became so acute that enterprising women commenced a profitable business as water carriers, charging from one to three pence for a large pot. Various proposals (such as the sinking of Artesian wells and the conveyance of water from Apapa), were examined and abandoned but in 1908 the plan was accepted to bring water into Lagos from the Ilo river (about 19 miles from Lagos). The scheme envisaged a supply of 500 000 gallons of water per day or 10 gallons per head per day for a population of about 50 000. Arrangements were made to provide for street and private services. The cost of the scheme was estimated at £120 000 and the annual cost of maintenance and pumping at £3 000. The big question was how the necessary funds were to be procured. The Colonial Office indicated that it would endorse the project on the understanding that the first cost would be met by a loan and a rate levied to pay the interest and sinking charges on the loan and to cover the cost of working the scheme.[55] The Lagos government decided to levy a water rate on householders and put forward the Lagos Assessment Ordinance to provide for an assessment of the annual value of property in Lagos and Ebute-Metta of which the rate was to be fixed.

While the enabling law was being awaited, the newspapers expressed misgivings. The *Standard* conceded that the scheme was 'a very desirable measure' but warned that it would not meet with popular favour if it involved the payment of a 'water tax'. What government should do to save the project was to follow the precedent of the electricity-supply scheme and erect standposts in the principal streets and squares where water could be got free and those wanting private supply should pay the charges.[56] The *Record* thought the government lacked 'the spirit of broadmindedness' in ignoring the difficulties of 'the poorer class'.[57] At the Legislative Council, Nigerian opposition was feeble and uninspiring and the initiative for practical resistance passed to the traditional elite and subsequently to the People's Union led by Dr Randle and Dr Obasa. On 3 November, a public demonstration led by White Cap Chiefs invaded the office of the Colonial Secretary. The official report speaks of 'a disorderly crowd . . . shouting out that they were too poor to pay for water'.[58] The demonstration was applauded by the *Record*, although with a mildness of language and brevity of thought which tended to suggest that someone was deputising for John Jackson.[59] In spite of the opposition, the Assessment Ordinance had a quick passage in the Legislative Council on 26 November.

The passage of the measure proved to be the signal for impassioned resistance by public and press. That same day a rally was held at Enu Owa which resulted in a petition to the Secretary of State. Two days later, the *Record* began a series of pungent criticisms which ran until September the following year. The *Standard* also entered the lists and the *Chronicle*, which was established in the middle of the crisis, soon waded in with its resources of economic jargon.

A common endeavour of the newspapers was to contest the official argument that the people of Benin paid for the installation of water in Benin City and that there was no reason why the people of Lagos should not do the same. The newspapers argued that costs at Benin were met principally by the chiefs who were rich enough to afford such expense. Lagos chiefs – 'thanks to the steady and persistent curtailment of their former rights and privileges' – had been reduced to 'a state bordering on penury'.

The view that the scheme was unnecessary now found advocacy among those who had supported it in principle. In Lagos where drinking water could be had in abundance underground, to say nothing of the rivers of fresh water encircling the town, it was falsely claimed the water scheme went beyond 'the unreasonable and partook of the nature of absolute folly'. According to the *Chronicle*, it was a fundamental theory in political economy that whatever was useful and could be obtained free and by all had no monetary value. 'The air we breathe, the light of the sun and water in the form of rain' were instances of this. Furthermore, although the rate was low, it was not sufficiently low for the generality of the people. In this respect, it was 'a Burden not a Benefit'.[60]

But the most persistent contention was that the government did not take the people into its confidence. Questioning the constitutional competence of the Legislative Council in introducing the principle of direct taxation, the *Record* remarked:[61]

> the principle of direct taxation under the customs and usages of British Government and law carried in its application certain fundamental and indispensable conditions which were of the nature of rights and privileges the abrogation of which was always guarded against whenever and wherever the principle was sought to be applied in practice.

The expropriation of land in the Iju Valley for the purposes of the water scheme in January 1909 helped to accentuate public disaffection which found expression in the press. This situation was not improved by public knowledge in March 1909 of the Secretary of State's refusal to grant the petition of 26 November 1908. The reaction of the *Record* was headlined 'Colonial Government and its unintelligibleness'. The press tended to shift the arguments from the rights and wrongs of the project to a systematic analysis of its viability. The *Record*, on 20 April 1910, reviewed the finances of the Lagos Colony and concluded that the Water Supply Scheme was 'infeasible, unjustified and unwise'. By this time, authorisation had been given for the construction of the Water Works and it was not until four years later that the controversy was re-opened.

Opponents of the Water Scheme were still smarting under the failure of their agitation when the public was electrified by the announcement of a proposal to introduce a Municipal Bill in September 1909. The timing was most unfortunate having regard to the sensitive nature of the municipal issue. Not only that, it was in that same month that a draft seditious law intended to throttle the press was published in the *Gazette*. The idea of a 'Colonial Church' was also in the air. Never since the jurisdictional controversy of 1901–2 had the public experienced such proliferation of controversial legislation.

The municipal idea had never enjoyed popular support in Lagos. Governor Moloney's attempt in 1888 to introduce a municipal system was decried because it would involve the people in the payment of tax. The proposal was revived two years later but it proved unacceptable then as previously. Prince Ademuyiwa Heastrup, a reputed auctioneer and patriot, established the *Mind*, an occasional newspaper, expressly to fight the measure. When on 7 November 1899 MacGregor, in his address at the opening of the Glover Memorial Hall, expressed the hope that before his retirement from the colony he would see a Muncipal Council holding its proceedings in that hall, strong protests were voiced against such 'unproductive measure'.[62] Egerton's Municipality Bill, therefore, could not but inflame public feeling.

The Bill's aim was the creation of a Town Council in the form of a Municipal Board of Health with nominated African representation. The Ordinance which was passed on 8 October 1909 was planned to come into force on 1 January 1910. A noteworthy feature of the agitation against the proposed Municipal Board was the divergence of opinion on the part of the opposition newspapers – the first of its kind for a long time. Permanent dissent by a section of the press was still in the future but the lack of unanimity was a reflection of the conflict of attitudes which the issue of taxation produced. The agitation was furthered in the Legislative Council where Dr Obadiah Johnson and C. Sapara Williams unsuccessfully pressed for a postponement of the Bill until a more regular municipal government was established[63] but it was the press that symbolised the prevailing disaffection. To the *Standard*, a municipality was premature from the viewpoint of essential manpower and standard of enlightenment.[64] The *Record* objected to the 'unique and extraordinary' character which was imparted to the Municipal Board; its status was 'strange and extraordinary . . .

without precedent and principle'.[65] To many opponents of the proposal, the major issue was summed up in the observation of the *Record* in its issue of 5 February 1910.

> The principle involved in the power conferred on the Board is one which trenches upon the rights and privileges of the people as British subjects and as entitled of right to the privilege which by tradition and law is accorded the British subject of having a voice by representation in any system of direct taxation to which he is subjected. This principle expressed in the axiom 'no taxation without representation' and which constitutes the foundation and charter right of British government, obviously cannot be violated in part without entailing the subversion of the principle as a whole.

How consistent John Jackson's views were can be seen in the reasons which he gave for supporting a municipal government twenty years earlier. Because there was provision for election in the 1890 abortive proposal, John Jackson (then editor of the *Lagos Weekly Times*) remarked in private correspondence with the government that taxation was 'the only basis upon which an elective franchise can be founded ... and the *sine qua non* condition of its operation'. His view then, which was basically unchanged twenty years later, was that a municipality was 'the initiatory step for introduction of self-government' and that it 'would teach ... self-reliance and dependency'.

The *Record*'s contribution made a strong impression on James Bright Davies who considered John Jackson's ideas 'weighty and full of significance'.[66] James Davies, who conducted the *Nigerian Times* (founded in 1910), frowned at the constitution of the Municipal Board but favoured its establishment. An independent-minded and courageous journalist with a background of rich experience in Sierra Leone where a municipality established in 1895 had functioned successfully, he castigated the people of Lagos for fearing to take up responsibility and for their unwillingness to be inducted in the elementary principle of self-government. The view that the people were too poor to pay direct tax was to him entirely unwarranted because the society of Lagos was bedevilled by 'lavish expenditure in extravagance in dress ... gaudy shows and the most extravagant and injudicious display of gold ornaments and of flippery gewgaws'.[67]

Whether the divergence of opinion hindered the nationalist cause is difficult to say. The more important fact was that the agitation failed to change or modify the policy of government. It was to be nine years later before provision would be made for the election of members into the Lagos Town Council.[68]

RACIAL SEGREGATION

After his chain of victories over the forces of nationalism, nothing seemed to be able to stay Egerton's legislative progress – until the eruption of the Colonial Church Question. At issue was racial discrimination which Egerton had fostered and institutionalised and which now threatened to invade the Church. The issue dramatised the fact of civil inequality and struck at the heart of religious integration and equality. For once in so many agitations, the opposition won a measure of victory and the Nigerian press had cause to crow over what it considered to be a singular triumph.

Egerton was the arch-segregationist but the beginnings of the practice went further back to the early period of the Christian missionary contact which was scandalised by acts of racial discrimination that were at the root of the ecclesiastical tensions and secessions of the nineteenth century and after. By the beginning of the present century, a tradition of racial discrimination had been established in the Civil Service and in society generally. The thinking which had enabled Nigerians like J. Otonba Payne (Registrar of the Supreme Court), G. J. Cole (Postmaster), Adolphus Pratt (Superintendent of Police) to occupy positions of responsibility came to be viewed as an absurd and antiquated aberration. A disparity which could not be explained in terms of academic qualification or experience came to characterise the salaries and conditions of service of black and white public servants. The further prostitution of discrimination resulted from the doctrine of segregation preached by the schools of Tropical Medicine as a precaution to be taken by Europeans against malaria. Egerton's predecessor, MacGregor, was opposed to racial segregation arguing, to the astonishment of L. Antrobus of the Colonial Office, that it would be socially disastrous and 'most unwise' to start a 'racial question' in Lagos.[69]

Such scruples did not weigh with Egerton. In 1905, as will be seen shortly, he wanted a church built for Europeans exclusively. During the laying of the foundation stone of the British Bank of West Africa in May 1906, and also during the Amalgamation Day celebrations of that year, seats were arranged to emphasise the division between black and white.[70] In 1907, about 2 000 Nigerians were evacuated from the area of the race course and their landed property appropriated for a European reservation.[71] In that year four Nigerian medical officers were compelled to submit a protest against the denial to them of the privileges enjoyed by their white colleagues.[72] It was in consideration of such developments that the *Standard* observed on 2 January 1907:

> . . . a new spirit has been introduced into the administration, a spirit entirely strange to Lagos, and which is noticeable in every opportunity being taken advantage of to repress . . . the native.

By 1909, resistance to segregation, which was hitherto ineffective, found a significant focus in the Colonial Church Question. The impetus was provided not only by the enormity of Egerton's prejudices but also by the callous and detestable way he sought to accomplish his objective. The seeds of a colonial church and a colonial chaplaincy had fallen on barren soil in Lagos in the nineteenth century. In 1875 and 1884, the idea had been mooted and abandoned in the face of strong public opposition. Colonial churches were established in the other British West African colonies but they had almost all been abolished by the end of the nineteenth century. British policy itself was no more in favour of any institutional links between church and state.[73] Thus although the progress of local and imperial thought was against him, Egerton thought fit to revive the project in 1905 by proposing the appointment of a colonial chaplain on a salary of £100 per annum. The Colonial Office deprecated colonial chaplaincies but gave Egerton a free hand to bring the question before the Legislative Council. In Council, the proposal was defeated by 5:3 whereupon the Governor embarked on all sorts of devious manoeuvres to secure a resolution providing for the establishment of a colonial church and a colonial chaplain, the funds for which were to be a charge on public revenue. The Secretary of State was not impressed and Egerton's move was blocked.[74]

But Egerton was set upon having a European Church and in April 1909 an attempt was made by Bishop Herbert Tugwell to seek the support of the Christ Church congregation for the founding of a colonial chaplaincy as an extension of Christ Church. The proposal was rejected, as had been an earlier proposal to convert Christ Church to a colonial church. Egerton's next move was to issue a public notice in which he invited all those interested in the building of a colonial church and the appointment of a colonial chaplain to attend a meeting at Government House. Eighty-two persons, of whom fifteen were Nigerians, attended the meeting. The rest were mostly European officials.[75] The attempt to deceive the Secretary of State and the British public by presenting evidence of multiracial support apparently succeeded and a Bill to legalise the setting up of the church and chaplaincy was ultimately passed by the Legislative Council. The church, to be built exclusively for the use of Europeans, was estimated to cost £10 000 of which £5 000 was to be paid by the public. A European chaplain to officiate only to Europeans was to be appointed and his salary, together with the upkeep of the church, was to be met from public revenue. In October, 1909, the Rev. L. S. Noble, an English clergyman, was appointed colonial chaplain and a large hall of King's College which had just been built, was used as a temporary church. By 1911, the church was already under construction.[76]

The battle against the colonial church was waged on various fronts both in Nigeria and in Britain. Members of the Legislative Council, the People's Union led by Dr John Randle and Dr O. Obasa, church dignitaries, members of the British Parliament and several other influential bodies and societies, all played vital roles. But there can be no doubt that the vanguard thrusts were made by the newspapers. Flabbergasted by the multiplicity of measures prolific of public outrage (Seditious Offences Ordinance, Municipal Board of Health, Native House Rule Ordinance and Colonial Church – all introduced around September, 1909), the newspapers unleashed a fusillade of attack which was sustained up to the end of 1910. Their accounts of developments in Nigeria aroused widespread attention in England and evoked strong protests by Members of Parliament, the National Free Church Conference at Hull and the Society for the Liberation of Religion from State Patronage and Control whose influential Vice-President, Dr John Clifford, was an avid reader of the *Nigerian Times*. The newspapers published or reprinted countless contributions from Lagos and abroad demonstrating widespread disgust with the Lagos administration. The role of the press in the controversy proved so unsettling to the Lagos government that it openly accused it of instituting 'a malicious campaign of misrepresentation'.

The primary target was the employment of public funds in the building of a church that practised racial segregation. The principle of a European Church was not contested so long as it was financed by Europeans. For the Nigerian taxpayers, made up of indigenous worshippers, Muslims and Christians, to finance such an exclusive building for European Christian worship was intolerable. As the *Standard* put it, 'why Africans should be saddled with the burden of providing for the religious needs of one class and that a very small class and one which contributed the least to the general revenue, was most unintelligible'.[77]

A point frequently emphasised was that the proposed church was being built to accommodate at most fifteen worshippers. It was alleged that as the European population of Lagos comprised Germans who were Lutherans, Scots who were Presbyterians and Irishmen who were Catholics, the episcopal 'white-only' Church would be attended by about fifteen Englishmen who, whenever it had pleased them to attend services at Christ Church, always had the best seats reserved for them.[78]

The iniquity of the segregationist church scheme was underlined by references to the Governor's inconsistency in the use of public funds for places of religious worship. In 1908, the Muslim community had collected £4 000 out of an estimated sum of £5 500 for building a Mosque. Egerton was approached for a loan of the outstanding £1 500 to complete the building but he declined to grant their request on the ground that public funds could not be used for building places of worship.[79]

All these arguments were re-emphasised and amplified in and outside the British Parliament. The extent to which the newspapers influenced opinion in England can be seen in the questions and speeches of some of the Members of Parliament. They quoted with relish such Nigerian newspaper expressions as 'robbery for burnt offering' and 'building the house of God by unrighteousness and maintaining the chaplaincy by extortion'.[80]

In response to all this pressure, the Colonial Office imposed certain restrictions on Egerton's proposals. It ruled that only £1 500 was to be devoted to the church scheme from the public revenue and that when the church was completed, it was not to be reserved for any patricular denomination of European Christians but to be open to the use of all of them. The *Record*'s view that the ruling portended 'a moribund condition for the project'[81] probably did not reckon with Egerton's mulish character; he persisted with his crippled plan but there was no doubt that he had been worsted in the encounter.

The Nigerian press almost always showered congratulations on itself whenever its agitation ended on a note of success. For example after the agitation for the separation of the Colony of Lagos from the Gold Coast Colony which the press successfully led, a newspaper had remarked: 'Truly, and we greatly rejoice over it, the power of the Press is beginning to be felt.'[82] But this was a mere smile compared with the glee of 1910. The prevailing mood is best seen in the review of the crisis by the *Nigerian Times*. After condemning the government for conducting a campaign of 'denunciations and vituperations' against the Nigerian press, an attitude which was 'unworthy, undignified and highly discreditable', (the government was 'pouring out the vial of its wrath' against the newspapers 'in a tirade replete with most undignified epithets and completely exhausted the vocabulary of objectionable adjectives and expletives on the devoted head of the press'), it asserted that the press welcomed this temper of the government for it was 'the surest indication of the effectiveness of its assault on its stronghold. It declared, '(The newspaper press) ought to congratulate itself if, after months of wearying toil and struggle and strenuous endeavour to draw the attention of the British public to the grave abuses and enormities which are being enacted in Southern Nigeria in the name of the British Government and people, its efforts have at last been crowned with success. . . .'.

If the *Nigerian Times* exaggerated the achievement of the press, its views should be seen against the background of its passionate involvement in the segregationist agitation [1]as well as the implacable hostility which its owner and editor, James Bright Davies, developed towards the Governor. No one feature of Egerton's policy had an equal influence in determining the character of Davies's opposition. Whereas by February 1912 when Egerton left Lagos to take up appointment as Governor of British Guyana other editors were inclined to concede some achievements to the Governor, such as the promotion of commercial and industrial activities, the development of the railway system and the founding of King's College,[84] James Bright Davies probably remained inflexible in his hatred. In May 1910 he wondered how long the people of Southern Nigeria would remain further 'under the rule and the cruel, oppressive and despotic tyranny' of Egerton.[85] In July, on the eve of the Governor's departure on leave, he reviewed his administration and remarked.[86]

Walter Egerton's attitude is that of blind and obstinate persistency combined with a dogged determination to carry out his purpose. He is a man incapable of brooking a defeat or admitting an error and making an honourable retreat from an untenable situation. He has no experience of the sobering influences which defeats caused by grave mistakes or errors of judgement have tended to exert on the conduct of public men and of those in active political life.

He mockingly wished Egerton 'bon voyage' but would rather remain in 'blissful ignorance' as to whether he returned or not, which in the latter event, would be for the good of Nigeria. The *Nigerian Times* disappeared about four months before Egerton left Nigeria,[87] but James Bright Davies must have considered his departure good riddance.

LAND TENURE

The tense political atmosphere in Lagos particularly in the last four years of the Egerton era had little opportunity for any relaxation. Egerton was to be succeeded by Frederick Lugard who was well known by reputation in Lagos. The prevalent feeling was described in a reminiscence by one of the newspapers:[88]

> . . . ninety percent of the people of the country had their misgivings of him and entertained doubts as to the approachability of a man who has seen such varied and bold services in different parts of the Empire and the report of whose doings in Northern Nigeria has set the ears a-tingling for long. A man whose walking stick is a pistol and whose thought by day and dream by night are punitive expeditions and military patrols. Stirring tales have been told of his negrophobia, his anti-black proclivities, his distant attitude, to all men in general . . . he was said to have arranged for the Emirs and Potentates to do him royal homage by throwing themselves in the dust at his approach and to cry ZAKI!!!

The primary object of Lugard's appointment was well known – the preparation of the groundwork for the proposed amalgamation of Northern and Southern Nigeria. Apart from sensitivity to the personality of the new Governor, the amalgamation scheme aroused apprehensions about the possible extension into Lagos of the 'despotic' political structure of the North. An important feature of the Northern System was the complete subversion of indigenous land tenure and land tenure had become an extremely sore issue since 1912. The responsibilities that awaited Lugard required, in the words of a newspaper, a man 'liberal in his views and gifted with a statesmanlike ability of organisation and control'. Obviously, these attributes were not found in the new incumbent but this was mildy reflected in the welcome he got in the press after he arrived in Lagos on 3 October 1912. In the arrangements for Lugard's wharf reception, a 'strong' colour line had been drawn between black and white in the Egerton tradition. The *Chronicle* took advantage of this incident to warn against any further provocation by policies which indicated a 'bias to racial classiness'. The *Standard* considered that the 'onerous and delicate' duties facing the Governor required a man who possessed 'qualifications of a high order'. The *Record* avoided any customary editorial welcome; it merely mentioned the fact of Lugard's arrival and admonished him to promote the welfare of the people.[89]

Lugard reprobated the audacity of the Nigerian press[90] and would give more than ample cause for more direct confrontation. But if he showed alarm at the tone of the press during his first few months in Lagos, he certainly had some justification. This is because his appointment coincided with the explosive Land Tenure Question which began in July 1912 and persisted beyond the end of the year. The event was a landmark in the development of the newspaper press for on no other occasion had the press demonstrated such initiative and energy. In the way it stimulated thought and practical action and in the way it sought to foster a general spirit of unrest and agitation not only in Lagos but throughout Yorubaland, the newspaper press confirmed its emergence as a powerful force.

The Land Tenure Question was caused by the decision of the British Government in July 1912 to appoint the West African Land Committee to inquire into land tenure in West Africa and to see how far the Northern Nigeria system could be applied elsewhere. The setting up of this committee was prompted by a number of British Members of Parliament and other public figures among them E. D. Morel, Noel Buxton, J. Ramsay MacDonald, Phillip Morrell, Albert Spicer and J. C. Wedgwood who suggested that 'an experienced Committee' be appointed to inquire into the problem of land policy in British West Africa. It was contended that in these colonies, the people were in danger of losing their lands to European capitalists if the indiscriminate method of land alienation by Chiefs was not halted. It was urged that to check the tendency, the control of the lands should be vested in the Governor as 'paramount authority', as in Northern Nigeria where the Land

and Native Rights Ordinance, 1911, vested all land in the government and declared that the indigenous people had no individual right of freehold in the land or house they occupied.[91]

Nigerian opinion was enraged particularly in view of the increasing consciousness of the educated Africans that they were a 'negligible quantity' in the British political programme. For, as the thinking went, if having been denied the right to representation and having been subjected to racial discrimination and segregation, they were also deprived of 'the most cherished right' to their homesteads, 'whither was the African to take refuge?' Land is a highly sensitive issue in Africa and from the 1890s to the beginning of the second decade of the present century, a number of government measures concerning land had infuriated the Nigerian people. For example, a proposed Forest Law was abandoned in 1897 following objection in the press and in 1899 the appropriation of land at Ebute-Metta provoked much public anger. Two years later, as has been mentioned earlier, the resuscitated Forest Law precipitated a prolonged agitation. In 1907, land appropriations at the race course had to be carried out with the help of armed men. That same year, the Ijebu-Ode timber concession dispute created much public ill-feeling. The official announcement in 1912 which, on the basis of certain decisions of the Supreme Court, set out conditions to be satisfied for claims to rights of property in land was also condemned without reservation.[92] And in that year, the proposed Forest Law in the Gold Coast (Ghana) provided sympathetic agitation in Lagos.[93] It was small wonder that the institution of the Land Committee was greeted in Lagos with an outburst of rage.

The educated Africans were particularly apprehensive as it seemed to them almost obvious that the Northern system would be introduced into the South. The Northern land law of 1911 had been passed immediately after a Commission of Inquiry had investigated land tenure in that area, and Lord Lugard, who had once administered the North (1900–6) was soon to assume the Governorship of the two Protectorates in Lagos. What was more disturbing, the representations which led to the setting up of the Land Committee originated from influential 'friends of Africa' such as E. D. Morel, the distinguished Afrophile editor of the *African Mail* (formerly *West African Mail*), who not only was credited with being the 'brain behind the land question' but was also a member of the committee.

The educated Africans, infuriated at what seemed to them a naked and gross betrayal on the part of Morel and others, were determined to block the importation of the Northern land system to the South. To this end, they mounted an ambitious press campaign which aimed at educating the British public on the nature of indigenous land tenure in Lagos and Yorubaland and at fostering in these areas a general spirit of resistance to what was regarded as an 'unprecedented innovation'.

Rumour-mongering about the proposed new land policy actually began in May 1912 but it was after the rumours were confirmed in July that agitation began in earnest. Initial newspaper reaction was to urge all people to take a positive stand in strong protest. It was thus a suspicious and unsettled atmosphere created by the the press that formed the background to the public meeting summoned by the White Cap Chiefs on 7 July. At this meeting, resolutions were adopted one of which called for a delegation to be sent to the hinterland 'to inform the people of the burning question'. The delegation comprised John Jackson, who was leader, Rev. D. A. Hughes of the United Native African Church, Sule Giwa, Abdullah Giwa and two *Ogbonis*.[94] They left Lagos on 5 September and spent five months touring to Abeokuta, Ibadan, Ilesha, Oyo, Oshogbo and Ife. In public meetings with the Obas, Chiefs and people, the delegation inquired into customs relating to land tenure and informed of the Land Committee, emphasising what dangers loomed up before the people. On their part, the indigenous authorities related their traditional systems of land tenure and vowed to resist any subversion of those systems. The progress of these meetings and their proceedings were given maximum publicity in the press alongside lengthy reports on the various land systems brought to the attention of the delegation.

Meanwhile, the Lagos Auxiliary of the Anti-Slavery and Aborigines' Protection Society, which had been established on 30 August 1910 in response to T. Fowell Buxton's appeal, had begun to make strenuous efforts to frustrate the motive behind the setting up of the Land Committee. They met almost weekly and notwithstanding serious internal differences of opinion ultimately sent a deputation to London to give evidence before the committee.[95] The delegation which left Lagos on 12 March 1913 was hailed as unique. As a newspaper remarked: '. . . never before in the history of West Africa has a deputation so strong in character, so representative in body, so varied in tribe, visited England on a common topic and a single aim'.[96] Among its members was James Bright Davies, who was the Secretary for Foreign Correspondence.

Apart from their involvement in the more practical aspects of the agitation, the newspapermen employed their profession with extraordinary zeal. The ferocity, volume and variety of their articles and contributions defies description. So all-absorbing did they make the issue that it was alleged that there was hardly any house an educated man could enter in Lagos without hearing the question '*Akowe, jo so fun wa bi oro ile tin lo si*' (literally, 'Bookman, please tell me how the land question is going on').[97]

Times without number, the newspapers stressed the danger in interfering with customary law relating to land. As the *Standard* put it:[98]

> . . . anyone who has the slightest acquaintance with the peoples of West Africa, knows that there is no question in which they are more keenly alive to their interests and more jealous of interference than the question of land ownership. Any proposed alteration of the immemorial and time-honoured laws and customs affecting the ownership of land has always met with the strongest opposition as being directed against their dearest and most cherished rights. . . .

The all-pervading chorus was the fundamental principle underlying the land tenure system in Southern Nigeria. Week after week, the newspapers literally screamed themselves hoarse about the communal nature of land ownership and the role of the Chiefs as trustees for the people. As the *Record* once put it 'the whole order of native life is communal and all its institutions are accordingly of a communal order'.[99] The individualistic notion of the European made this hard for him to understand and it was necessary to explain what was highlighted as his muddled thinking on the subject. The basis of the Northern System was the view that the Chiefs did not themselves own the land which they held in trust for the community, that the structural law of tenure was not ownership but occupancy, that the Chiefs granted the right of occupancy in exchange for a payment which was virtually a rent, that the right of occupancy was perpetual provided the land was used and that the occupant committed no crime against the state. Under this system, the Governor of Northern Nigeria as 'paramount chief' through conquest, became the sole trustee and exercised all control over the land. To some of the newspapers, to reason this way was 'to propound . . . a contradiction or a fiction'.

For if the structural law was occupancy, all the would-be occupier needed to do was simply to occupy a piece of land without reference to anybody. Such reference formalised in the payment of rent signified the existence of a landlord – which the indigenous Chief was not. The significant fact was that, except in the odd cases of certain migrant farmers, in no part of Southern Nigeria was rent paid for the use of land.[100]

Also disputed was the view, which Morel was at pains to justify,[101] that land would otherwise be indiscriminately alienated to European speculators with calamitous consequences for the economic future of the people. The newspapers hastened to point out that the government, even in Southern Nigeria, had become the greatest and most unscrupulous speculator of all. Concessions had been granted by the government to various ex-government officials and there was no knowing what would happen if the entire control of the land was vested in the Governor.[102]

As the newspapers charged the proponents of land reform and published progress reports and detailed essays on land tenure systems furnished by the Jackson delegation, they also reprinted relevant material from outside Nigeria in support of their cause. E. J. P. Brown's speech entitled 'Land Question on the Gold Coast' which was first published in the *Gold Coast Globe* and which was an indictment of British land policy, was serialised by the *Chronicle*. Articles contributed to British newspapers by Sir W. N. Geary were reprinted and Geary was hailed for his 'valiant stand' in defence of African interests. E. D. Morel became the whipping-boy of the press. Objections were raised to his membership of the committee and every opportunity was seized to denounce him.

Morel himself noted that he was 'the best abused person' in the West African Press at the time. The strictures came not only from Nigeria but also from the Gold Coast where a running fire was also directed against the philosophy behind the appointment of the Land Committee.

The West African Land Committee was so divided at the end of its inquiry that it could not issue a report. The Lagos Auxiliary of the Aborigines' Protection Society under the leadership of James Johnson had every reason to congratulate themsleves. But it was probably a greater victory for the Nigerian newspaper press. However, by a tragic irony, the land tenure campaign ended ultimately in a mournful note. Its leading spirit, John Jackson, had contracted the illness during the Yoruba-wide tour which eventually led to his death. The details of this tragedy are not very clear but the available evidence indicates that John Jackson retired from active life soon after the tour and died two years later on 1 August 1915 at the age of 67.

CONCLUSION

During the period 1900-13, the Nigerian newspaper press undoubtedly exerted considerable influence on the policies of the colonial administration and the attitudes of the people. By 1913, it seemed prepared to face the future confident of its power as 'the guardian of the rights and liberties of the people as well as the interpreter of their ideals and aspirations'. It would be straining the evidence to hold that the political achievements of the period can be attributed solely to the pressure of the newspaper press. Vital and sometimes crucial roles were played by private and group opinions in Nigeria and Britain but there can be no doubt that the newspaper press at all times occupied the centre of the stage. It was a crucial agency in the overall strategy for meaningful participation in government and for the dissemination of political awareness and nationalist consciousness. In success and perhaps more so in failure, it succeded in spreading disaffection and thus laid a good foundation for the new epoch of nationalism which began in 1914. A clear evidence of its achievements in this regard was the uneasiness and irritation felt by the government. Some colonial administrators tolerated severe criticism but others were less accommodating and replied with prosecutions and repressive legislation. In the next chapter, we shall focus on the relationship between the newspapers and the government; this would provide the necessary backdrop for the role of the newspaper press in the movement of nationalism associated with the First World War.

Notes

1 See *Lagos Standard*, 11 January 1899.
2 14 March 1899.
3 *Lagos Standard*, 7 March 1899; 24 January, 7 March 1900.
4 6 March 1895. Also 2 September, 23 December 1896. 22 March 1899;

7 March 1900; 11 April 1900; 10 August 1904; 15 June 1904. *Lagos Weekly Record*, 9 January 1897; 27 February 1897.

5 C.O. 147/112, Stallard to Chamberlain, 19 January 1897. *Lagos Standard*, 27 February 1907.

6 C.O. 147/100, Denton to Chamberlain, 27 August 1895.

7 *Lagos Standard*, 8, 15 May; 14 August 1895.

8 The circulation of the *Record* rose from about 26 000 a year in 1895 to 30 000 in 1900. The *Standard* climbed from 16 000 in 1895 to 30 000 in 1900.

9 Lynch, *Edward Wilmot Blyden*, pp. 232–4.

10 *Ibid.*

11 *Ibid.*

12 For details, see Fred I. A. Omu, 'The Newspaper Press in Southern Nigeria' in B. I. Obichere (ed.), *Aspects of the History of Southern Nigeria* (forthcoming).

13 Minutes in C.O. 147/157, MacGregor to Chamberlain, 2 October 1901.

14 31 August 1901.

15 T. N. Tamuno, *The Evolution of the Nigerian State*, London, 1972, p. 254.

16 Minutes in C.O. 147/157, MacGregor to Chamberlain, 2 October 1901.

17 *Ibid.* Also Tamuno, *op. cit.*, p. 254.

18 20 November 1901. Also 11 December 1901.

19 Minutes in C.O. 147/157, MacGregor to Chamberlain, 2 October 1901.

20 C.O. 147/158, MacGregor to Chamberlain, 13 December 1901.

21 MacGregor may be believed but the point is that it was Jackson's opposition which led to the withdrawal of the subsidy. The opposition preceded the subsidy cancellation; therefore to restore the subsidy would only have brought the situation to the status quo before 1900.

22 Minutes in C.O. 147/157, MacGregor to Chamberlain, 13 December 1901.

23 Tamuno, *op. cit.*, p. 255.

24 *Lagos Standard*, 26 February 1902.

25 'In no way can Sir William MacGregor be considered the 'corresponding part' of the late Sir John Glover except in the fact that the one is the complete antithesis of the other. The one is a *talker*, the other was a *worker*'. 'Lagosian On Dits' in reply to the *Weekly News* of Freetown which remarked that MacGregor was the 'corresponding part' of Glover. *Lagos Standard*, 5 March 1902.

26 Certain further amendments were advised by the Colonial Office. In order to prevent the illegal importation of rubber into Lagos from Southern Nigeria, the Governor was to be empowered to prohibit the export of rubber without requiring the consent of all the Native Councils in the Colony and Protectorate of Lagos as originally provided. The Ordinance was duly amended and finally passed in December 1902. C.O. 147/161, Chamberlain to MacGregor, 31 July 1902; MacGregor to Chamberlain, 20 October 1902, 5 December 1902.

27 *Lagos Weekly Record*, 20 May 1899; 10 June 1899.
28 *Lagos Weekly Record*, 30 June 1900. See also Open Letter; 'Junius' to MacGregor, 13 March 1900 in *Lagos Standard*, 14 March 1900. *Lagos Standard*, 27 June 1900, 4 July 1900.
29 *Lagos Weekly Record*, 31 May 1902.
30 See Chapter 6.
31 Tamuno, *op. cit.*, p. 770.
32 C.O. 147/165, Chamberlain to MacGregor (telegram) 18 June 1903.
33 *Lagos Weekly Record*, 20, 27 June; 4, 11, 18, 28 July, 1 August 1903.
34 *Lagos Standard*, 1, 22 July 1903.
35 C.O. 147/166, MacGregor to Chamberlain, 25 July 1902. Enclosure I (James Johnson to MacGregor, 23 July 1903).
36 C.O. 147/166, Chamberlain to MacGregor, 21 August 1903.
37 See *Lagos Weekly Record*, 20 June 1903.
38 1 August 1903.
39 *Lagos Standard*, 12 November 1902; 5 April 1905; 12 April, 19 April, 12 July 1905; 18 July 1906; 1 July, 28 October 1908.
40 *Lagos Weekly Record*, 8 October 1904, 1 April 1905, 6 May 1905; 22 July 1905, 18 November 1905. *Lagos Standard*, 19 July 1905. See also *Lagos Weekly Record*, 4, 11 October 1902.
41 *Lagos Weekly Record*, 3 June 1905.
42 *Lagos Standard*, 28 June 1905.
43 *Lagos Weekly Record*, 1 July 1905.
44 C.O. 520/47, Elgin to Egerton, 19 July 1907. For details of the agreement, see enclosures in C.O. 520/47, Egerton to Elgin, 14 July 1907.
45 C.O. 520/48, Elgin to Egerton, 22 August 1907.
46 23 May 1881; Also 9 March 1881.
47 24 January 1883.
48 3 July 1886; 10 July 1886, 7 August 1886.
49 See *Lagos Standard*, 21 April, 1897. A columnist of the Standard, Janus, considered the *Record*'s remarks 'entirely out of place, uncalled for . . . and most uncomplimentary'.
50 3 April 1897.
51 *Lagos Weekly Record*, 24 December 1904; *Lagos Standard*, 7 October 1903; 4 December 1907; 12 February, 29 April 1908.
52 The complaint was made in 1902 that while Moloney did not dismiss a single Nigerian from the civil service, Carter only two and Denton two and MacCallum none, there were no less than 20 dismissals by MacGregor in 24 months. See *Lagos Standard*, 22 January 1902; 26 November 1902.
53 Other officers were: Shitta-Bey, Second Vice-President; D. A. Taylor and S. S. Davies, Financial Secretaries; W. R. Harding, Auditor. Other unofficial members were Dr Kasunmu Giwa, Alli Balogun and L. A. Cardoso. The APS appears to have collapsed after a short time but was revived in 1910 as the Lagos Auxiliary of the Anti-slavery and Aborigines' Protection Society.
54 C.O. 147/77, Moloney to Knutsford, 27 December 1890. Also J. P. Jackson to Oliver Smith (Ag. Colonial Secretary) 5 April 1890 (enclosure).

55 C.S.O. 1/22/2, Crewe to Egerton, 26 February 1909.
56 24 June 1908; 29 July 1908.
57 25 July, 8 August 1908.
58 C.S.O. 1/21/3, Egerton to Crewe, 16 November 1908.
59 7 November 1908.
60 *Nigerian Chronicle*, 27 November 1908; *Lagos Weekly Record*, 8 January, 19 March 1910; 25 July 1908; *Lagos Standard*, 9 December 1908; 27 January 1909.
61 5 December 1908.
62 *Lagos Standard*, 29 November; 6 December 1899.
63 Legislative Council minutes, 7 October 1909.
64 29 September 1909.
65 2 October 1909.
66 *Nigerian Times*, 26 April 1910.
67 *Nigerian Times*, 12 April 1910.
68 The Lagos Township Ordinance of 1919 provided for three elected members of the Lagos Town Council. In the elections of 29 May 1920, the following were elected – H. Folarin, Dr R. A. Savage and G. D. Agbebi.
69 C.O. 147/155, MacGregor to Chamberlain, 8 July 1901. Antrobus remarked that 'there was a curious vein of sentimentalism' in Mac-Gregor. See minute in C.O. 520/20. Egerton to Elgin, 27 December 1907.
70 Africanus to *Lagos Standard*, 23 May 1906; Also Herbert Macaulay to *Lagos Standard*, 16 May 1906.
71 C.O. 520/58, Egerton to Elgin, 27 January 1908.
72 C.O. 520/50, Egerton to Elgin, 30 December 1907.
73 E. A. Ayandele, 'The Colonial Church Question in Lagos Politics, 1905–1911', *Odu*, iv, 2, January 1908, pp. 53–73.
74 *Lagos Standard*, 6 October 1909; *Nigerian Times*, 5 April 1910.
75 *Ibid.*
76 Ayandele, 'The Colonial Church Question'.
77 *Lagos Standard*, 6 October 1909.
78 *Ibid.*
79 *Lagos Weekly Record*, 23 April, 4 June, 24 December 1910. *Lagos Standard*, 6 October 1909.
80 See report of London Correspondent of the *Nigerian Times* in issue of 20 August 1901.
81 28 May 1910.
82 8 November 1886.
83 8 November 1910.
84 *Nigerian Chronicle*, 23 February 1912; *Lagos Weekly Record*, 2 March 1912; *Lagos Standrd*, 13 March 1912.
85 3 May 1910; Also 31 May 1910.
86 19 July 1910.
87 Egerton left Nigeria on 27 February 1912. The *Nigerian Times* was suspended on 30 October 1911.
88 *Lagos Weekly Record*, 8 March 1913.

89 *Nigerian Chronicle*, 3 October 1912; *Lagos Standard*, 12 October 1912; *Lagos Weekly Record*, 12 October 1912.

90 M. Perham, *Lugard, op. cit.*, p. 390.

91 *The Times*, 6 June 1912, reprinted *Lagos Standard*, 10 July 1912; *Lagos Weekly Record*, 20 July 1912. Morel's 'Open Letter to West African Friend' on the subject of 'The future of the peoples of West Africa in relation to the forces of European capital and industry, with particular reference to the occupancy and enjoyment of the land'. *Lagos Standard*, 25 September 1912; *Nigerian Chronicle*, 13 September 1912; William Neville Geary to *African Mail*, 16 July 1912 reprinted in *Nigerian Chronicle*, 30 August 1912.

92 The order was issued by Colonial Secretary Boyle to the effect that in view of decisions of the Appeal Court on 14 March 1910 that Dosunmu ceded to the British all lands not subject to pre-existing rights of private ownership, (i) no right of property in lands acquired after 1910 was to be recognised by government by way of Crown grant; (ii) rights acquired between 6 August 1861, and 14 March 1910, except those that were covered by Crown grants, would be considered purely on merit. *Lagos Weekly Record*, 30 September 1911; *Lagos Standard*, 15 October 1911.

93 The Gold Coast Forest Ordinance, 1911, evoked widespread indignation and a deputation was sent to London under Casely Hayford *Lagos Standard*, 22, 29 May, 5 June, 21 August 1912. *Lagos Weekly Record*, 22 June 1912.

94 The *Ogboni* were an influential secret cult.

95 C. Sapara Williams, Vice-President of the Auxiliary, supported the rival People's Union in their opposition to a delegation going to England. Criticism of Williams in the *Standard* resulted in a libel suit *C. A. S. Williams, v. G. A. Williams and J. B. Benjamin*, 1913, in which damages of £300 were awarded. What happened was as follows: 'Lasore' wrote an antidelegation article in the *Standard*. This was severely criticised by 'Watchman' (J. Blackall Benjamin) who not only revealed that 'Lasore' was Sapara Williams but went on to suggest in innuendoes that Sapara Williams was privy to the murder of Otonba Payne. Sapara Williams's suit for £600 was heard by Justice R. J. B. Ross who awarded £300. The money was quickly subscribed by the public.

96 *Lagos Standard*, 14 May 1913.

97 J. G. Campbell to *Lagos Standard*, 21 August 1912.

98 24 July 1912.

99 3 August 1912. Also 13, 20 July, 17, 24, 31 August, 14, 21 September 1912. *Lagos Standard*, 22, 29 May, 5 June; 10, 24, 31 July, 21 August, 25 September; 2, 9, 23, 30 October 1912. *Nigerian Chronicle*, 5, 12, 19 July 1912.

100 *Lagos Weekly Record*, 3 August 1912; *Lagos Standard*, 24 July 1912. *Nigerian Chronicle*, 9 August, 6, 13, 20, 27 September 1912.

101 See Morel's Open Letter.

102 *Lagos Standard*, 25 September 1912. *Nigerian Chronicle*, 27 September 1912.

6 Liberty versus authority

In the first chapter, we drew attention to the dilemma of press freedom which provided the key to the relations between news-papers and the government in Sierra Leone and the Gold Coast in the nineteenth century. The point was made that the colonial administrators had to seek an accommodation between ex-pediency, local official necessity and the supervisory uncertainties of the Colonial Office. The problem is important for the Nigerian press because the history of the relations between it and the government in our period is the story of attempts to control the newspapers and the unremitting efforts of the press and the public to safeguard freedom of expression. Few issues united the people of Lagos and excited their wrath as much as the threat to press liberty. In defence of it, they quoted English principles, asserted rights and privileges, mounted agitation and made sacrifices in contributions to offset libel costs.

References to established principles were made in support of the case for a free press as an essential instrument for 'vindicating the cause of the oppressed'. John Milton's remonstration against press censorship in which he contended that 'in a free and open encounter' truth would always triumph over falsehood; the idea prevalent in the eighteenth century that liberty was the source of England's greatness, that a free press was the most valuable of British privileges, 'the great palladium of the British freedom'; the arguments of the Philosophic Radicals or Benthamites – the influential intellectual element in the British liberal movement of the nineteenth century – which gave great intellectual support to advocates of press freedom: all these were cited and quoted in support of press freedom in Nigeria.[1] The famous declaration of *The Times* of London in 1858 became an article of faith:

> Liberty of thought and speech is the very air which an Englishman breathes from his birth; he could not understand living in another

atmosphere. Nor when you once allow this liberty can you restrict the range of its subjects. The principle must have free exercise, or it dies. . .

The educated Nigerians were English citizens by law as much as by cultural attitudes and naturally expected that the principle should apply to them. They did not seem to have realised the implications of the colonial situation for such British democratic principles as press liberty.

Apart from the concept of the role of a free press in a democratic society as the instrument for the scrutiny of government policy as well as for obtaining redress and checking abuses, there was the more pragmatic viewpoint which saw freedom of expression in a Crown Colony situation as a permissible outlet for the 'inevitable fumes of discontent'. As John Jackson put it:[2]

> The tendency on the part of the educated native to ventilate his grievances ought. . . . to be regarded as an advantage as it is of the nature of an escape valve and has the helpful effect of affording vent for the escape of the effervescence of feeling which if kept continually smothered might develop into a violent outburst.

Although the struggle for a free press was a patriotic cause, contradictory statements and notes of warning were often given by Nigerians in circumstances of indignation due to severe criticism of themselves. 'Liberty of press and free speech', observed Obasa of Ikija, 'is justified only in a community where there is a public opinion educated sufficiently to guide and direct such liberty so as to prevent degeneration into licence';[3] Dr Akinwande Savage lauded the British patriots whose sufferings and sacrifices made possible the freedom of the press and warned: 'We must take care that the freedom we are enjoying is not allowed to degenerate into a licence capable of being utilized as a cloak to prosecute personal vendetta and for the ventilation of grievances born of disappointed hopes.'[4] Such sour remarks, however, did not detract from the unity of purpose and action which underpinned nationalist efforts to secure press liberty.

EARLY RESTRICTIVE EFFORTS

It was not until the first decade of the twentieth century that regulations were for the first time introduced to control the press. Before this time, however, a number of governors had manifested much desire to control the newspapers. In 1862, Governor H. S. Freeman, on hearing that a newspaper was about to be established in Lagos, sought permission to impose a newspaper tax. Robert Campbell had purchased a second-hand printing press from England and was making preparations to launch the *Anglo-African*. Freeman informed the Secretary of State about the danger which a newspaper would constitute in the colony and drew his attention to the 'dispute and ill-feeling' which the 'worse than worthless' periodicals published at the other colonies on the West Coast had caused. Freeman feared that though there was little ill-feeling exhibited between the different sectors in Lagos, there was a strong undercurrent which would break out when journalism gave it a vent. To prevent any trouble, the Governor requested that any newspaper published should be taxed to prevent it from succeeding as a monetary speculation. In the alternative, he suggested that one paper might be allowed in which government notices would be inserted and which would thus be a government paper and free from tax. He trusted that the Secretary of State would sanction his putting 'this trifling check' on the liberty of the press which, he claimed, was a 'dangerous instrument in the hands of semi-civilized Negroes'.[5] The last nail had only the previous year been driven into the coffin of newspaper taxes in Britain, and the Drape-Hill controversy in Sierra Leone in the 1850s was still fresh in the minds of Whitehall officials, as was revealed in copious minutes. It was hardly surprising that Newcastle, the Secretary of State, rejected Freeman's demands.[6]

In 1866, Governor John Glover apparently wished he had the power to control the London-based *African Times*. He had one edition of the newspaper confiscated by the Post Office, and eventually arranged for slow deliveries whenever politically convenient.[7] In 1882 (May 19) J. B. Benjamin of the *Lagos Observer* was taken to court and convicted for contempt of the judiciary even though the crucial ingredient in the case did not appear to have been proved. The article which occasioned the charge was as follows:[8]

> Our courts of law, although just at present all conducted by a learned and efficient judge, are generally presided over by amateur Lawyers, often, by delay, maladministration and expense, to the sorrow of unfortunate suitors who are obliged to resort to them. Some of these amateurs are known to be men steeped in the most

bitter Negro hatred such as is often found in vulgar West Indian plantation overseas. And yet, black men are interested in ninety-nine per cent of the cases tried before these people. We do not wish to assert that where a case is clear, the party to whom it is due does not receive justice; but where the right is nearly balanced, we do not hesitate to say that prejudice would be allowed its influence, and in such case, if allusion is made by an advocate to what is manifest to everyone, he is threatened with all the penalties of the court, so as ever after to keep quiet.

The prosecution rested its case on the evidence of the police officer who testified that he bought the offending newspaper at Benjamin's office with money given to him by C. G. Blackburn, the district commissioner. Benjamin pleaded fair comment and contended that the ownership of the newspaper had not been established in court. This gap in the law would be filled more than twenty years later with a law compelling proprietors to register their names with the government; nonetheless, the district commissioner ruled that the issue of ownership was immaterial to the case and in his judgment held that the passage charged amounted to 'an imputation of improbity and corruption against those who administered justice in the colony'. He observed that such an imputation was 'beyond the bounds of frank and honest discussion and of liberal criticism'. It was 'calculated to bring the administration of justice into distrust, hatred and contempt' and was 'certainly unlawful'.[9] Benjamin was convicted and, evidently to intimidate him, he was requested to appear for judgment whenever he was summoned. His appeal against this decision was thrown out.

The Official Secrets Ordinance was introduced in 1891 but it was of no significance for the newspapers. Recommended for enactment by the Colonial Office because two years earlier the British Government found that no legal proceedings could be taken against a civil servant who had divulged important State Secrets to a newspaper, it was not expected to hinder press freedom either by the newspapers or the African members in the Legislative Council and it never in fact did so.[10]

THE NEWSPAPER ORDINANCE, 1903

The heightened tone of press criticism which marked political opposition from the last years of the nineteenth century to the eve of the First World War could not but irritate the colonial administration. The policies and persons of the governors were attacked unceasingly and a regime of hostile propaganda was established which presumably complicated the problems of government and widened the gulf between the administration and the people. Governor Henry McCallum apparently rode out the newspaper storm but his successor, William MacGregor, was less accommodating and must have wished he could control the newspapers. In the manner of Governor Hill of Sierra Leone and William Drape, he sought to intimidate John Jackson by discontinuing the subsidy arrangement but this drove the latter to attack the government harder than before. MacGregor must have begun to consider how best to control the press when, to his pleasant surprise, a draft Newspaper Ordinance arrived from the Colonial Office.

This seemingly mysterious event had its origin not in the Colonial Office but in the Protectorate of Southern Nigeria. Ralph (later Sir Ralph) Moor, the High Commissioner and a soldier, deprecated the vigour and influence of the Lagos Press, and was afraid that it might mislead what he termed 'an ignorant population' in his area of authority. He disliked the tendency which appeared 'to lead to the position that the native element . . . determine the legislative action that can be taken by the administration' and feared that if the position advanced a step further, the territories of Nigeria would be 'ruled piecemeal by and for the native . . .' He therefore called the attention of the Secretary of State to the fact that education was spreading throughout the territories and that the educated and semi-educated elements would no doubt be guided in their views and opinions by the local press. As he was later to put it, 'The education of the natives of this Protectorate is practically only just beginning and I have been already had experience of difficulties created by natives with elementary education taking the statements in the press as actually true and in future years there can be no doubt that the opinion of not only the better educated but also the half educated natives will be formed to an extent from the local newspapers.' He therefore thought it was well that 'such restrictions should be put on the press as will require that facts are duly authenticated before publication and that the Government may have some reasonable control over the press'.[11]

Chamberlain, the Colonial Secretary, was probably already

prejudiced against the West African newspaper press. The Freetown government's attribution of the 1898 insurrection in Sierra Leone to subversion and treason on the part of the press had been discredited by Sir David Chalmers but a harmful image of the press might have been created. In Lagos, in despatches between 1900 and 1901, the press had been described by MacGregor as 'ill-formed and mendacious' and 'ignorant and malevolent'.[12] It is no wonder, therefore, that the Secretary of State granted Moor's request; he transmitted to Calabar a copy of a press law passed in Trinidad in 1894 for regulating the printing and publishing of newspapers. Chamberlain went a stage further: he sent a copy of all this correspondence to the Governor of Lagos for his 'observations and suggestions'.[13] We shall not concern ourselves with the progress of the measure in the Protectorate of Southern Nigeria, for, up to 1906, when it was amalgamated with the Colony and Protectorate of Lagos, it had no African-conducted newspaper. It is sufficient to point out that in his anxiety to make the law more drastic, Moor went into disagreeable arguments with Chamberlain which redounded to his discredit.[14]

The Trinidad law provided for the registration of the owners, publishers and printers of newspapers. Newspaper proprietors were required to deposit £200 caution money with the government in the form of a bond. This sum of money was a guarantee for the payment of fines or damages. The restrictive nature of the stipulation is illustrated by the fact that in Trinidad, as an official later pointed out, it killed the *Tobago News* because the owner was unable to furnish the amount of the bond. For obvious reasons, the law suited MacGregor's desires, but the Governor felt that the bond should be increased to £500. A number of Colonial Office officials thought that £200 was enough considering what the provision had 'accomplished' in Trinidad; but some others argued that a newspaper which would be killed by having to give security for £500 had no title to exist. The Secretary of State agreed with the latter view, but chose to leave the amount to the Governor's discretion.

Nigerian journalists were quick to anticipate the government. Samuel Harden, who wrote the column 'Lagosian On Dits' in the *Standard*, was first to alert the public: 'It is contemplated to enact a law to establish a censorship over the press. At least so goes the rumour . . .'[16]

Harden took the rumour seriously enough to express his

anxieties about the need to safeguard press freedom, His speculation, even though misleading was good 'watchdog journalism' but
the 'subterranean rumbles' which it reportedly stimulated proved
incapable of staying the Governor's hand. On 23 April 1902, the
the Newspaper Bill was introduced into the Legislative Council.
The great outcry which it elicited found its outlet in the *Standard*
and *Record* which were now engaged in a battle for their own
survival. The *bête noire* was the bond. The *Standard* condemned
it in the strongest possible terms and described the principle as
'vicious' because it discriminated against 'a weak class of citizens
in favour of a large majority'. The paper reminded the government of the importance of the press in European countries where
it was a power in the way it educated the masses, corrected abuses,
instituted reforms and generally safeguarded the interest of the
people. If the press was so valuable in highly developed countries,
its value in West Africa was inestimable. Enlightened opinion in
West Africa, the *Standard* urged, knew full well the value and
importance of the newspaper as a public educator, the advocate
of the rights of the people and the medium through which they
might make known their grievances with the chances of receiving
redress. Then in words which were to ring out in the Legislative
Council, the paper declared, 'Without universal suffrage, without
representation of any kind – without a municipality or other
agency by which it may be said that the people have any voice or
hand in the government, the press is the only means, feeble and
ineffective as it often is, still it is the only means there is for
restraining or checking abuses. . . .'[17]

Three days later, the *Record* declaimed against the proposed
law which it described as 'inequitable and vicious in principle'.
Denouncing it as 'a tyrannical measure designed to fetter the
press and stifle public opinion', the *Record* remarked that it was 'a
superfluous piece of legislation lacking warrant and . . . wisdom
and opposed to reason and equity'.[18]

The critical views expressed by the newspapers were embodied
in a petition to the Governor and the Legislative Council on 13
May, signed by three hundred people including thirteen chiefs.
Prominent signatories included J. P. L. Davies, A. W. Howells,
J. B. Benjamin, A. B. Cole, George Alfred Williams, Dr John
Randle, W. B. Macaulay and John Payne Jackson. The petitioners
described the bond as 'a restraint without any reason on liberty'
and contended that in a British Crown Colony like Lagos which

lacked adequate representation, the press was the principal instrument by means of which they were enabled to express publicly
their opinions and grievances. It was therefore more desirable in
the public interest that the working of the newspaper should be
unimpeded and every facility given for public complaints to
be freely heard consistent with reasonable protection against
libellous productions. Attention was also drawn to the fact that
the proposed law did not take into account that the interests of the
local press were not limited to the individual owners but extended
to the public who had always identified their interests with those
of the press by their readiness to share in any financial burdens
imposed as a result of libel suits.[19] C. J. George and Dr Obadiah
Johnson made powerful speeches but the case for the press was
put most admirably by C. A. Sapara Williams.[20] Disposing of the
government's argument, which in retrospect was misleading, that
the West Indian people had accepted a similar measure without
protest, he declared:

> In the West Indian colonies Europeans settle in large numbers with
> their families, circumstances might be produced from such a state of
> society which justified Government in passing such a law in order to
> protect themselves. In Lagos the case is different. We all know that
> many newspapers in England have become defunct in consequence of
> heavy damages and costs being awarded against the Proprietors and
> publishers of such newspapers for libel actions. Has the Government
> of the day in consequence thought fit to bring in a bill to compel every
> newspaper proprietor, printer and publisher to enter into such a
> Bond as that contemplated by this Bill before the commencement of
> the printing and publication of newspapers? Certainly not. Why so
> in the colonies? . . . The Bill seems to savour of class legislation
> which is most undesirable and objectionable. I have been severely
> criticised by these newspapers but I think nothing the worse of
> them.

MacGregor had a high opinion of Sapara Williams, whom he
had unsuccessfully recommended to the Colonial Office for
appointment as Queen's Advocate.[21] In the public struggle against
the press law, Williams's influence must have been an important
factor in the Governor's indecisiveness, which was again shown in
the decision to drop further consideration of the Bill. Meanwhile,
the Lagos press continued the struggle against it. The *Record*,
while blaming the proposed law on 'official bias and official
arrogance', underlined the paradox of intolerance to criticism:

Susceptibility to criticism on the part of those who govern is always looked upon as a bad sign for the reason that when those in power would presume themselves to be infallible and would brook neither interference nor criticism, the outcome is sure to be maladministration, and it is the consciousness of misdoing which engenders apprehension and develops a sensitiveness to inquiry and criticism the latter growing more acute as the tide of popular sentiment rises in opposition to misgovernment.[22]

MacGregor thought over the issue for another five months before he made up his mind to go ahead with the Bill. In the Legislative Council, a determined fight was fought by the African members but their verbal blows did not avail to block its passage. After the Bill was passed, newspaper editorials began to multiply their appeals to 'all lovers of freedom' in England and elsewhere who had always championed 'the cause of the down-trodden and oppressed in Africa' to help the people of Lagos in their hour of 'grave peril'.[23] In West Africa, the *Gold Coast Leader* and the *Sierra Leone Weekly News* had earlier waded into the agitation. The former which headlined its comment, 'The People of Lagos gagged' described the law as a 'piece of oppressive, iniquitous and gagging legislation'. The *Weekly News* drew attention to the failure of Governor Hill to control the Sierra Leone press and the rejection by the Chalmers Commission of Cardew's impeachment of the Sierra Leone press.[24] In England, the *African Review*, the *Truth* and *Reynolds' Newspaper* ('Imperialism and Tyranny go hand in hand'), appealed to the Secretary of State to withold assent.[25]

The last battle from Lagos was fought by a petition having two hundred signatories and praying for disallowance. In forwarding the petition, MacGregor expressed surprise that the signatures should be a mere two hundred out of a population of a million and a half. To be worthy of some attention, he contended, the petition should have borne two thousand signatures. Furthermore, it was his view that £250 was a moderate security which would provide some defence to private or official persons against 'reckless and irresponsible misrepresentation'.[26] A Colonial Office official suggested that they should 'stick to (their) guns', and Chamberlain did.[27] In his reply to the petition, the Secretary of State informed the Lagos Community that the provisions of the measure were necessary and these provisions in no way interfered with or hampered the free discussion of events in a legitimate manner.[28] This ruling greatly disappointed the *Record* which continued to demand that the law be repealed.[29] The Newspaper Ordinance ran into twenty-two clauses the significant sections of which were as follows,

> *Section 2* (definition of a newspaper). A newspaper was any paper containing public news, intelligence or occurrences, or any remarks, observations or comments thereof printed for sale and published in the colony periodically or in parts or members at intervals not exceeding twenty-six days between the publication of any two such papers, parts or members.

The term also meant

> any paper printed in order to be dispersed and made public weekly or oftener or at intervals not exceeding twenty-six days containing only or principally advertisements.
>
> *Section 3* (registration and bond)
> From and after the commencement of this Ordinance no person shall print or publish or cause to be printed or published within this colony any newspaper unless he shall have previously
> (1) made, signed and sworn before any police Magistrate or District Commissioner or any Commissioner of Oaths or registered in the office of the Chief Registrar of the Supreme Court an affidavit containing the several matters and things following, that is to say
> (a) the correct title or name of the newspaper.
> (b) a true description of the house or building wherein such newspaper is intended to be printed and
> (c) the real and true names of abode of the person or persons intended to be the printer or printers, publisher or publishers, proprietor or proprietors, of the same; and
> (2) given and executed and registered in the office of the Chief Registrar of the Supreme Court a bond in the sum of £250 with one or more sureties as may be required and approved by the Attorney General on condition that such printer or printers, publisher or publishers, proprietor or proprietors, shall pay to His Majesty, His Heirs and Successors every penalty which may at any time be imposed upon or adjudged against him or them upon any conviction for printing or publishing any blasphemous or seditious or other libel at any time after the execution of such bond, and also any damages and costs of any judgement for the plaintiff in any action for libel against such printer, publisher or proprietor, and all other penalties whatsoever which may be imposed upon or adjudged by the Court against him or them under the provisions of this Ordinance.

The penalty for failure to comply with the above provisions was a fine of twenty-five pounds. It was also declared an offence to publish a newspaper which did not carry at the foot of the page, the address of the printer and publisher. Penalty for this offence was fifty pounds. Printers and publishers were compelled to deposit with the Chief Registrar within six days a copy of every newspaper published. Such subscriptions were to be paid for quarterly. Non-compliance was liable to a fine of five pounds.[30] Some of these provisions were to be slightly altered fourteen years later when the 1903 law was replaced by another which proceeded upon different and more extreme principles.

The government's intention in passing the newspaper law despite the volume of opposition was never hidden. It came out clearly in debates in the Legislative Council. Contributing to the debate on the second reading of the Bill, the Acting Chief Justice said that the object of the Bill was to impose some responsibility on the press. 'If the press is to be of any value', he stated ,'it must have some responsibility which would impart some weight to it.' MacGregor scoffed at the idea that the press was a medium of instruction. In his view, a lecture at the Lagos Institute was a far more real means of instruction for the people. After a visit to the eastern districts, he felt pleased that the area had not yet been 'reached by the local press'. According to him, he found people to be most loyal and it could not be said that the people needed the assistance of the newspapers. Criticism, he admitted, was permissible in certain circumstances but it brought a great deal of harm to young officers while it proved embarrassing to the government.[31]

The Newspaper Ordinance was capable of hindering the growth of the newspaper press in two ways. The Bond of £250 made the newspaper business a relatively expensive venture and the demand for sureties faced newspaper owners with new problems. It was not always easy for proprietors to get sureties because it would seem that people in high places were reluctant openly to identify themselves with the critics of the government. Furthermore, potential sureties apparently did not want to be involved in the frequent quarrels between proprietors and contract-printers. For if after a Bond was executed, the proprietor and the printer parted company, the surety was required to join in executing a fresh Bond. This was amply demonstrated in the case of the

Daily Telegraph which came under five different printers in ten years in the twenties and thirties.[32]

It is difficult to determine how precisely these considerations affected the growth of the newspaper press. Prosecutions under the Ordinance were few and they did not take place until the 1930s.[33] But perhaps the significance of the law lay not in the number of newspapers prosecuted but in its subtle effect in limiting the proliferation of newspapers. It must have dissuaded persons with limited resources from venturing on journalism. It is perhaps significant that while up to 1901 (the year in which the measure was mooted) the longest interval between two new newspapers was four years, there was a corresponding gap of eight years (1900–8) during the first decade of the present century. It would be reasonable to explain this difference in terms of the initial apprehension caused by the Newspaper Ordinance.

However, if the press law did limit the proliferation of newspapers during the period immediately following its passage, it did not succeed in reducing the mounting press attacks. On the contrary, it provoked the newspapers to step up their opposition; by 1909 the Attorney-General felt convinced that the Lagos press was guilty of 'a good deal of misrepresentation', and Governor Egerton, MacGregor's successor, accused the press of continually and deliberately stirring the Yoruba people against the Europeans. His introduction that year of the Seditious Offences Ordinance reflected the extent to which he found the situation intolerable.

THE SEDITIOUS OFFENCES ORDINANCE

The occasion for the introduction of the Seditious Offences Bill was the publication by Herbert Macaulay of a pamphlet entitled 'Governor Egerton and the Railway' in September 1908. The Macaulay Pamphlet, about 1 000 copies of which were sold, levelled serious charges of maladministration against the Governor. It drew attention to the Governor's 'disregard' of serious allegations of scandals in the Railway, his 'personification of prejudice', his permitting minor considerations to take precedence over momentous issues, his neglect to direct that criminal prosecutions be commenced against an alleged friend of his who was involved in the scandals. Other charges included 'wicked expropriation' of lands.

Egerton was so upset that he promptly sought legal opinion. The Attorney-General, A. R. Pennington, was then on leave and the Acting Attorney-General, J. Ernest Green, was requested to submit 'advice on the liability of Macaulay's pamphlet to criminal proceedings.' Green advised that there was nothing in the pamphlet that could be construed as seditious. He could see that there was an undercurrent of general attack on the administration of the Railway Department as a whole and of government officials but nothing that could be construed into 'an attempt to subvert the Government . . . and excite rebellion and disorder.'

Meanwhile the Governor had sent a minute to the Acting Chief Justice, Edwin Speed, to seek his opinion on the matter and also recalled the Attorney-General from leave. Speed, in a letter marked 'private and confidential', gave his opinion that the pamphlet was 'seditious libel from the first paragraph to the last'. Back from leave, Pennington had no hesitation in saying that the pamphlet was a seditious libel 'under both English law and also under the Indian Penal Code'.[34]

With the majority in favour of prosecution, Egerton wrote to the Secretary of State urging the enactment of a Seditious Ordinance. He reported that Herbert Macaulay had been notorious for his violent attacks on the Governor and the government generally in letters and articles published in the newspapers, contributions 'of a nature calculated to do infinite harm by the unscrupulous misrepresentation of facts', among a people who were 'apt to accept anything that appears in print'. He submitted that the government should be strengthened by the law relating to seditious, unlawful assemblies, resistance to civil power, etc. Such legislation, he pointed out, would allow reasonable freedom of discussion of government measures but would give the government 'power . . . to punish publications and speeches designed to inflame an excitable and ignorant populace the bulk of whom are absolutely under the control of Headmen and Chiefs who themselves have only recently emerged from barbarism and are still actuated by the old traditions of their race'.[35] Egerton indicated his preference for an Indian precedent and requested that he should be supplied with copies of the latest edition of the Indian Penal Code and of recent enactments dealing with sedition and seditious publications in newspapers.[36]

It may be asked why Egerton desired the enactment of a law when he could have successfully instituted a criminal action against Herbert Macaulay, and also why he wanted the law to be based on the Indian Penal Code. The Governor was probably afraid that such a prosecution might lead to disturbances because tempers were running high over land appropriation, water rate and the European church and chaplaincy. He presumably calculated that the passage of a harsh legislation, which he was probably not anxious to enforce, could have the effect, even if temporarily, of checking the mounting hostility. Alternatively, it might be that the Governor was much more concerned to exploit the opportunity to tighten control of the newspapers. He preferred an Indian precedent because in that country sweeping and severe laws had been passed in the last century to control newspapers which preached open violence and even gave instructions on how to manufacture bombs and organise secret societies in opposition to the government. Typical of the severity of these laws was the Seditious Offences Ordinance of India which carried the penalty of transportation for life. The Nigerian press did not preach violence or subversion, but the government picked its own weapon.

Opinion differed at the Colonial Office as to whether the Governor had taken the right step. An official, although he disdainfully thought that the Nigerian press was 'a wholly contemptible thing', nevertheless submitted that it would be 'a retrograde step' to introduce Indian laws at that date in Southern Nigeria where conditions were very different. Another was 'clearly' of the opinion that 'undue sensitiveness' on the part of governors should be deprecated. 'Much worse things are said and done in Ireland and no action is taken.' A view more sympathetic to the Lagos government which emphasised the difficulties of a colonial administration as the target of all attacks, found favour with the Colonial Secretary who signified his support for Egerton's proposals concurring in the view that the proposed Ordinance should be based on the Indian Penal Code of 1860 but as amended up to 1903.[37] In Lagos, the draft Ordinance was accepted as 'quite suitable' to the local conditions[38] and was published in the *Gazette* on 22 September 1909.

The Bill, entitled 'An Ordinance to make provision for the punishment of Seditious Offences', was divided into eight sections. Under sections three, four and five, anyone who excited hatred towards the government or between classes in the community or caused an officer to fail in his duty, was punished with imprisonment 'which may extend to two years' or with a fine (no amount stated) or with imprisonment and fine. Section three was a restatement of the existing law.

> Whoever by words, either spoken or written, or by signs, or by visible representation, or otherwise, brings or attempts to bring into hatred or contempt or excites or tries to excite disaffection, disloyalty or feelings of enmity towards His Majesty or the Government established by law in Southern Nigeria, shall be punished with imprisonment which may extend to two years, or with a fine or with both imprisonment and fine.

It did not constitute an offence under this section to criticise the government provided that such criticism did not excite hatred. . . .

Section 4
> Whoever . . . promotes or attempts to promote feelings of enmity or hatred between different classes of the population of Southern Nigeria, shall be punished. . . .

It was lawful under this section to point out, without malicious intention, anything which tended to produce feelings of hatred between different classes of the population.

Section 5
> Whoever makes, publishes or circulates any statement, rumour or report,
> (a) with intent to cause, or which is likely to cause any officer of the Government of Southern Nigeria or any person otherwise in the service of His Majesty to disregard or fail in his duty as such officer or servant of His Majesty
> (b) with intent to cause or which is likely to cause fear or alarm to the public or to any section of the public whereby any person may be induced to commit an offence against the State or against the public tranquillity, or
> (c) with intent to incite, or which is likely to incite, any class or community of persons to commit any offence against any other class or community, shall be punished. . . .

It did not amount to an offence within the meaning of this section if the statement published was true.

In addition to these sections, provision was made for the precautionary apprehension of an offender by the judiciary. Under Section Six, authority was given to district commissioners and police magistrates to check seditious publications in their areas of authority, by requiring offenders to execute a bond for good behaviour for a maximum period of one year.

The new Bill was to be introduced into the Legislative Council in the first week of October but before then, the newspapers had denounced it unreservedly. It came at a difficult time for them because they had to divide their energy between continuing attacks on the water rate project, delivering attacks on the newspaper measure and storming against the introduction of the municipal system and the proposed erection of a European church. The *Standard* published the text of the Bill and a letter from a correspondent who in a lengthy criticism observed that 'a more mischievious, wicked and diabolical measure than this to goad the people unto rebellion could not be devised'.[39] Commenting editorially, the paper regretted that such a Bill should be introduced in a peaceful and law-abiding community like Lagos whose loyalty had been several times 'severely tried and never found wanting'. It strongly objected to Sections three and four of the Bill, remarking that if there was any attempt to promote feelings of enmity or hatred between the classes, it had been noticeable since the arrival of the Governor with his policies of segregation and discrimination against black people. The paper saw no substance whatsoever in the proffered exemptions because everything hung upon the interpretation acceptable, not to a jury, but to a judge and assessors. Comparing the spirit of the 'oppressive enactment with the Inquisition and Star Chamber, the *Standard* accused the government of attempting to gag the people and muzzle the mouth of public opinion in an era of intense opposition activity. It therefore urged the people and the African members of the Legislative Council to resist the 'deadly blow' and prevent a 'dreadful catastrophe'.[40] Published simultaneously with the *Standard* editorial was a lengthy stricture which seems to have the cadence of Herbert Macaulay.

> . . . If by any degree of possibility this bill should ever be passed and be placed on the stature book of the Colony and Protectorate of Southern Nigeria, it will be the darkest page in the story of an Administration which already contains many dark pages in regard to the treatment of the native races in this portion of Western Africa under British rule during the past five years – the intention is simply to gag the people; to effectually gag the public press of the country; to suppress and extinguish all lawful assemblies; to discourage and suffocate all constitutional agitations against unpopular and oppressive measures of the government. Under such a law . . . newspaper editors must either talk platitudes or indulge in fulsome adulation of

government officials. . . . The worst form of slavery will then be established, namely the bondage of the mind. . . . A more mischievous, wicked and diabolical measure than this, to goad the people on to rebellion could not be devised.[41]

Two days later, the *Chronicle* condemned Clause 5 of the Bill which sought to prevent the criticism of white officials, as 'an aggression on the liberty of the press'.[42]

Either because the *Record* was too engrossed in the other agitations or because the editor had quarrelled with Macaulay over his decision not to publish the article which subsequently appeared in the controversial pamphlet and so refused to join in protesting against a situation which the pamphlet had contributed to bring about, it did not comment on the Bill until after it was passed.[43] But the stand of its two contemporaries clearly indicated the feelings of the people, including the chiefs. Lagos Chiefs threw themselves into the agitation as never before; they demanded and got a Yoruba-language translation of the law, and, at public meetings summoned by them, they objected strenuously against the measure and informed the government accordingly.[44]

In the Legislative Council, debate on the Bill was heated. Sapara Williams and Obadiah Johnson were actively supported by Kitoyi Ajasa who complained that the bill tended to equate the people of Lagos with Indians and the Irish.[45] The government's determination to rush the Bill and its disregard of all shades of African opinion on the matter decided Sapara Williams and Johnson to force a showdown. So when the Bill came to committee they promptly packed their papers and walked out of the chamber.[46] When they resumed their seats, the council had returned from committee and the three African members continued their attack on the Bill.

All this time, criticism of the Bill was going on in Britain. The *Christian World* attacked it and in Parliament C. R. Buxton, Member for Ashburton, drew from Colonel Seely, the Under-Secretary of State, the statement that the people of Lagos were law-abiding and that their loyalty to the British Crown had never been in doubt.[47]

Nevertheless, the Bill was passed (9 November 1909) and confirmed; but it would seem that the legislation did not immediately have the dire consequences feared. Although the press was unrelenting in its criticism of Egerton, so much so that Kitoyi Ajasa saw the need to reproach the opposition newspapers for exceeding 'the bounds of fair and legitimate criticism' and transcending 'the limits of propriety',[48] yet until he left Lagos in 1912, the Governor did not direct a single prosecution. It is remarkable that the only libel case during that period was a private suit instituted by an official of the Government Railway, and therefore, 'a protected person'.[49]

It is possible that Egerton did not really intend to use the law. As suggested previously, he might have wanted the measure as a sort of scare-crow to reduce press criticism. Coming only six years after the introduction of caution money, the law could reasonably have been expected to achieve this aim. Alternatively, he might well have been faced with the problem of whom to prosecute and whom to leave out. All the newspapers said virtually the same thing and that with the same verve. To have prosecuted one newspaperman would have exposed the government to the charge of bias and to have taken all the offending journalists to court would have aroused the wrath of the Colonial Office.

During the quarter-century which followed the passing of the law, there were three prosecutions for sedition – two during the First World War. These cases, which ranged from incitement of Africans against Europeans to incitement of a local political faction against another, would seem to indicate that the measure was capable of wider interpretation than for the most part was thought at the time it was passed. In other words, it was the kind of instrument which could meet the needs of Egerton's successor, Lord Lugard.

Lugard was a dictatorial former soldier with a strong dislike of the educated African: '. . . I am not in sympathy with him. His loud and arrogant conceit are distasteful to me. . . '. [50] Newspapermen saw his assumption of office as presaging a much more bitter public struggle to safeguard press freedom. Yet the newspapers welcomed him to Lagos with ridicule and warnings and, until the outbreak of war when they voluntarily imposed a censorship on themselves, continued to scrutinise his policy in a manner which provoked him beyond endurance. But surprisingly enough, Lugard complained about the liberty of the Nigerian press in a way which suggested that he was totally powerless to deal with it. On 16 October 1913, in one of those memorable letters to his wife, the Governor referred to the 'scurrilous local yellow press' and decried what he called its 'monstrous freedom' which, according to him, he was powerless to deal with 'for the Colonial Office . . . would never tolerate any infringement of the right of the press to be as libellous and seditious as it pleases.'[51] The following year, he described the opposition to the Provincial Courts Ordinance as 'virulent' and marked by 'plentiful abuse'.[52] That same year, he claimed that popular criticisms of the inadequacies of the system of education were 'substantiated by the bitter and at times almost libellous tone' of the newspapers. Stressing the need for character training in self-discipline, self-control and truthfulness in Nigerian schools, he averred that education had not brought 'happiness or contentment' to Nigeria if the performance of the newspapers was taken as a criterion. To his mind, it should be the aim of the educational system 'to train up a generation who shall exchange this bitter hostility for an attitude of friendly co-operation'.[53] In 1915, the Governor-General felt that a newspaper ought to be established which would explain government policies and the following year, he felt convinced that the 'Lagos Rags' were partly responsible for the Iseyin riots.[54]

Lugard undoubtedly exaggerated his powerlessness and mis-represented the Colonial Office; and his assessment of the quality of Nigerian journalism was prejudiced. However, if he genuinely feared that the Colonial Office would not support vindictive press prosecution, this might help to explain why he carried out no prosecution until he could exploit the special circumstances of war time. In 1916, he prosecuted an editor twice and that same year, under the pretence that he was codifying the existing criminal laws, he inserted a strange and vague paragraph under which it was possible to send editors to prison for criticising government policy. It was stated to be an offence to do 'any unlawful act calculated to interfere with the free exercise by the Governor or a Lieutenant-Governor of the duties or authority of his office or with the free exercise by a Member of the Executive or Legislative Council of his duties as such member'. The penalty was three years' imprisonment.[55]

REX V. JAMES BRIGHT DAVIES, 1916

Lugard had gladly welcomed the self-censorship which the newspapermen imposed on themselves soon after the First World War broke out in practical demonstration of Nigerian support for

Britain. At a meeting with F. S. James, the then Administrator of
the Colony, the editors had appealed to the government not to
introduce vexatious measures. The passage by the administration
of an unpopular Criminal Code Law and the re-opening of the
controversial water rate question in 1915–16 were scarcely the best
way to heed the editors' appeal. Most of the editors abided by their
undertaking and made only feeble attacks against the government,
but one of them, James Bright Davies chafed under the restraint.
He could not endure this apparently one-sided arrangement and
his positive reaction led to his first trial and conviction.

The first article complained of was an attack on British policy in
Lagos in December 1915:

> A policy . . . which threatens with ruin the progress and prosperity of
> the only town of importance in the so-called Colony of Nigeria . . . by
> the austerities and severities of a continuous series of measures and
> enactments which could only have been dictated by a rancorous
> negrophobism and which apart from German rule could only flourish
> under the British Crown Colony System of government or under a
> constituted and authorised autocracy.

The second article rejoiced with the people of Sierra Leone for
being rid of a 'negrophobist governor' and expressed the hope that
Nigeria would have such good fortune.

> The people of Nigeria, and of Lagos in particular, will take
> courage from this fact that someday or other, whether distant or
> near, their own relief from the iron and cruel rule of their own ad-
> ministration is sure to come and we shall be freed from the galling
> yoke of its iniquitous measures and laws.[56]

James Davies was charged with attempting to bring the government into hatred and contempt and to excite disaffection, disloyalty and feelings of enmity towards it. On 9 February 1916, he
was convicted on both counts and fined £100. In addition, he was
requested to enter into a recognisance, himself and two sureties in
£100 each, to be of good behaviour for twelve months. He would
go to prison for six months if he defaulted. He defaulted – or was
said to have done so. In August 1916, he attacked British firms and
his thinly veiled expression of sympathy for the Germans led to
his prosecution. The offending paragraph ran as follows:

> The system adopted by the British firms in the produce trade
> since the war . . . is responsible for the strong under-current of
> sympathy for the German cause which pervades the breasts of the

majority of the Native population. And the intensity of this feeling is such that one frequently hears the wish and the most sanguine hopes expressed in the daily conversations of the people about trade, that Germany should win this war, as they would prefer to come under German rule if only to escape and be saved from tyranny and exploitation of the British merchants.[57]

James Davies was this time accused of inciting the non-trading community to commit an offence against the trading community. Before the case was taken to court, the Governor had disagreed with the Chief Justice over the demerit of the newspaper article: Lugard thought that it was certainly seditious but the Chief Justice considered that the article was 'justifiable journalese comment'.[58] Nevertheless, the trial was authorised and on 6 November James Davies, now sixty-eight years old, was sentenced to six months' imprisonment, to the great delight of Lugard. The trial judge, however, held that the charge of inciting one class of persons against another was not proved, the question discussed by the paper being 'eminently a question between two sections of the trading community and the non-trading community'; on the second count of exciting disaffection, the judge felt that he could not ignore the fact that on two separate occasions within nine months, James Davies had 'chosen to publish wicked and malicious libels against the Government of Nigeria at a time when it (was) the obvious duty of every right-minded man to give to that Government his most strenuous and uncompromising support'.[59] James Davies was released from prison the following year in response to the intervention of persons of influence, including Kitoyi Ajasa and Thomas Jackson who based their plea on the editor's old age and poor health.

THE ABORTIVE CENSORSHIP LAW

In spite of the Criminal Code, Lugard continued his search for the most effective restraint on criticism. In 1917, he decided to introduce a permanent censorship ostensibly as a safeguard against any emergency. The proposed law was intended to repeal the Newspaper Ordinance of 1903. Both measures ran into twenty-two clauses and contained about the same general provisions. However, the new proposal stipulated that signed copies of newspapers were to be delivered or sent by post to the Central Secretary on the day of publication instead of to the Chief Registrar within six days of publication. In addition, the government was no longer to be required to pay for the copy of newspapers so deposited. Furthermore, the failure to comply with the provisions as to caution money (£250) was declared punishable not by a fine of £25 but £50. But what gave the proposal its special character was contained in Section 17. Not only was a censor of newspapers to be appointed in situations or threats of emergency but also the buildings and equipments of a convicted newspaper were to be liable to confiscation as Ralph Moor had proposed for the Niger Coast Protectorate at the beginning of the century.

(1) If and whenever an emergency shall have arisen or to be about to arise affecting the public safety the Governor may by notice in the Gazette
   (a) appoint a censor of newspapers
   (b) require the submission to the censor of a copy of every newspaper before the publication thereof.
(2) The censor appointed as aforesaid may alter, amend or delete any part of such copy without assigning any reason thereof.
(3) The proprietor, printer and publisher of any newspaper which shall be published, sold or issued to the public before a copy of the same shall have been presented to and passed by the censor, or in a form differing from that passed by the censor, and every person who shall knowingly sell or distribute such newspaper shall on summary conviction before any magistrate be liable to a fine of £100 or imprisonment for 12 months or to both and every copy of such newspaper and the premises and all plant machinery and stock used in aid of the printing or publication or production of such newspaper shall be liable to forfeiture.
(4) On becoming aware that an offence has been committed under this section the censor shall inform the nearest Magistrate who shall forthwith order a warrant authorising the closing of such premises and the seizing of all such copies, plant machinery and stock pending the hearing of the case.[60]

Though horrified by the Censorship Bill, Nigerians exhibited a calm which contrasted strangely with their usually vigorous opposition to restrictive press legislation. It was either that the press and people were reluctant to abandon their attitude of co-operation with government while the war lasted or that the event coincided with a period of transition for the Nigerian press when the earliest and most experienced editors were either dead or senile, and their financially crumbling newspapers were being put together by a younger generation of newspapermen soon to distinguish themselves in nationalism and journalism. The *Standard* said nothing until after the Bill was passed whereupon it commented tamely on the withdrawal of six days' grace granted under the old registration law for the delivery of newspaper copies to the government. The view of the newspaper's own columnist, 'Dogmatist', that its editorial comment on the Ordinance was 'disappointingly amateurish and muddled' added to its discredit. The *Record* in an editorial headed 'The Newspaper Ordinance 1917 or Press muzzling as a fine art in Nigeria' stated its opposition to any 'crucifixion of the liberty of the press'.[61] The moderate tone of criticism was made all the more disquieting by the silence of the *Pioneer*, which by the middle of the following year would warn its contemporaries that the extravagance of exceeding the bounds of decency and moderation needed curbing.

Not until James Davies returned from prison did the traditional tempo of resistance find expression. In a petition to the Governor-General, he took serious objection to the provision for the delivery of copies of newspapers, describing it as 'too hard and fast and rather exacting'. Listing numerous factors which could make it impossible for an editor to deliver a copy of his newspaper to the Central Secretary on the day of publication (momentary oversight, delay or negligence on the part of a messenger; completion of printing after the official hours necessitating immediate publication; hurry to catch an outgoing mail which closed at 6 p.m. or mail train going to the North; early closing on Saturday) he argued that no injury or inconvenience was likely to be caused to any public or private interest which might be advanced as a reason justifying the substitution of an absolute and unconditional provision for the liberal provision of six days in the 1903 Ordinance. On the refusal to pay for copies delivered, Davies deemed it 'inequitable'. He contended that if it were a case of supplying a museum for purposes of record, there would be something to be said for the government's decision. 'In this case', he asserted, 'it was a case of furnishing the Government material for legal proceedings.' But the proposal Davies considered intolerable was the censorship. He argued that censorship was never a permanent right of government. Any law which established it was 'transient'; it was called into being for a specific purpose and under special circumstances. When the occasion which gave rise to it had passed, the measure must expire automatically. He believed that the censorship in England was not established upon a distinct law but upon regulations framed under the provisions of the Defence of the Realm Act, a temporary measure called forth by the Great War which would cease to operate when the war ended.[63]

In his reply to the petition, Lugard stated that the points raised in it did not possess sufficient weight. In answer to the criticism of non-payment of newspapers delivered, Lugard explained that in most countries the publisher of a book, however costly, had to furnish copies to the government free of charge. He affirmed that the censorship was 'a permanent provision to be called in aid whenever necessity (arose)'.[64] Davies was not satisfied with this reply and in a second letter to the Governor-General, he reiterated his main arguments, warning that the censorship was in conflict with the law in England and that the British people would not tolerate its restrictive implications.

The Newspaper Bill seems to have passed the Legislative Council without much difficulty. Presented on 29 June and read a second time on 13 July without opposition by the three African members, Eric Moore, Ajasa, and S. H. Pearse, it was passed on 3 August. In the Colonial Office, however, it was studied critically on the basis of James Davies's petition to the Secretary of State. No precedent could be found for Clause 17 as a piece of permanent legislation. Lugard claimed to have based that section on the Nyasaland (Malawi) Ordinance of 1914 but it was found that the Nigerian Ordinance differed from it in two important particulars. First, the Nyasaland Ordinance was essentially a war measure, which provided for the censorship of both telegrams and newspapers to be established in an emergency. There could, therefore, be no censorship of newspapers until there was a situation grave enough to justify censorship of telegrams. (Sierra Leone had a similar law in 1916.) But Section 17 of the Nigerian Ordinance had omitted all reference to the censorship of telegrams, and under it it would be possible to establish a censorship of newspapers on occasions not serious enough to justify a censorship of telegrams. Secondly, the Nyasaland Ordinance required action by the Governor in council, while the Nigerian section gave the power to the Governor alone. A further important point was that the Nyasaland Ordinance had been repealed because the British Protectorate (Defence) Order in Council, 1916, had been passed, thus rendering the Nyasaland law superfluous. Consequently, in November 1917 the Secretary of State, Walter H. Long, instructed Lugard to withdraw the provision. He advised him that if during the war and during any other grave emergency censorship was required in Nigeria, it would be provided by means of the existing Imperial Regulations.[65]

Lugard was notoriously impatient of Colonial Office supervision, and the rejection of his censorship law must have confirmed his worst fears about Colonial Office attitude to colonial newspapers. Blocked in his oversmart and extremist plans for press control, the Governor forgot the Newspaper Ordinance until a long time afterwards when the Colonial Office called his attention to the matter. To avoid the disallowance of the Ordinance, an amending Ordinance repealing the permanent censorship provision and effecting other necessary emendations was rushed through the Nigerian Legislative Council in September 1918. The two Ordinances were simultaneously confirmed in December.[66] By this time the war had come to an end, and even if it had not it seems fairly obvious that Lugard would not have established a temporary censorship.

The eve of Lugard's departure from Nigeria coincided with the real emergence of the new generation of newspapermen. Relieved from voluntary political restraint by the end of hostilities and determined to settle old scores with the Governor-General, they pounded him with abuse and thus served notice of what unpopular successors should expect.

'HERBERT MACAULAY MUST BE GAGGED'

Few administrations in Nigeria were greater victims of press criticism than that of Governor Hugh Clifford who succeeded Lugard. His reactionary and negative role in the Congress movement and the Eleko Affair invited a torrent of abuse which must have proved unsettling. But he did not initiate any repressive measures probably because he was the sort of person who gave as much as he took. The situation was different under Graeme Thompson whose administration saw at least four prosecutions, the most significant of which was the so-called Gunpowder Plot Rumour Case involving Herbert Macaulay and others. The sedition case arose out of Herbert Macaulay's crusade on behalf of the deposed and banished Eleko. On 19 June 1928, a cable arrived in Lagos announcing the decision of the Privy Council that the

Supreme Court in Lagos was wrong in holding that the Eleko could not test the validity of the Deportation Order under which he was banished to Oyo. The news that the Eleko's appeal had been allowed was greeted with public jubilation as groups of men and women danced about the town, singing and drumming abusive songs. In the midst of this excitement, Macaulay's newspaper, the *Daily News*, gave prominence to a rumoured allegation that there was a plot to assassinate the ex-Eleko who, it was incorrectly reported, was soon to return to Lagos. The 'plot' rumour was spread a few months before the 323rd anniversary of London's Gunpowder Plot of 5 November 1605 which inspired the headline 'Gunpowder Plot Rumour' in the issue of 29 June. Public excitement ran so high that outrages were allegedly perpetrated on some important anti-Eleko personalities in the community. Chief Obanikoro, an inveterate enemy of the Eleko, was reported to have been jeered at and called a murderer in Tinubu Square. The Eleko's successor, Ibikunle Akitoye, was said to have been hissed.

On 6 July, J. A. Olushola, editor of the *Daily News* was charged to court for publishing a rumour with intent to incite one class of the community against another. The Police Magistrate, H. A. Young, who heard the case was so hostile to counsel for the defence (Kushika Roberts) that the latter after examining witnesses on both sides, refused to address the court. The magistrate, however, proceeded to find Olushola guilty and imposed a fine of £50 or three months' imprisonment. The fine was paid. Shortly afterwards, Herbert Macaulay and Dr Caulcrick, proprietors of the *Daily News* were charged to court for the same offence (13 August). No case in Lagos had been followed with such keen public interest, particularly as it was the eve of the second elections into the Legislative Council and it was widely believed that the objective was to get rid of Caulcrick, Vice-President of the NNDP and a possible candidate for the elections, and generally to demoralise supporters of the party. As was predicted, the defendants were found guilty, Caulcrick being directed to pay a fine of £50 or go to jail for three months; Macaulay had six months' imprisonment without the option of a fine. They appealed to the Supreme Court but their convictions were upheld. Macaulay stayed in prison for 185 days and had little praise for the prison authorities.[67]

The imprisonment of Herbert Macaulay apparently brought much satisfaction to his political enemies whose sentiments were reflected in the reaction of the *Daily Times* which opposed the view that the sentence was too severe. Attributing the 'diabolical rumour' to the 'tortuous and unscrupulous working of Herbert Macaulay's mind', it asserted that Macaulay's record generally was such as made him an 'altogether undesirable person'.

> He is a seditious-monger, an exploiter of the poor and ignorant in the name of patriotism and an agitator of the down-right low type whose diabolical influence requires not a temporary check but complete eradication from the community, and no measure the Government could take to effect this can be considered too drastic or rigorous. . . . [68]

The offensive of the *Daily Times* in the murder plot sensation actually started earlier on 3 August with a comment headlined 'Herbert Macaulay must be gagged'. The newspaper accused Macaulay of spreading 'rank sedition and sentiments of defiance of constituted authority' and lamented the 'sublime in-activity' on the part of the government. The climax of the newspaper's intervention was an impassioned plea for the restriction of press freedom. In the issue of 4 April 1919 and notwithstanding that it was narrowing the scope of its privilege, the *Daily Times* called the attention of the government to the Spanish dictator General Primo de Rivera's view that 'the freedom of the press cannot be a dogma, not even an axiom' but must be examined in reference to existing circumstances. The Spanish dictator's habit of 'watching over and exercising the strictest control over the press' as well as the restrictive practices in Italy and France were held up as worthy of emulation in Nigeria.[69] Fortunately for the Nigerian people, nothing was achieved by this reactionary campaign.

Between 1929 and the outbreak of the Second World War it would appear that there were no prosecutions for seditious libel. The relative political placidity of the period which compelled newspapers to print more foreign news reduced the chances of newspapermen clashing with the government. As African nationalism acquired momentum and inspired constitutional changes which produced African participation in government, and as the nationalist parties increasingly turned against one another, British administrators apparently became less disposed to limit the freedom of the press. However, contempt of law cases served to remind the newspapermen that they were subject to the consequences of law.

CONTEMPT OF COURT

In the British system, the freedom of the press was limited not only by the laws of sedition and defamation but also by the jurisdiction vested in the courts to safeguard their integrity against what was called 'scandalising a court or a judge' by dealing summarily with such contempt. The attitude of the newspapermen to the judiciary was coloured by the belief of the Nigerian people that the principle of the independence of the judiciary did not always enjoy in the colonies the same reverence with which it was regarded in Britain and that both the administration and judiciary were intimate areas of government. This explains why the *Observer* reacted to its conviction for contempt in 1882 with a strong plea for the freedom of the press. The available evidence indicates that there was no prosecution for contempt until *Rex vs. Thomas Jackson, 1925*. In the article entitled 'The Dangers of the Judicial System in Nigeria', Thomas Jackson held that the judges of the Supreme Court were under the subjection of the Executive and would not give a decision unfavourable to the government, and that they had been compelled to invent plausible arguments in order to be able to record decisions compatible with official wishes.[70] The Chief Justice (Sir R. M. Combe) remarked that if similar 'wicked aspersions' had been written in England, or were read in Nigeria by only 'the more intelligent and advanced members of the communities', the Court would be satisfied to leave the 'scandalous reflections' to public opinion which was likely to take an opposite view. But Nigeria comprised 'a large majority of populations . . . (which) consist of primitive people, who until the recent advent of the British administration had but little reason for trusting in the integrity of the courts which adjudicated in their affairs'. They would be misled by Thomas Jackson with serious implications for the integrity of the judiciary in the eyes of the public. Thomas Jackson expressed his profound apologies but was sentenced to two months' imprisonment 'to purge his contempt'.[71]

There were two other noteworthy cases in our period: *Rex vs. Herbert Macaulay and two others (1929)* and *Rex vs. Victor Babamuboni (1931)*. In the first, Herbert Macaulay was charged with Dr Caulcrick and J. A. Olushola, co-proprietor and editor of the *Daily News* respectively, on the basis of articles published between May and August 1929.[72] They were all fined five guineas by the

Acting Chief Justice, A. F. C. Webber. Macaulay greeted the judgment with an eulogy of the Nigerian Bench.[73] In the second case, Victor Babamuboni, acting editor of the *Nigerian Daily Telegraph*, took the Chief Justice to task for allegedly refusing to prevent an Englishman cited in a case in Lagos from escaping from the country and was jailed for two months while the proprietors of the newspaper, the Nigerian Press Limited, were fined £50. A further case, *Rex vs. Ajasa, 1936*, was withdrawn after the accused apologised in court for contempt of court – publication of matter that was *sub judice*.

Although these cases contributed to increase the feeling of the press that it was subject to arduous restraint, it was obvious that the courts could not have systematically enforced its jurisdiction in the same way as the government could not have enforced all the restrictions. Irregularity and uncertainty in prosecutions and other attempts at press control stemmed primarily from the government's incapacity to restrain the increasing boldness of the opposition press. Backed by the unflinching support of the people who enthusiastically contributed money towards the payment of fines or damages imposed or awarded by the courts,[74] the newspapers stimulated a firm tradition of fearless comment which was to underpin the propaganda of the independence movement.

Notes

1 G. Rude, *Wilkes and Liberty*, Oxford, 1962; Francis Williams, *Dangerous Estate, The Anatomy of newspapers*, New York, 1958; *History* of The Times, Vol. II, Edwin Emery, *The Press and America*, 2nd ed., Prentice-Hall, Inc. New Jersey, 1962,

2 *Lagos Weekly Record*, 25 April 1903.

3 'An open letter to the Lagos Standard'. See *Nigerian Chronicle*, 23 November 1913.

4 See *African Messenger*, 21 May 1925.

5 C.S.O. 1/1, Freeman to Newcastle, 28 January 1863.

6 C.O. 147/1, Newcastle to Freeman, 28 January 1863.

7 *African Times*, 23 April 1866.

8 *Lagos Observer*, 18 May 1882; Also 1 June 1882.

9 See Report of Proceedings in *Lagos Observer*, 1 June 1882. Also 6 July 1882.

10 For the provisions, see E. A. Speed, *Ordinances and Orders and Rules of the Colony of Lagos* (revised edition), vol. 2, London, 1902, pp. 657–9.

11 C.S.O. 1/16/3, Chamberlain to Moor, 20 August 1901 which mentions Moor to Chamberlain, 14 December 1901 (missing). See also C.S.O. 1/15/3, Moor to Chamberlain, 27 May 1902, 28 November 1902.

12 C.S.O. 1/1/30, MacGregor to Chamberlain, 19 June 1900; C.S.O. 1/3/5, MacGregor to Chamberlain, 2 October 1901.

13 C.S.O. 1/16/3, Chamberlain to Moor, 20 August 1901.

14 Moor accepted the Trinidad law as a good precedent but was of the opinion that there should be a provision that the right of printing and publishing should cease from the moment conviction took place. His reason was that a great deal of harm could be done by a newspaper before the provisions in the law which were designed to prevent illegal printing and publishing could come into force. Another suggested alteration concerned the best way to check misleading information. Although he admitted that 'it was unwise to restrain criticism however severe or however illogical or ill-judged it may be', he nevertheless thought that the legitimate liberty of the press would not be interfered with if power was given to inflict a penalty for the publication of mis-statements of facts 'which the editor at the time of publication knows to be a mis-statement had he made reasonable enquiries'. These proposed amendments did not impress the Secretary of State. The 'mis-statement clause', in particular, appeared to him 'not only too drastic but also an altogether unusual provision in a press law'. Moor, however, refused to yield ground; he made a pretence of reconsidering and modifying the two main areas of dispute but desperately sought to show that he was right in refusing to accept Colonial Office ruling on the matter. Records of further correspondence on the matter have not been found but it seems certain that Moor could not have escaped a reprimand. Whatever happened, his repressive enthusiasm was effectively checked because he ultimately promulgated the Newspaper Proclamation No. 26 of 1903 which excluded his harsh amendment proposals. C.S.O. 1/16/3, Chamberlain to Moor, 20 August 1901; C.S.O. 1/15/2, Moor to Chamberlain, 12 October 1901; C.S.O. 1/15/3, Moor to Chamberlain, 28 November 1902; C.S.O. 1/16/4, Chamberlain to Moor, 31 July 1902.

15 Minutes in C.O. 147/160, MacGregor to Chamberlain, 4 January 1902; Chamberlain to MacGregor, 19 March 1902.

16 *Lagos Standard*, 27 November 1901.

17 30 April 1902.

18 3 May 1902.

19 See *Lagos Weekly Record*, 3 June 1903.

20 *Government Gazette*, Colony of Lagos, January–December 1903, pp. 174–7. *Lagos Standard*, 18 February 1903.

21 MacGregor was instructed to forward the opinion of the Chief Justice; this did not seem as favourable as that of the Governor.

22 13 June 1903

23 *Lagos Standard*, 10 June 1903; *Lagos Weekly Record*, 6, 13 June 1903.

24 See *Weekly Record*, 1 July 1903; *Standard*, 15 July 1903.

25 See *Standard*, 12 August 1903.

26 C.S.O. 1/1/43, MacGregor to Chamberlain, 5 July 1903. On signatures, cf. Monster Petition of 1923. Governor Clifford felt that 17 000 signatures were not enough in a population of 99 000. Governors tended to capitalise on the issue of signatures whenever it suited their purpose.

27 Minute by H. B. Cox in C.O 147/167, MacGregor to Chamberlain, 5 July 1903.

28 C.S.O. 1/2/74, Chamberlain to MacGregor, 26 August 1903.

29 3, 17 October; 1 December 1903.

30 *Laws of Southern Nigeria* (Lagos), 1908.

31 Legislative Council Debates, 1903–1907. See also *Lagos Standard*, 13 June, 1 July 1903.

32 Between 1927 and 1937, the *Nigerian Daily Telegraph* was printed by the following – (1) Akibomi Press (2) Awoboh Press, 1927–29 (3) Tika Tore Press 1929–30 (4) Tanimola Press, 1930–37 (5) Karaole Press, 1937. Another example was the *Akede Eko*. Early in 1929, the editor, I. B. Thomas, contracted for printing with the Awoboh Press. He broke the contract in June (which led to a breach-of-contract suit in which S. H. Pearse of Awoboh Press unsuccessfully claimed £33 10s and had to execute a fresh bond. *Awoboh v. I. B. Thomas*, 1929. *Akede Eko*, 31 October 1929.

33 In 1930, Coulson Labor, of the *Dawn*, was at Aba sentenced to six months' imprisonment for breach of the registration law. In 1935, D. O. Oke abandoned the *Abeokuta Weekly News* following prosecution for offence against the registration law.

34 C.S.O. 1/21/3, Egerton to Crewe, 27 November 1908. Enclosure No. 2, Green to Egerton, 29 September 1908; No. 4, Pennington to Egerton, 26 November 1908.

35 *Ibid*. Also C.O. 520/50, Egerton to Elgin, 2 December 1907.

36 *Ibid*.

37 C.S.O. 1/22/2, Crewe to Egerton, 24 February 1909.

38 C.S.O./1/21/4, Thorburn (Ag. Gover.) to Crewe, 25 March 1909.

39 29 September 1909.

40 *Ibid*.

41 *Ibid*.

42 1 October 1909.

43 6 November 1909. Macaulay, in hand bills, stated that he first gave the article to the *Standard* which was unwilling to publish. (The *Standard* considered its language 'quite unfit for publication'. See issue of 15 September 1909.) He then took it to the *Record* but the latter, after sending in proof sheets, allegedly withdrew from publication because some European friends of the Railway officials attacked in the article had intervened. (*Lagos Weekly Record*, 3 October 1908.) J. P. Jackson, in a disclaimer, asserted that Macaulay's allegations were 'absolutely untrue' and claimed that the *Record* had never accepted articles from Macaulay. (*Ibid*.) Heratio Jackson, whom Macaulay had accused specifically, denied most emphatically the charges levelled against him and in a letter to the *Standard*, literally blazed away at Macaulay. The latter was represented as a 'professional patriot' and a past master in

the art of misrepresentation. He had a 'peculiar knack for making history, for saying or writing things which are hopelessly inconsistent with facts'. On the quality of the article in question, Horatio Jackson commented: '[It] was . . . lacking in journalistic ethics and I could not prostrate the columns of the *Record* to anything that savoured of yellow journalism or the fire-brand type. I deemed discretion the greater part of wisdom and was more inclined to respect the cherished convictions of my father rather than violate them. . . .' T. H. Jackson to *Lagos Standard*, 7 October 1908. See also *Lagos Daily News*, 6 April 1929.

44 See *Lagos Standard*, 17 November 1909.

45 *Legislative Council minutes*, 6 October 1909. See also *Nigerian Chronicle*, 22 October 1909.

46 See *Nigerian Chronicle*, 22 October 1909.

47 See reprint in *Nigerian Times*, 3 May 1910; 26 April 1910.

48 The *Weekly Record* (12 November 1910) described Ajasa's remarks as 'a refrain of sycophantic brayings'.

49 H. S. Hewitt v. Chris Johnson (*Nigerian Chronicle*), 1910. Johnson was fined £100 plus 30 guineas costs.

50 See Perham, *Lugard, op. cit.*, p. 390.

51 *Ibid.*, p. 597.

52 *Ibid.*, p. 591.

53 F. D. Lugard, *Education in Colony and Southern Provinces of Nigeria* (16 April 1914).

54 Perham, *op. cit.*, p. 593.

55 Criminal Code No. 15 of 1916. *Nigeria Gazcttc*, January–June, 1916.

56 *Times of Nigeria*, 7 December 1915.

57 *Times of Nigeria*, 29 August 1916.

58 See Perham, *op. cit.*, p. 598.

59 Chief Registrar's Criminal Record Book, No. 18.

60 For the draft Ordinance, see C.S.O. 1/32/12, Lugard to Harcourt, 17 August 1917.

61 *Lagos Standard*, 17 October 1917; *Weekly Record*, 21 April 1917.

62 31 May 1918.

63 See C.S.O. 1/32/12, Lugard to Long., 17 August 1917, Encls. 4, 5, 6.

64 *Ibid.*

65 C.O. 583/59, Long to Lugard, 21 November 1917.

66 C.S.O. 1/33/60, Harcourt to Lugard, 23 December 1918; *Nigeria Gazette* (1918), p. 50.

67 He spoke of 'the singular courtesy which camouflaged the relentless exercise of the most rigid discipline and fine administration of the Statutory Regulations of His Majesty's prisons over my physical frame'. See *Daily News*, 11 March 1929.

68 28 August 1928.

69 See also 30 April 1929. The most admirable reaction was by I. B. Thomas of the *Nigerian Evening News*. '. . . . The suggestion for press censorship savours of cowardice and is generally made by those whose selfishness is as great as their weakness and self-delusion'. July 8, 1929.

70 *Weekly Record*, 26 September 1925.

71 Chief Registrar's Criminal Record Book, Vol. 29, pp. 38–47.
72 11 May, 6 August and 9 August 1929.
73 See *Daily News*, 10 October 1929.
74 A few examples can be given. In Samuel Percy Jackson v. Chris Mason, 1900, the £5 11s damages were publicly collected. The same was true of £65 19s awarded against the *Lagos Weekly Record* in 1912 for a libel against Akadiri Ishara, a policeman.

7 A New Dawn and Dissent

At the beginning of 1914, the outlook for political journalism seemed auspicious. In January, Thomas Horatio Jackson took over the management and editorship of the *Record* from his ailing father. The following month, James Bright Davies revived his defunct *Nigerian Times* and renamed it the *Times of Nigeria*. That same month, Kitoyi Ajasa established the *Pioneer*. The appearance of progressive new men in the editorial situations as well as old men with reanimated perspectives, coinciding as it did with the emergence of dissenting voices, foreshadowed an epoch of uncompromising opposition and ideological confrontation. The situation found a helpful atmosphere in the greater complexity of the problems of administration. With the Lugardian amalgamation, Lagos became the capital of an extensive country stretching from the coast to Lake Chad. As the headquarters of the new Governor-General under whom the administrative systems of North and South were unified, it was the nerve-centre of diverse political activity. A national community audience had formally come into being to which the newspapers now had to address themselves.

'THE NEFARIOUS NIGERIAN SYSTEM'

In Chapter 5, we drew attention to the suspicion and resentment with which Lugard was viewed in Lagos before and after his arrival on 3 October 1912. The initial reception was perhaps a little cautious but the temper of public feeling was not disguised for long. On 8 March 1913, on the eve of Lugard's departure to England on leave, the *Record* gave him a rude send-off: 'His Excellency Sir Frederick Dealtry Lugard . . . is a disappointment to Southern Nigeria'. The *Chronicle* joined in the execration, adding that Lugard's amalgamation plan would be awaited before a general attack would be directed as necessary. 'We promise him that we shall do so fearlessly, conscientiously, constitutionally and with the powers we possess.'[1] By 1914, Nigerian detestation of Lugard as an autocratic person became an important ingredient in the animosity against the policies of his government.

A further ingredient was scepticism and apprehension regarding the amalgamation. In the first place, the enlightened public was doubtful if Lagos would derive any benefit from the exercise. The thinking went like this. Lagos was a stagnant community as part of the Gold Coast Colony and it was not until the 1886 separation that the economy began to grow. The 1906 amalgamation resulted only in the expansion of the European bureaucracy imbued with racial bigotry and enjoying vast sinecures. As the *Standard* summed up the situation in 1909, 'the history of amalgamations and their disastrous results' were sufficient to discourage any proposal to amalgamate Southern and Northern Nigeria.[2] In the second place, the view was strongly held that the system of indirect rule as adopted in Northern Nigeria was inconceivable and dangerous in Southern Nigeria. Educated Nigerians in Lagos expressed in vague terms the way the Northern System was operated, emphasising the incompatibility of the 'democratic industrious and peaceful South' with the 'autocratic, hectoring, rough and ready' systems of the North and the 'moral darkness' that pervaded the 'place of despotism'. Amalgamation itself thus became one big scare. The scare was not assuaged by Lugard's proposal, early in 1914, to transfer the capital of 'United Nigeria' to Kaduna. This did not happen but the mere idea created great alarm in the press and public.[3] It would be fascinating to speculate on how the Nigerian press and people would have reacted to amalgamation had it been carried out by a popular governor like Gilbert Carter. Lugard's position as the creator of the Northern System, as an undesirable administrator in Lagos and yet as the chief amalgamator, helped to cast a shadow upon the amalgamation and to stimulate opposition to his administration which, in the words of a newspaper, was characterised by 'a multiplicity of laws which were not only depressing in their outlook and irksome in their provisions but were also intended to break the morale and discourage the legitimate aspirations of the natives for social expansion'.[4]

Given this background of disparagement, fear and uncertainty, the response of the educated Africans to the 'three-fold legislation of [Lugard's] amalgamation scheme',[5] comes into proper focus. The measures were (1) the Supreme Court Ordinance, (2) the Native Courts Ordinance and (3) the Provincial Courts Ordinance. The object of these measures was to bring about a re-organisation of the judicial structure to make it conform to the northern pattern.

Under the Northern System, the Residents and the executive officers under them, in addition to their administrative duties, carried out judicial functions through what were known as Provincial Courts. In this system, political officers, most of whom had no legal training, sat as judges and allowed no legal representation for accused persons. Other aspects of the judicial structure were a Supreme Court under a Chief Justice whose jurisdiction was restricted to Europeans and Customary Courts presided over by *alkalis* (in Muslim areas) and by the emirs and elders (in non-Muslim areas).

The judicial structure was one complement of Lugard's concept of indirect rule, a framework which was to constitute him the final arbiter in all aspects of government. The traditional forms of administration in which the Fulani aristocracy wielded despotic power, were retained, the emirs constituting 'an integral part' of the British superstructure. Units of local government called 'native administration' were set up with the Emir at the centre of each unit, advised and guided by the Resident, the highest British official in the area. A logical outcome of this administrative system was the creation of local treasuries. The institution of the treasury in Northern Nigeria pre-dated Lugard's assumption of office but the latter, by upholding the Emir's right to direct taxation, gave the revenue system method.[6]

By the new arrangement in Lagos, the Supreme Court, whose jurisdiction hitherto covered Southern Nigeria, was now confined to Lagos colony and, outside the colony, to a few urban areas. This 'reform' as well as that dealing with the constitution of customary courts, did not evoke much comment from the newspaper press. The explanation was that the Provincial Courts Ordinance was central to the entire change and the heavy attack upon it implied a rejection of the new judicial structure.

The Provincial Courts Bill provided among other things, that 'Each Provincial Court shall consist of the Resident or Commissioner, all District Officers and their Assistants and Persons appointed as Justices of the Peace for that province. Every member of a Provincial Court shall exercise civil and criminal jurisdiction as provided by this Ordinance and vested in the Court which jurisdiction may be increased or revoked by the Governor-General. . . .' The common law in force in England on 1 January 1900 was, so far as applicable, to be in force in the Protectorate. Along with this, 'native law and custom as obtained in any province and not repugnant to natural justice, equity and good conscience', could be applied where necessary. The courts were also empowered to try offences, punishments for which did not exceed imprisonment for a term of six months, a fine of £50 or 12 strokes of the cane. No legal representation was allowed nor were appeals permissible but the court was required to send to the Governor-General a report upon any case on which the decision needed to be confirmed. Every such list transmitted both in civil and criminal cases was to operate as appeals leaving it with the Governor-General to confirm or decline to confirm the decision of the court.[7]

Many educated Nigerians were flabbergasted by the Provincial Courts Ordinance but it is significant that there seemed to have been considerable public apathy which the newspapers were at pains to discourage. The common view was that the measure affected only the members of the legal profession and had nothing to do with the rights and privileges of the people. To the *Chronicle*, those who reasoned in this way were 'in the main illiterates and men who cannot reason for themselves'. In the opinion of the *Record*, for 'any reasonable Nigerian' to sit down with arms folded in the belief that the measure affected only lawyers was 'nothing but to bug a great delusion'.[8] The newspapermen were better placed to see the problem in its proper perspective but it was also true that the lawyers not only formed an influential group in society but also readily gave moral, professional and intellectual assistance to the newspapers. Their anxiety to protect the financial and social interests of the lawyers was no doubt motivated by the purest of nationalist motives but it would be misleading to pretend that self-interest was totally absent.

Notwithstanding the public apathy, the newspapers mounted a vigorous attack against what was seen as an attempt to perpetuate 'that autocratic and despotic sway' identified with 'the notorious Northern Nigerian System'.[9] The most exasperating implication of the law was the augmentation of the powers of the Commissioners or Residents. The *Standard* complained that as a class they had, 'with the already too extensive powers possessed by

them, displayed a disposition to be so haughty, despotic and over-
bearing in their dealings with the natives in the Protectorate',
and had shown 'such utter disregard of justice and fair treatment
in their judgements, that the most serious consequences [were] to be
dreaded from any increase to their authority'.[10] The *Record*
shared this view when it lamented three days later that if the
Ordinance became law, the Commissioners would have 'almost
absolute power' to try and decide any action within their districts,
including those involving capital punishment 'without adequate
check upon them as the way they use their powers'. This check was
necessary particularly as most of the administrative officers had
had no special training for their work.[11] As the *Standard* put it,
'. . . they are not all of them lawyers, but are recruited from
different professions, the Army, Navy, Medicine, Engineering
and even the Church . . .'.[12]

It was to show that the law would prove 'a dangerous engine of
oppression' that the *Times of Nigeria* began on 24 February to run
a disheartening story under the rubric 'Foretastes of its operation',
about one Thomas Williams, described as a contractor to the
Government Railway, who would have been imprisoned at
Abeokuta but for the prompt intervention of a lawyer.

That the new measure made a mockery of the independence of
the judiciary was also stressed. The *Record* considered it 'ano-
malous' to vest the confirmation of sentences, not in the Supreme
Court but in the Governor-General. In the opinion of the newspaper, Lugard wished to curtail all the rights of the people so that
if he allowed some concessions to be squeezed out of him, he
might appear to be magnanimous. The people 'must be made
political slaves in order to have a chance of freeing them'.[13]

How practicable were the judicial responsibilities imposed on
the Governor-General? The *Standard* was concerned that the
concentration of powers in the Governor-General would impair
efficiency.

> Considering the number of Provincial Courts there are in the colony
> and the number of cases that are likely to be tried in them in the
> course of a month, the task imposed upon the Governor-General of
> wading through accumulation of document, minutes and notes of
> evidence is not only Herculean but impossible of being satisfactorily
> performed by a single man.[14]

The newspapers were almost unanimous in their condemnation
of flogging. It was argued that flogging was foreign to Yoruba

people and that its introduction was clear evidence that the 'despised native' had greater regard for what was 'right, just and humane' than the 'civilised' white man.[15]

An important question was raised by the *Chronicle* when it drew attention to the absence of codified customary law in the Southern provinces. With what reasonableness could justice be dispensed, whether by the foreigner or the indigenous person when, 'unlike the Islamic system of the North, the rules of customary observance are not of universal validity throughout Yorubaland'?[16]

> The . . . difficulty . . . is that Native law is to be administered side by side with English law and that power is given to Commissioners to enforce the observance of any law or custom existing in the Protectorate. The English common law which is peculiar to the English nation has been codified and the maxims and procedure widely known and applied by men who have made it their special study. In the case of Native law, the customary law of Northern Nigeria . . . is far different from the customary law of the people inhabiting the Southern Province. In the case of the former the fundamental principle of law is founded on the Mohammedan religion with its tenets and doctrines of resignation and fatalism. In the case of the latter where paganism is the prevailing religion, the maxims of law are drawn from their ideas of the Divine as embodied in their ethical codes which are matters of common knowledge among them. Starting from such divergent basis it will be admitted that the end of positive law must be differently served for what is regarded as happiness by the one cannot be regarded as happiness by the other.
>
> Now by the amalgamation a mechanical and outward union of the two peoples has been brought about. But a union of name does not mean or involve a union of customs and manners, a similarity of usages and idiosyncrasies such as this Provincial Courts Ordinance is labouring to establish. . . . The Native customary law of the Southern province has still to be reduced to writing to make its canons known and its principles appreciated by Europeans who are going to sit as Dispensers of justice in these courts. It will be criminal to place a Foreign or Native Judge on the Bench without the knowledge of the principles of the law he has to dispense especially men who have been imbued with the Zaria idea.[17]

In addition to these strictures against the judicial changes or what Duse Mohammed Ali was later to call an 'extraordinary pseudo-judicial contraption',[18] signed and anonymous letters to Lugard were published week after week in the newspapers. 'Cicero', for example, spoke of the 'anarchy and chaos' which would result from the operation of the ordinance.[19] A mass meeting was held on 3 February and a petition was drawn up which repeated the arguments advanced in previous editorials on the matter. In addition, delegations which included some of the editors were sent to interview the Governor-General. In England, the Anti-slavery and Aborigines' Protection Society took up the issue with Lugard and the Secretary of State, and questions were asked in Parliament. Sir N. Geary wrote articles and pamphlets against the measure. All these were without doubt a strong factor in deciding Lugard to publish in the *Gazette* a defence of the change of system by Chief Justice E. A. Speed. But this 'apologetic memorandum' did not impress the agitating newspapers and in its 'Public comment on the Chief Justice's memorandum re the Provincial Courts Ordinance', the *Chronicle* carried out a detailed refutation of the points advanced by Speed.[20] The Ordinance was passed in March but the agitation continued until the thirties when the system was revised by Governor Cameron. After 1914, insistent attacks on the measure stopped but occasional indignant references to it showed how much the issue was alive in the minds of most of the editors.[21]

In this account of the press agitation against the Provincial Courts Ordinance, it is remarkable that the *Nigerian Pioneer* did not feature prominently even in a negative way. If the public had expected a press war between the *Pioneer* and the opposition newspapers, they were sadly disappointed for the *Pioneer* was virtually silent throughout the crisis. Dissent was reflected only in a brief statement under 'Rambling Notes and News'.[22]

> We are voicing the opinions of men of very opposite views and sympathies when we say that the impression and feeling is that His Excellency will not knowingly permit the oppression of any class of the community of Nigeria or will permit their liberties to be in any way interfered with. . . .

The newspaper went on to inform its readers that 'important amendments' had already been made and with one or two more, the opposition should be satisfied. It seems obvious that Kitoyi Ajasa was working behind the scenes to secure some compromise but it has not been possible to establish what these 'important amendments' were and whether they were actually carried out as claimed. But perhaps the *Pioneer*'s credibility was not the important question. The silence of the newspaper when it was expected to give punch for punch in defence of the government creates a puzzle. Why did Kitoyi Ajasa disappoint supporters of Lugard in what should have been his first major encounter with Thomas Horatio Jackson, George Alfred Williams, James Bright Davies and Chris Johnson? One reason is that Kitoyi Ajasa, himself a lawyer, was not in support of the judicial changes (as seems evident from his sole remark on the issue) and therefore chose the path of silence. His dislike of the Ordinance was revealed not only in the statement quoted above but also in remarks made in 1918 and 1919 in which he called attention to the haste with which Northern precedents were introduced into the South.[23] A second and more important reason related to Kitoyi Ajasa's style of journalism. As pointed out in Chapter 2, he always fought shy of open controversy. A man of quiet disposition and personal dignity, he was incapable of resolving the contradiction in the nature of his personality and the demands of political journalism in an era of crisis and controversy. His moderation inclined him in June 1914 to see in strong criticism of the government a 'tendency towards the coming into existence of disloyal citizens and the paving of the way for sedition'. Such a view, which an opponent promptly dismissed as 'most mischievous, wicked, shameful, scandalous and infamous' and as 'the idiotic conception of a fatuous brain and imbecile mind',[24] needed to be amplified but to expect this was not to appreciate the *Pioneer*'s extreme brevity.

BREAKDOWN OF A TRUCE

Before the agitation against the Provincial Courts Ordinance raged itself out, the First World War broke out. The outbreak of the war dramatised a contradiction in contemporary Nigerian thought as vociferous Nigerian nationalists turned ardent supporters of the British Empire. As has been continually emphasised in this study, the early educated Nigerians, in spite of their vigorous criticisms, stood for the acceptance of and submission to the rule of the British Government. They considered British Colonial policy definitely more acceptable than the policies of the other European powers. 'As British subjects', the *Standard* remarked in 1899, 'we have ever found British rule the least irksome compared with other colonies.'[25] French Colonial rule 'partook more of the nature of martial law than civil administration' and the Germans believed that 'a successful colony can be trained into existence under the same conditions as a Hussar regiment'.[26] In declaring war against Germany, therefore, Britain seemed to Nigerians not only to be fighting to ensure her own survival and consequently the survival of those ideals which Nigerians cherished so fervently; she appeared also to be fighting Africa's battle against one of the representatives of outrageous colonialism. Nigerians in Lagos inaugurated a Committee of Emergency with Dr Obadiah Johnson as chairman and Dr Obasa as secretary, to educate the public about the war and to co-ordinate local assistance to the British war effort. And their newspapers threw themselves into helping Britain to liquidate Germany. They attacked Germany and helped to advertise the British Empire as a diverse entity united against a common foe.[27] They gave considerable attention to campaigns for contributions towards various funds inaugurated to promote operations in various theatres of war. Persistent appeals were made to the people to support the Great National Relief Fund organised by the Prince of Wales. In mid-1915, the *Pioneer*, inspired by an appeal for fresh meat for the two battalions in the Duala front in the Cameroons where Nigerian soldiers saw action against German colonial troops, masterminded, with some success, the Cameroons Meat Fund. And in 1917, the *Record* dropped its anti-imperialist role and urged the public to 'think imperially' by supporting the Nigerian Overseas Contingents Comforts Fund. Discordant notes were not lacking and some questioning of the popular support for Britain soon found expression in the *Times of Nigeria* with unfortunate consequences for the editor who was prosecuted and sent to jail. However, the Nigerian press played a noteworthy role in the Great War and it was not surprising that they all greeted the end of hostilities with an outburst of enthusiastic comment.

At the outbreak of war, the newspaper editors, with the exception of Kitoyi Ajasa, met and undertook on their own initiative to impose a censorship. Subsequently, the Administrator of the Lagos Colony, F. S. James, invited the editors to a conference where they formally proclaimed their intention to suspend attacks on the government provided no vexatious measures were introduced. Lugard was then on leave and when he returned, he embarked upon unpopular measures in disregard of the mutual undertaking. On 8 July 1915, he published the Criminal Code Bill and opened the second phase of the Water Rate Question the following year. These measures inflamed the public but the news-papermen resolved to honour their undertaking and to adopt a pacific line of action while doing their best to assist with the war effort. Actually, their position was not an enviable one because they were caught between two stools. The problem was clearly stated by the *Record*:

> As a public journal, the difficulties that confront us at the present crisis are manifold: for in endeavouring to express adequately the bitter acrimony manifested by the people . . . and the dismal cry of anguish and pain wrung from their unwilling lips. we stand a chance of running the gauntlet of seditious agitation; whilst on the other hand to attempt to repress the turgid current of their rage by suggesting some reasonable compromise . . . would expose us to the charge of partisanship with the government. . . .[28]

It was in an effort to resolve this dilemma that the *Record* enun-ciated a new editorial policy. Politically, it would stand fearlessly for 'Truth, Right, Liberty and Justice' deprecating as bigotry 'any uncompromising hostility towards governmental measures irres-pective of their propriety or impropriety' and as toadyism 'any blind subservience' to the authorities. What this meant was fully explained:

> where proposed governmental measures appear detrimental to native interests, it will be our sacred duty to oppose them vehemently and incessantly. But where the measures claim some degree of rational justification and only novelty of experience constitutes the one possible objection, we shall endeavour to enlighten and educate public opinion.[29]

The Criminal Code Ordinance was a revival of an earlier pro-posal which had been abandoned in 1899 following strong op-position. At that time, the newspapers declaimed against the measure particularly as it did not stop at codifying existing criminal laws but also aimed at introducing new regulations which were obsolete in Britain. The 'abstruseness and elasticity' of the 1899 code exasperated many Nigerian men of influence at the time.[30] The Lugardian Code was also couched in overelastic terms and contained provisions which threatened the freedom of expression. However, while the *Pioneer* applauded the Code, the *Standard* ignored it completely while the *Record* raised only a feeble protest. It 'respectfully' urged upon Lugard the necessity of being 'a little more sympathetic' towards the legitimate wishes of the people particularly at such a 'critical period of the Empire's existence' when all sections of the Empire were gearing themselves for 'the final issues of the contest of Armageddon'.[31]

In 1916, the government provoked severe public outcry and unrest when it indicated its determination to enforce the levying of the water rate which the people had consistenly opposed since 1908. The assessment of the capital and rental value of houses commenced in spite of a general refusal to co-operate and arbitrary estimates were distributed in what were known as Blue Notices. The Notices contained provision for appeal against excess taxation. House of a capital value of not more than £50 (later raised to £80) and a rental value of not more than £4 (later raised to £6) would be exempted from paying the water rate.[32] When the issue was mooted in 1914, opposition to it was strong. The *Record* moaned that direct taxation had been 'revamped from the shades of oblivion and now reappeared 'as a hydra-headed monster, inspiring all classes of the community with terror and dismay'.[33] In 1916, newspaper opposition was muted even though the chiefs and people manifested a determination to offer strong resistance evidenced by the hard speeches of Chiefs Obanikoro, Aromire, Suenu, Ologun, Oluwa, Eletu, Oloto, Ojora and other White Cap and War Chiefs, Muslim leaders and sectional headmen at their open meeting on the Water Rate Question with Acting Administrator Colonel H. C. Moorhouse on 6 May 1916.[34] Extracts from a few of the speeches are instructive.

> Giwa Agoro: . . . we do not want your water. We would rather die than admit taxation among us. Taxation is against our national tradition.
> Taba Thomas: You invited us to come and at the same time ordered your soldiers and policemen to be lined up and to guard the place and the people you have invited . . . But we are not afraid.
> Chief Obanikoro: . . . we are determined not to pay water rate even at the risk of our being killed. . . . If my being killed will free the people of Lagos from paying this taxation or water rate, I very freely offer myself to be taken down to the Lagoon and slain there.

The divergence between public opinion and newspaper opinion is best seen in the attitude of the *Record*. It appealed for restraint and respect for established laws. In a lengthy comment which covered nearly two pages, the newspaper reviewed the history of the agitation and remarked that one might not blame the illiterate masses if in their ignorance they defied constituted authority but the position was different with the educated class. For, by virtue of their educational training ,'they are under some legal obligation to obey any law whether good or bad until it has been repealed, modified or suspended by any spontaneous act of the Government or on the strength of any constitutional representation or agitation by the people'.[35] On the face of it, this was a reasonable and responsible attitude to take but in the context of the development of Nigerian political journalism, it exemplified the extent to which some of the nationalist newspapers, apparently overwhelmed by the war emergency, had become nervous and mealy-mouthed.

'A TANTALIZING PROBLEM'

Although the truce of 1914 was ignored by Lugard, there was a saving grace brought about as a result of the initiative of Lieutenant-Governor Arthur Boyle. Apparently anxious to find some basis of accommodation with the newspaper press, Boyle had initiated a system in 1915 by which the newspapermen first held a dialogue with the government on any public grievances which came to their notice and which they thought required redress. It was only when satisfactory settlement could not be effected that the newspapermen resorted to agitation. The system would seem to have worked well; after about a year, the *Record* described the policy as 'progressive and highly satisfactory' and was later to assert that over a hundred cases were successfully handled.[36] One of these was the case of the Akarigbo of Ijebu Remo who was sentenced to twelve months' imprisonment in July 1915. On representations from the editors, the case was reinvestigated and the Akarigbo was released from prison in September 1915.

However, there were disagreements which provoked agitation. One of the most significant of these was in connection with the introduction of direct taxation into Egbaland in January 1918 which led to the incident known as the Adubi Rising. At a meeting of 'accord and understanding', the editors impressed upon the government the advisability of withdrawing the measure in view of the stout opposition of the Egba people and particularly in veiw of the Colonial Office ruling that the scheme should be proceeded with only if it was willingly accepted by the people.[37] The government was adamant and an opposition campaign ensued. In waging the verbal war, the newspapermen were particularly irritated that the restraint and prudence shown by them since the outbreak of the First World War had failed to make a decisive impression on this occasion. Seeing themselves in the guise of 'experienced mariners' successfully manoeuvring in the 'stormy sea' of journalism and 'dodging the innumerable shoals and sandbanks of the Criminal Code and Seditious Offences Ordinance',[38] they remembered with displeasure their failure to dissuade Lugard from attempting to convert a temporary war censorship into a permanent censorship in 1917.[39] Indeed, the failure of the censorship proposals and in particular the public knowledge that the Colonial Office had little sympathy for Lugard's despotism and his hatred of press freedom, contributed to rousing the newspapers from their muffled vigilance to a condition of alertness and candour. Thus a current of re-animation in the newspaper press was the background to the crisis in Egbaland which marked the end of Lugard's administration.

To see the events of 1918 in their proper perspective, it would be necessary to sketch certain developments in Egbaland since 1914. British involvement in the First World War created in the minds of the educated Africans the impression that all nationalities, however small, had a right to their independence and also a right to expect respect for the sanctity of treaties. Britain was understood to have declared war on Germany in defence of the treaty guaranteeing the political independence and territorial integrity of Belgium. Educated Nigerians took seriously the advertisement of British resolutions emphasising her 'inflexible determination to continue to a victorious end the struggle in maintenance of those ideals of Liberty, Justice and Freedom' which were said to be the common cause of the Allied Powers.[40] Hence, the educated Nigerians failed to appreciate the abrogation of the independence of Egbaland in 1914 in consequence of an unrest for the suppression of which the Egba government had to rely on foreign troops from Lagos.[41]

The loss of Egba independence exasperated educated Nigerians, many of whom had seen independent Egbaland as a certain special symbol. In 1898, the *Standard* had exulted: 'A wishful smile plays across our face at the mention of the fact that the Egba kingdom stands alone today, the only independent native state in this part of West Africa'.[42] The *Record* remarked in 1913: 'Abeokuta is sailing as a self-dependent barque on the ocean of politics … we in Lagos take a special pride in the autonomy and progress of the Government of Abeokuta as demonstrating to the world at large the resources for self-government . . . possessed and practised by the Native and sincerely pray that nothing may ever happen to weaken that autonomy or hinder that progress'.[43] It is small wonder that the abrogation by Lugard on 16 September 1914 of the 1893 treaty which guaranteed the independence of Egbaland rankled in the minds of many educated Nigerians.

A consequence of the termination of Egba autonomy was the extension to the area of the principles of Indirect Rule. The ground for the change of system was prepared early in 1918 when Adegboyega Edun, Secretary of the Egba United Government, visited Kano and Zaria at Lugard's suggestion to learn at first hand the financial system in operation there. The plan was to divide Abeokuta into seven districts under resident district heads with native courts. A consolidated tax was to be levied in place of the customary tributes and forced labour. But the rumour that taxation would be introduced in the area caused considerable unrest and the radical newspapers were quick to harden the minds of the Egba people against the new system. Five years earlier, the *Record*, for example, had warned that the introduction into Abeokuta of any system of direct taxation was fraught with grave dangers. In March 1918, it again warned:

> There can be no question that the attempt to foist upon the people of Egbaland the pernicious Northern Nigerian System was destined *ab initio* to produce the most disastrous results. . . . It was expecting the impossible to hope that the Egba native authorities could have been induced to abandon the less irksome and indirect method of raising revenue by the well-tried system of inland tolls and thus plunge themselves recklessly into the rude uncertainties and unexplored danger of direct taxation. . . .[44]

As tension mounted, the *Record* and the *Chronicle* volunteered compromise measures aimed at resolving the crisis while the *Pioneer*, although recognising differences between the indigenous systems in Egbaland and Northern Nigeria, nevertheless appealed for co-operation. ('We must abandon a lot of our old conservation and take in new ideas.')[45]

On 3 June 1918, violence erupted in Egbaland. The telegraph was destroyed and a section of the railway lines uprooted. There was serious fighting between Egba insurgents and Lagos troops. More than 500 Egba were said to have been killed. A newspaper was later to allege that the rising 'was attended by Germanic barbarism, brutish outrage and inhuman cruelties'.[46] As was to be expected, the Lagos newspapers leapt into the imbroglio, taking the opportunity to vent their pent-up emotions.

Most active was the *Standard* whose owner, George Alfred Williams, took great pride in his Egba origin. The newspaper presented in six lengthy articles what it considered to be the factors which accounted for the insurrection and came to the conclusion that it was 'a violent symptom of a disease of long standing'. Among the factors analysed were 'the substratum of deep distrust' in the public mind as a result of the incident of 1914 and the abrogation of Egba independence, the disruption in the pattern of social, political and administrative life consequent upon the introduction of the Lugardian Indirect Rule, forced labour and its effect on the farm economy and the introduction of direct taxation. This time the crux of the issue was not evaded.

> There is not the slightest doubt that the administration of Sir Frederick Lugard is very unpopular among natives of this part of Nigeria... Ordinances upon Ordinances have been passed . . . native freedom under British law restricted. . . .[47]

The *Record*, which was to remark ten years later that Egbaland had been 'a tantalising problem' to the Nigerian Government 'since 1914', was in general agreement with the above analysis but it reserved its strictures for the Secretary to the Egba Government, Adegboyega Edun. In previous quarrels over Edun's role in Egba affairs, enemies of the Secretary had employed the *Chronicle* while his supporters defended him in the *Record*. Now the *Record* called for the impeachment of Edun whose administration it compared to 'czarist autocracy'.[48] A different position was taken by the *Pioneer* which saw the crisis as 'a diabolical conspiracy' engineered by the Egba intelligentsia in Lagos. To the distress of its contemporaries who answered back with abuse, the *Pioneer* disputed all the advertised causes of the disturbances which it attributed to 'intemperate and mischievous conversations'. What it meant by this was not clear but the charge was presumably that of incitement by Egba leaders in Lagos.[49]

However, all the newspapers were united in demand for a Commission of Inquiry. The *Pioneer* called for a 'thorough and very searching inquiry' and the *Standard* settled for a 'full and impartial' one. The latter suggested, in addition, that a special committee of Lagos-based Egba prominent people be set up to undertake the work of reconstruction at home. On 23 July the

Egba Society was formed under the chairmanship of J. K. Coker 'to watch and promote the interests of Egbaland'. Eric O. Moore was Vice-Chairman, Dr R. A. Savage, Secretary and Phillip Coker, Assistant Secretary. A Commission of Inquiry was eventually appointed, consisting initially of Dr (later Sir) John Maxwell, a Resident, (chairman), Eric O. Moore and MacGregor, a member of John Holt's Company. On the suggestion of the *Pioneer* that a European clergyman who possessed a thorough knowledge of Yoruba be added to the panel, the Rev. O. J. Griffin of the Wesleyan Church was later appointed to the commission.[50] The findings of the Maxwell Commission were awaited with interest but its report was not published. Many had thought that since, to the chagrin of the people, the report of inquiry on the Ijemo crisis of 1914 was not published, the situation would be different in 1918. All such hopes were disappointed and opportunity was given to the newspapers to snipe at the government even after Lugard had left Nigeria.[51]

A SIGH OF RELIEF

Lugard left Nigeria at the end of the war; in late January 1919, his retirement was announced. Never in the history of Lagos had the news of a retirement created such great excitement. The community was thrown into ecstasies of delight and the newspapers mirrored the public mood in severe criticisms of Lugard's administration. The *Record* took the lead in a two-page assessment.[52]

> Sir Frederick is a huge failure . . . a hopeless anachronism . . . the victim of exaggerated personality. . . Opinionated, unswerving from a purpose if even it be irrational when it was once formed, and brooking no interference with his imperious will, . . . Sir Frederick flagrantly disregarded the sage advice of those who were in sympathetic touch with the natives and paid the greatest courtesy to those satellites who . . . flattered his reactionary schemes and wild ambitions with the result that he found himself enmeshed in a series of blunders and violent misrule which constitutes the indelible stains of his inglorious administration. . . .

The newspaper spoke of the 'multiplicity of laws' which were distinguished more for their 'repressiveness and brutality' rather than for their enlightened statesmanship and of Lugard's hatred of the educated Nigerian and 'constant dread' of the newspaper press. It concluded:

> As far as the natives of Nigeria are concerned . . . Sir Frederick departs from the stage of West African activities 'unwept, unhonoured and unsung'. Let us hope he will be the last of military governors to disgrace the annals of British Colonial history in West Africa. . . Let us hope that with [his] departure . . . the Nigerian System – the product of his exuberant imagination – will be consigned to the limbo of oblivion where embedded in the historical strata of British imperial colonisation it will exist as the fossilated remains of an administrative experimental failure. . . .

Distressed by the maladministration of Lugard, Nigerians had prayed for change, any change which would afford some degree of relief, however brief or temporary. The answer to their prayer was a double blessing for not only did Lugard go but he was to be succeeded by Hugh Clifford whose fame had preceded him to Nigeria. Clifford had been Governor in the Gold Coast from 1912 to 1918 and had been known throughout West Africa for his liberal and statesmanlike policies not to mention his literary interests. In 1918, he had published a booklet entitled *German Colonies: A plea for the Native Races* in which he condemned certain aspects of British Colonial policy. 'Of all the appointments that His Gracious Majesty has ever been pleased to make', commented a newspaper, 'this is undoubtedly one of the very best'.[53]

Clifford arrived in Lagos on 8 August 1919 to a welcome reception unprecedented in scale and grandeur.[54] Peace celebrations were on but were eclipsed by preparations for the Governor's arrival. The atmosphere portended an era of peace and public contentment and many regretted that the new and promising administration had to succeed to a legacy of 'blundering ineptitude' and 'a hot-bed of seething discontent'.[55] However, it was widely believed that Clifford would easily clean 'the augean stable of Lugard's confusion' and place the country on a new path of progress and prosperity. It was in an attempt to assist the new Governor, the 'ideal administrator', in his work of reform that the *Record* published a Fourteen-Point Programme.[56] It was a wide-ranging administrative survey which emphasised the immediate steps the new Governor should take and proposed guidelines for the future. The programme of change represented by implication the most comprehensive newspaper press indictment against the administration of Lugard.

1. The removal of the Judiciary from the control of the Executive.
2. The complete jurisdiction of the Supreme Court in the Colony and Provinces with the rights of automatic appeal in civil and criminal cases from all the courts provincial or otherwise.
3. The admission of Barristers and legal practitioners to all the courts of the Colony and Province in civil and criminal cases.
4. The decent burial of the Criminal Code and the immediate return to the principles and practice of the Criminal Law of England.
5. The rehabilitation of the right of the Legislative Council to legislate for the Colony and Protectorate.
6. An increase in the number of native unofficial members and the introduction of liberal constitution with a view to gradual representation.
7. The extinction of the Nigerian Council which is as useless as the fifth wheel of a coach.
8. The sweeping away of the Provincial System whereby a District Officer wields in the provinces the power of life and death over any native whatever his education or standing. . . .
9. The rectification and scientific adjustment of provincial boundaries in consonance with the wishes and historical traditions of the communities affected. . . .
10. The abolition in the Southern Provinces of the Northern Nigerian method of direct taxation. . . .
11. The clearing of the Abeokuta muddle . . . and the permanent removal of Mr. Edun . . . from every phase of Egba politics. . . .
12. The regrading of the Civil Service – both European and Native; the concession of liberal emoluments . . . the institution of a policy of promotion by merit . . . the admission of natives to higher plums of the service and the removal by retirement or transfer to other colonies of political officers who are wedded to the Nigerian System. . . .
13. The neutralisation of the nefarious principles . . . by which natives are being swindled out of their immemorial rights to their ancestral lands. . . .
14. A network of motor roads to the principal agricultural and industrial towns. . . .

All this fervour, however, was destined to be shortlived, for barely three months after Clifford's arrival, he became enmeshed in the sensitive and intractable problem of the position of the indigenous monarchy in Lagos represented by Prince Eshugbayi

(Eleko), head of the Dosunmu-Oyekan House. By the end of the following year, he had compounded the Eleko Question and also revealed his antagonism for the African nationalist movement.

'QUESTION OF QUESTIONS'

Educated Nigerians in Lagos showed an especial interest in the fortunes of the House of Dosunmu. Since the death of Dosunmu in 1885, the question of the emoluments and political stature of the head of the House had received the eager attention of Nigerian members of the Legislative Council as well as the newspaper press. With the death of Oyekan in 1900 and the succession of Eshugbayi the following year, the issue assumed a new dimension and was to reach a turning point in 1920.

The strenuous support of the Lagos intelligentsia for the House of Dosunmu calls for explanation because it reveals a contradiction in their thinking. They rejected Indirect Rule which denied their claim to be the true representatives of the Nigerian people but wished to enhance the power and prestige of the indigenous monarchy in an urban centre like Lagos where such institutions were more anachronistic. Generally, the low fortunes of the House of Dosunmu were seen to symbolise the injustice and lack of fair play which were concomitants of colonial rule; more important, however, was the fact that the Eleko became a pawn in local power politics. Factional politics in Lagos, which went back to the beginning of British rule, entered a new phase in the course of the Water Rate agitation of 1916. Dr Randle and Dr Obasa compromised their leadership of the community by their unsatisfactory conduct and practically sold Lagos to Herbert Macaulay who identified himself more reliably and resolutely with the public cause. The leaders of the Peoples' Union were alleged to have induced the community in 1914–15 to subscribe large sums of money (about £11 500) ostensibly to fight the water rate and the Criminal Code which was then being proposed.[57] The accession of Herbert Macaulay to popular leadership, however, aroused bitter divisions and dissensions which conditioned political activity for a long time. As Herbert Macaulay rose as the strong man of local politics and the chief spokesman of the Eleko movement, his opponents became supporters of the Eleko's opponents such as Chief Obanikoro. In the logic of the new polarisation, the progressive newspapermen like Thomas Jackson, James Bright Davies and Ernest Ikoli (later to change camp) were on the side of Herbert Macaulay and the House of Dosunmu whereas Kitoyi Ajasa, Henry Carr, Dr Randle, Dr Obasa and their friends supported the government.

Before 1919, Prince Eshugbayi had fallen foul of the government twice, the first time in 1908 when he supported the opposition to the water rate. When the issue was revived in 1916, he had his allowance suspended for refusing an instruction to send his bell-man round the town to order the striking traders to end their strike. The allowance was however restored the following year. In October 1919 three months after Clifford's arrival, Acting Governor Colonel Moorhouse suspended Prince Eshugbayi from his position on the ground that he conferred chieftaincy titles on certain Muslims contrary to 'local custom and precedent' and in defiance of the government. What happened was that the Eleko gave recognition to some persons whom the Jamat Muslims, a faction of the then squabbling Muslim Community, put forward as leaders. The other faction had supported the government over the water rate issue. On his return from tour in November, Governor Clifford held discussions with thirteen Nigerian leaders, among them Henry Carr, Kitoyi Ajasa, Dr Randle, Dr Obasa, S. H. Pearse, Dr R. A. Savage and Coker who advised that the disciplinary action on the Eleko be upheld. Consequently, the suspension was confirmed and the White Cap Chiefs were constituted into a Council of Regency.

This development provoked public wrath and strong protest by the newspapers. In an article entitled 'An Impending Disaster', the *Record* lamented that 'a great calamity' was threatening the House of Dosunmu and called on those who had pride in Nigerian indigenous ruling institutions to rally round and avert 'an imminent danger'. The previous day the *Standard* had demanded fair play and justice.[58] On 17 November, a mass meeting was held at Enu Owa at which a deputation of twenty was selected to wait on the Governor. As a result of all this pressure, Clifford decided to reinstate the Eleko and to authorise the payment of his arrears of salary. For this decision, he was hailed as 'a great governor' evincing a desire to 'hold up the balance of justice without fear or favour'.[59] But perceptive observers must have seen that Clifford was not after all the super-governor of popular imagination and that he could also make mistakes. The reversal of an earlier decision was no doubt an abandonment of the 'white man's prestige' theory of colonial administration but it could also be a mark of uncertainty and indecision. Probable doubts about Clifford's excellence were confirmed a year later when another crisis erupted on the same issue.

The occasion was Prince Eshugbayi's refusal to repudiate what purported to be 'certain absurd statements . . . made to the people of England' by Herbert Macaulay who was in London with Chief Oluwa in connection with the latter's appeal to the Privy Council in the famous Apapa Lands Case.[60] The government alleged that in an interview which Herbert Macaulay had with the *Daily Mail*, he claimed that Prince Eshugbayi was 'King of the 17 million people of Nigeria'. When requested by the government to repudiate this 'offensive' statement, the Eleko published a disclaimer in the *Record*. But this was considered insufficient and the Eleko was ordered to broadcast the disclaimer through a town-crier. He declined to do such a humiliating thing; instead, he requested that the matter be deferred until Chief Oluwa returned to Lagos and also that he should be allowed to travel to Britain, with some members of the family and two lawyers, in order to check the facts and correct any misstatements there if necessary. This offer was rejected and a decision was taken to withdraw official recognition from him even though it had come to be known that what Herbert Macaulay actually said was that Eshugbayi was acclaimed as 'the titular King of Lagos' by the 17 million people of Nigeria.[61]

The withdrawal of recognition meant the loss to the prince of his small annual allowance of about £300 but it was not the financial implication that mattered. Rather, it was the injustice of the decision and, more importantly, the suspected manoeuvres of Herbert Macaulay's enemies. The *Record* was later to describe the ensuing crisis as 'the question of questions' and the *Nigerian Advocate* was to compare Eshugbayi's chequered career with those of Mary Queen of Scots, Louis XVI of France and Czar Nicholas I of Russia.[62] Indeed, the Eleko controversy was a development of significance for in its social and political repercussions, it was without precedent in Nigerian political history. It raised political consciousness to new heights and sealed the fate of many a politician.

The newspaper press played a key role in the unfolding of events. In opposition to the *Pioneer* which had wondered that the government had waited so long to sever relations from 'a useless mischievous official friendship' and which was later to represent Prince Eshugbayi as inheriting his father's character of 'rogue and fool', the *Record* and the *Times of Nigeria* flayed Governor Clifford, the former newspaper describing his policy as that of 'Mess and Muddle'. It accused the governor of 'gross indiscretion and ridiculous partisanship' and appealed to him to rectify the confused state of things.[63] Throughout 1921 while Clifford was on leave, the *Record* and the *African Messenger* intensified the campaign. And when the rumour spread that the Eleko's enemies were exerting pressure on the government to deport him, the *Messenger* pressed for an immediate inquiry.[64]

When Clifford was due to arrive back from leave in December 1921, there were campaigns in some newspapers that there should be no public welcome. Moderate opinion, however, prevailed and a Welcome Address was presented on 21 December. The address travelled so far outside the customary route of such exercise that the view was expressed that it was more of a Grand Remonstrance. Written by Thomas Jackson, it was an ingeniously worded catalogue of grievances and suggestions for redress. Three months later (on 15 March 1922), Clifford replied irritatingly to the address, much to the satisfaction of the *Pioneer* which congratulated the Governor on his 'courageous stand' while its opponents expressed dismay. '. . . Here is a prince', moaned the *Messenger*, 'the descendant of a long line of powerful kings, literally thrown into the streets to beg his bread'.[65]

All this time, since November 1921, efforts were being made to collect signatures to a petition to the Governor on behalf of the Eleko. By the end of November 1922, a total of 17 000 signatures had been obtained. Thomas Jackson played the leading role in the preparation of the petition as well as in the collection of signatures. The document, which was christened the 'Monster Petition' because of the large number of signatories, was forwarded on 28 November 1922 to Governor Clifford through the Resident of the Colony of Lagos, Henry Carr. The presentation of the petition was carried out in an atmosphere of 'sensation and fanfare'.

The petition, however, made little impression on Clifford who ridiculed the efforts of the educated Nigerians. Publishing his reply in an equally spectacular way – by employing policemen to distribute the leaflets – he dismissed the Monster Petition movement as worthless.

I feel both surprise and regret that any persons of presumed intelligence and respectability should have wasted time and money during
the period of twelve months in laboriously collecting signatures
to a Petition which they must have known was certain to be barren
of result and was therefore not worth a moment's effort or a single
penny-piece.[66]

Clifford even doubted the genuineness of the signatures, remarking
that 17 000 signatures were even a poor showing in a community
of about 100 000. Newspapers were quick to point out that the
Constitution of Jamaica with a population of one million had been
amended by virtue of a petition signed by 3 000 persons but this
achieved nothing. For the pro-Eleko newspapers, Clifford had now
reached the nadir of his unpopularity. His failure to live up to the
expectation of the press had produced complete disillusionment. So
pronounced was the revulsion against him that the newspapers might
well have said that Clifford 'the Good' had become Clifford 'the Fool'.

The passage of the next two or three years would do nothing to
revive the Governor's crumbled popularity. By 22 May 1925,
when he finally left Nigeria, differences of opinion about himself
and his administration which had begun to crystallise in 1919
were in no way near reconciliation. The *Pioneer* gave him a send-off
eulogy but the *Record* fired a parting shot of rhetoric ('Sir Clifford
is the only discourteous individual who has represented British
sovereignty in Lagos . . . and whose administration of the Government of the Colony has been remarkable for official squandermania,
intolerable partisanship, autocratic obstinacy, persistent dis-
courtesy and irrational blunder').[67] The next six years after
Clifford's departure would see the deposition and banishment of
Prince Eshugbayi to Oyo, a development which led to protracted
litigation until the Prince was allowed to return to Lagos in
1931. The newspapers were to follow the course of events with
relentless vigilance and to hail the end of the crisis with self-
congratulation.[68]

The Eleko Question constituted the graveyard of many a
reputation and also the acme of the aspirations of the early
nationalist press. Even if the newspapers failed to change the
attitude of the government to Prince Eshugbayi, they nevertheless
succeeded to some extent in intensifying public wrath sufficient to
cause uncertainties in official minds and to delay a final decision
for a long time. They also strengthened political awareness among
the people and diffused destructive propaganda about enemies of

Herbert Macaulay whose political eclipse was confirmed thenceforth. If eye-witnesses are to be believed, sales of pro-Eleko newspapers rose sharply at the height of the crisis between 1920 and 1922 as marketwomen and many other loyal but unlettered followers of the indigenous monarchy bought newspapers which they asked to be read to them. They read about their fellow countrymen whose intrigues were allegedly behind Eshugbayi's fall. Thirteen of these whose advice was followed in the suspension of Eshugbayi in October 1919 had earlier been nicknamed 'The Thirteen Contemptibles' and 'The Despicable Thirteen'. They and their friends were now pilloried, and in popular thinking, confirmed as evil men.

ELECTIVE FRANCHISE AND EPOCH OF ELECTIONEERING

It is remarkable that it was at a time when criticism was mounting against the government of Governor Clifford that he introduced the principle of elective representation in the Legislative Council which had the effect of diverting attacks away from the government to the ranks of feuding personalities and political groups. For, the introduction of the Clifford Constitution in 1923 and the advent of electioneering the following year, not only revealed a crisis of loyalties in press and public but also marked the beginning of the attempt to mount propaganda expressly aimed at advancing political party interests. Whether the introduction of elections was a calculated ploy to make the government a less convenient target is difficult to establish but it might well throw some light on the paradox of the introduction of elective franchise at a time when the Governor himself had indicated his strong opposition to the concrete expression of African nationalism. Views regarding the underlying factors in Clifford's constitutional reform may be in conflict[69] but all are agreed that the pressure of Nigerian opinion for elected representation was very strong. What is not often sufficiently stressed is the fact that the representation campaign was largely the work of the newspapers and the newspapermen who formed both the weapon and the vanguard of the battle. Their campaign of post-war nationalism, in which elective representation formed a major plank and which culminated in the National Congress movement, provides a fruitful point of reference for the developments in 1922-23.

Early in 1919, the *Record* published a long editorial article aimed at bringing together and consolidating the strands of post-war Nigerian thought. Entitled 'Post-war ideals and the Educated Native in Nigeria', the article examined the character of the post-war ideological ferment and enunciated what was described as 'principles of advanced native thought' which were stated as follows: politically, political franchise must be won through acts of 'heroism and self-sacrifice' in constitutional as opposed to violent agitation; educationally, efforts must be made to change the Nigerian Educational Code which was 'hopelessly deficient and peculiarly distasteful'; economically, the realisation of commercial or industrial independence was to be sought through co-operation or combination; socially, social revolution was to come about not through complete Africanisation but by following the 'social mean or scientific pathway' which lay in the 'Africanisation of Western ideals'. This was further explained to mean 'the adaptation of Western ideals to African environment by a process of selection and assimilation'; religiously, the establishment of African National Churches, the African Church Movement being the 'Protestantism of Africa directed against the Europeanization of Christianity'.[70]

In June 1919, the newspaper again focused on the theme of constitutional reform in its Fourteen-Point Programme. Paragraph 5 demanded the rehabilitation of the Legislative Council to legislate for the Colony and Protectorate and to assume the control of Estimates and Expenditure with the consequent re-organisation of the Council which was 'nothing short of a glorified board'. Paragraph 6 called for an increase in the number of Nigerian members of the Legislative Council and the introduction of a liberal constitution with a view to gradual representation. The seventh paragraph demanded the extinction of the Nigerian Council which was 'as useless as the fifth wheel of a coach'.

A milestone was reached in the propaganda of the franchise movement when the National Congress of British West Africa (NCBWA) was inaugurated at Accra in March 1920. Elective representation formed the core of the agitation of the National Congress. The Congressmen demanded the establishment of a Legislative Council in each territory of British West Africa one half of whose members would be elected Africans and the other half nominated. This and other resolutions (African vote over taxation; the appointment of Africans to judicial offices; abolition of racial discrimination in the Civil Service and the establishment of a West African University) as well as details of proceedings and general activities found much inspiration and publicity in the Nigerian newspaper press. It was small wonder, therefore, that the Congress passed a resolution recording its condolence with the families of George Alfred Williams (founder of the *Lagos Standard*, died in June 1919) and James Bright Davies (proprietor of the *Nigerian Times/Times of Nigeria*, died in January 1920) who were described as 'prominent West African journalists who did noble work in upholding the rights of the race'. Indeed, the National Congress itself was the brainchild and product of the newspapermen in Nigeria and West Africa.

The persistent controversy about who originated the Congress idea, whether Dr Richard Akiwande Savage or Dr Randle, has tended to obscure the true origin and growth of the idea. What proponents of the Savage and Randle hypothesis fail to realise is that the notion of a 'West African Conference' did not originate in any part of former British West Africa. It was given expression in Monrovia, Liberia, between 1900 and 1905. During this period, Monrovia newspapers generated interest in the subject throughout West Africa and newspapers in Nigeria and the Gold Coast showed particular enthusiasm for the idea to which they gave some publicity. It all started with the *Cape Palmas Reporter* which, probably in 1903, mooted the idea of a 'Conference of West Africans'. The following year, the *Living Chronicle* published a letter from 'A West African' calling attention to the need for 'a consolidation of sentiments'. The writer suggested that there should be a Conference of West Africans about once in every five years 'at which time matters that appertain to the Africans can be discussed freely, whether commercial, political, religious or social'. The 'leaders and best men' on the coast, from Gambia to Lagos might meet at a specified place and be presided over 'by some discreet men with liberal views'. The author of the letter invited the editors of West African newspapers and 'the thinking minds of West African negroes' to take up the subject and hold a debate upon it.[71]

Commenting on the scheme in August 1904, the *Lagos Standard* asserted that there could hardly be any question as to its desirability. The 'suggestions and recommendations' of such a conference would carry a 'weight and prestige' which would be lacking in isolated efforts.[72] In the Gold Coast, the *Advocate* and the *Gold*

Coast Leader saw the Conference idea as 'a crying necessity of the times'.[75] Meanwhile the *Living Chronicle* (Liberia) had taken up the idea with greater vigour, making constructive suggestions about the venue of the conference (mid-1905 in Monrovia) and the choice and number of candidates (six from each country). The *Lagos Standard* much preferred the Gold Coast as a more central place and also put forward the suggestion that local committees be formed in the different territories to facilitate the effectuation of the scheme. The very existence of such committees could not fail to arouse interest in the scheme in the localities in which they were situated and the committees would be in communication with each other and thus expedite the arrangements for a General Conference. It was an indication of the seriousness with which the *Standard* took the subject that it made a special appeal to the Nigerian educated public in January 1905.[74]

> What we would like to impress upon our readers. . . is the fact that at no time was the necessity for union and co-operation among members of the race so urgent as at the present moment and that unless the African awakes to his responsibilities and putting aside all feelings of petty jealousies, selfish interests and other evil influences that have so long retarded his progress, determine to combine and co-operate for the general good of the race, he must be content to bear those ills which are inseparable from a condition of such culpable in difference.

By March, 1905, the *Standard* rejoiced that the Conference idea was 'on a fair way towards realization' in contemptuous reaction to the hostile views of the British journal, the *African World*, which opposed the sentiments of the *Standard* on the subject, warning British administrators to watch the conference movement as 'a movement of disaffection and disloyalty'.[75] In April, evidence of public support was indicated in a communication.[76] Then nothing more was heard about the conference scheme, at least in Nigeria, until the idea was revived in 1913. There is no evidence that the administration of Governor Egerton took the *African World* seriously which suggests that there probably was not enough public support. But there can be no doubt that the scheme was not a new discovery by Dr Savage or Dr Randle, nor was it a new idea to the educated public in West Africa by 1913. Dr Randle and Dr Savage were prominent local figures in Nigeria and the Gold Coast respectively, places where the conference idea was well publicised in 1904–5, and could not have been unaware of such important pan-African developments at the time. It seems obvious that what Randle or Savage 'pioneered' was not the conference idea itself but the more realistic truncation of it to embrace people with similar social and political experience.

Between 1913, when the conference idea was resuscitated, and 1920, when it took concrete form, it owed its progress almost entirely to the newspapers which propagated it with characteristic vigour. Soon after Dr Savage and Casely Hayford issued their circular letter at Cape Coast in 1915 appealing to prominent West Africans to support a West African Conference, the Nigerian press took up the issue and by examining all the possible problems in a dispassionate manner, helped to prepare the way for the smooth inauguration of the National Congress five years later.[77] It is worth noting that it was the propaganda of the Nigerian press that brought about the summoning of the first Conference meeting in Lagos where a committee, with Dr Randle as Chairman and Thomas Jackson and Dr Savage as joint-secretaries, was set up to take up the matter with Africans in the other colonies.[78] As the war progressed, Nigerian editors continued to appeal for more positive action. They called attention to the 'spectacular progress' of the India National Congress which 'by giving articulate expression to Indian national aspirations in a tone of increasing strength and firmness' had forced India to the forefront of 'Imperial politics';[79] they applauded the organisational achievements of Afro-Americans in the United States, emphasising the racial significance of the first Pan-African Congress held in Paris in 1918–19 and the formation of the United Negro Improvement Association and its affiliate the African Communities League by Marcus Garvey.[80] Indications of public apathy did not dampen their enthusiasm as they sought additional ways of arousing popular interest. The newspapermen organised public meetings which failed and they tried public lectures which had poor attendance.[81] These depressing developments notwithstanding Patriarch Campbell, a freelance journalist and 'Professor' Adeoye Deniga, at the time sub-editor of the *Record*, joined three other Nigerians as the colony's representatives at the inaugural meeting in Accra.[82]

Apart from originating the Congress idea and advancing its growth and practicalisation, the West African newspapermen were also the staunchest defenders of the National Congress movement against the thrusts of its enemies. In Nigeria, Kitoyi Ajasa's frugal animadversions were easily discounted[83] but the major challenge came from Governor Clifford who, in his celebrated address to the Nigerian Council on 29 December 1920, subjected the National Congress movement to blistering criticism. Clifford's oft-quoted strictures against 'a self-selected and self-appointed congregation of educated African gentlemen who collectively style themselves the "West African Conference"' and the 'manifest absurdity' of a 'West African Nation'[84] could not but infuriate the educated Africans who found their able spokesman in Thomas Jackson. In a monumental retort which began on 29 January and ended in mid-July 1921, Thomas Jackson's *Record* subjected Clifford's address to searching analysis and criticism. The editorial articles which were given the Biblical title 'Mene Mene Tekel Upharsim' were unprecedented in their length (average of two full pages each), comprehensiveness and display of erudition.[85] They were not confined to the immediate question of Clifford's assault but ranged over related issues. The first aiticle was subtitled 'Progelomena'; the second, which started on 5 February, was headed 'The Political or Administrative Machinery'. The third, on 19 February, was 'The National Congress of British West Africa'. The fourth, subheaded 'The Eleko Episode and the Mohammedan Question', began with the issue dated 2–16 April. The fifth article, 'Abeokuta muddle and the Evolution of Native states', came out with the issue of 7–14 May. The sixth (21–28 May) was on 'Education and Other Problems'. The seventh, carried in the issue of 18–25 June, was on 'Social Evolution in West Africa'. The series was concluded in the publication of 2–16 July with 'Summary and Conclusions'. Given the initiative of the newspaper press in the campaign for elective franchise as well as for the formation of a West African Conference which gave a new urgency to the franchise agitation, it was quite reasonable for the nationalist press to claim the credit for the achievement of constitutional reform in 1922. And in the nature of things, the newspapers were bound to play an important role after the Clifford Constitution became effective.

The coming into effect of the constitution witnessed a remarkable political awakening and involvement which found new directions in political parties. Thomas Jackson co-founded with Herbert Macaulay the Nigerian National Democratic Party (NNDP). In fact, the available evidence indicates that the NNDP was the brainchild of Thomas Jackson. In one of his reminiscences in 1930, Thomas Jackson claimed that he originated the idea of a political party in 1923; when he visited Liberia in April that year, he seized 'the golden opportunity' offered by the Presidential elections there to study the workings of the party system with a view to adapting same to the Nigerian situation. Emphasising how much the formation of the party was owed to him, he averred that it was he who christened the party 'National Democratic Party' although Herbert Macaulay added the word 'Nigerian' which Thomas Jackson thought was 'somewhat superfluous'.[86] The constitution and rules of the party were also drafted by him. Indeed, the constitution was an abridged version of an earlier special editorial article in the *Record*. This can indeed be seen in the style and language of the stated aims of the NNDP: 'To secure the safety and welfare of the people of the Colony and Protectorate of Nigeria as an integral part of the British Imperial Commonwealth and to carry the banner of "Right, Truth, Liberty and Justice" to the empyrean heights of Democracy until the realization of its ambitious goal of "A Government of the People, by the People. . ." '[87] It was hardly surprising that on 9 June 1923, the *Record* launched the NNDP with great verve.

About three weeks after the NNDP was inaugurated, the Young Nigeria Party (The Union of Young Nigerians) was formed under the leadership of Dr Moses J. da Rocha, a medical practitioner and newspaper columnist. Ernest Ikoli was one of the main speakers at the inaugural meeting although he held no office in the party. In spirit, he probably belonged to the NNDP camp but he had parted company with Herbert Macaulay in 1921 following a quarrel which resulted from his refusal to publish a contribution by Herbert Macaulay. Herbert Macaulay did not usually tolerate such an 'affront' and did not hesitate, as was the case with John Jackson in 1908, to break an established friendship on that account.

The involvement of the newspapermen in the formation of these parties provide one explanation for the heated participation of the newspapers in the Legislative Council elections. Newspapers shifted their focus from that of political group supporters to organs of political parties. A second explanation was that certain people were aroused by the constitutional changes to establish their own newspapers expressly to fight the elections. Such newspapers, by the very nature of their birth, tried very hard to influence public thought and so introduced vehemence into the campaigns. A further reason was the natural disposition of newspapers to exploit political excitement for commercial ends. The

233

polemics inevitable in electioneering gave a boost to newspaper sales.

In the election battle, the newspapers fell into three main groups: pro-NNDP, anti-NNDP and 'uncommitted'. In the first category were the *Record* and the *Eko Akete*. Against these were ranged the *Pioneer*, the *Spectator* and the *Messenger*. The *Advocate* remained neutral, arguing persistently that to free the political atmosphere from bitterness, the politicians should present a common front and a common programme, that the NNDP, the Young Nigeria Party and other political groups should hold a round-table conference to iron out their differences.

Of the two combatant groups, the anti-NNDP were first to open active campaigns. The *Pioneer* spearheaded this move. Nine months before the elections were due (September 20 was Election Day) the paper began to preach that the qualification for voting and for being elected was a sense of responsibility. As the election drew near, it continually harped upon the theme of 'principled leadership' which was worthy of public emulation.[88] It published the 'election addresses' of two European candidates, A. H. Harvey and F. B. Mulford.

The *Messenger* saw Lagos society as a federation of two societies – one of principled men headed by Ajasa, and the other of dishonest men led by Herbert Macaulay. From August, the paper had nothing but scorn for the NNDP leader. It campaigned for independent candidates and especially for Adeyemo Alakija, a dissident member of Herbert Macaulay's party.[89]

The bitterness of the *Pioneer* and the *Messenger* was shared by the *Spectator*. The paper stated its determination 'to smash up the apathy and indifference' that prevailed among the educated sections of the community. But outside abuses, one looks in vain for more effective propaganda methods which would have given the paper's crusade the necessary impact.

The anti-NNDP newspapers lacked one advantage which the 'organs' of that Party had, namely, an affective vernacular newspaper. The anti-NNDP group had potential support in the *Eleti Ofe* whose owner and editor, Akintan, was an official of the Young Nigeria Party. But for unknown reasons, the paper refrained from effectively participating in the elections. It only published the manifestos of all the candidates. The *Eko Akete*, which at the time was rising rapidly in circulation (from 500 in 1922 to 1 000 in 1923),[90] campaigned in Yoruba, reporting NNDP rallies and encouraging the party to fight hard and win. But perhaps its most effective propaganda was its persistent adulation of Macaulay. It showered praise-names on him: he was the intrepid fighter, the unrelenting, the conqueror of the savannah (lion) etc.[91] Many of the praise-names became slogans and household words.

But of all the newspapers that took part in electioneering, the *Record* was the most organised. Entering the contest on 9 June with the accumulated vehemence of thirty-three years, it thundered week after week about the responsibilities of the electorate, emphasising the need for the exercise of constitutional rights 'in accordance with the accepted principles of Democratic government'. It gave full support to J. Egerton Shyngle, Eric Moore and Dr C. C. Adeniyi-Jones, the three candidates of the NNDP, publishing their manifestos and strengthening these with editorial eulogies. It reached the climax of its campaigns in the first week of September when it devoted a full page to a twenty-five line appeal which began as follows:

> Vote the straight Democratic Ticket
> And thereby
> Vote for the safety and welfare of
> the people.

Of the three candidates, it said:

> Vote for Councillor J. E. Egerton Shyngle,
> The Leader and Lion of the Bar
> And the stout Defender of the
> People's Rights and Liberties.

> Vote for Barrister Eric O. Moore,
> The Honourable Member of the
> Quondam Legislative Council
> and Father of
> Municipal Elective Representation.

> Vote for Dr. C. C. Adeniyi-Jones,
> The Apostle of child welfare
> and
> Staunch Advocate of Modern
> Sanitation for the masses[92]

The elections were, as was expected, a sweeping victory for the NNDP and the reactions of the newspapers were typical. Taking its defeat with ill-grace, the *Spectator* refused to congratulate the victorious party for it was firmly convinced that the future of Lagos was not safe in their hands.[93] The *Pioneer* denounced the 'wild jubilation' that greeted the results of the elections and asserted that Lagos had sold her birthright by electing 'three non-Lagosians'. Calabar also committed the same crime by returning 'a native of the Gold Coast'.[94] Ajasa's own uncertain background and the pressure which he exerted on behalf of European candidates combined to heighten anger at his remarks. Stung into a fierce retort, the *Record* urged the 'goody-goody utopians of the Ajasa group' to accept their defeat like sportsmen.[95]

Two other Legislative Council elections were held in our period – in 1928 and 1933. But there could hardly be a greater contrast between the fury which characterised newspaper participation in the 1923 elections and the apathy in the other two. In 1928, the *Daily Times* and the *Record* did little beyond publishing the manifestos of independent and NNDP candidates respectively. The strong opposition of the *Daily Times* to Herbert Macaulay was given weak expression in the electioneering campaign. In 1933, the *West African Sunday Digest*, the *Daily Times* and the *Pioneer* published a few comments which hardly added any colour to the elections. This dichotomy could be attributed to the fact that until the late thirties, no political organisation emerged to challenge the NNDP whose election successes were, therefore, taken for granted. Furthermore, the early thirties were marked by an acute dearth of 'powerful' newspapers. Most of the old radical or vociferous newspapers were either dead or decrepit. However, the nonchalant role played by the newspapers is best seen in the context of the climate of political activity from 1924 to the end of our period.

TWILIGHT OF THE POLITICAL PRESS

From the point of view of the newspaper press, 1924–37 were fourteen placid years. Excepting spasmodic, evanescent excitement aroused by re-opened political wounds, the years were relatively barren of major political developments. Perhaps the economic depression of the period had repercussions in the political field, creating an atmosphere of uncertainty, apathy and drift. The *Record* might have felt convinced in 1927 that the administration of Hugh Clifford's successor, Sir Graeme Thomas, was 'the reverse of enlightened statesmanship';[96] and the *Nigerian Daily Telegraph* might have considered in 1925 that Thomson's successor, Sir Donald Cameron had 'a certain fault of temperament' which relied on 'a policy of opportunism';[97] but such criticisms were no more than the occasional flash in a still sky. The vacuum in aggressive and stimulating journalism which resulted from the decline and demise of the veteran newspapers in the late twenties and early thirties, was no doubt an important factor. The *Record*, as well as the *Spectator* and *Advocate*, died in 1930 after a period of decline accelerated by the rise of daily newspapers in 1926. The *Lagos Daily News*, published by Herbert Macaulay, was a potential successor to the *Record* but it was most irregularly produced.

But apart from institutional weaknesses in the press, there were other possible explanations. Before the advent of electioneering, the government had been the convenient target of opposition attacks but things began to change with the escalation of local political strife during the Eleko Question. As this crisis merged into the epoch of electioneering, the government increasingly became a minor target. Personal feuds and political party antagonism became the paramount focus of journalistic activity. This departure of the newspaper press from its customary role of a government rival created much concern in many minds in Lagos to the extent revealed by the proceedings of a public debate on 22 February 1923. The motion 'that the influence of the Lagos press is not wholly for good' was carried by a large majority.[98] The inter-newspaper tension did not diminish after 1923; indeed, it increased resulting in frequent press wars which became the dominant feature of the political press in the late twenties and early thirties. The intermittent re-opening of wounds was the symptom of a significant malaise in society at large. A newspaper equated the social and political situation in the twenties with the 'nocturnal fracas and caterwaulings of the feline tribe'. The atmosphere, according to the newspaper, was 'surcharged with highly volatile and destructive elements of hatred, malice, envy, jealousy and all uncharitableness breathing the spirit of a Corsican vendetta'.[99] Some editors, disturbed by the thought that the newspapers would have no moral strength to attempt to remove the beam in the eyes of public men if there was a big mote in their own eyes, attempted to forge a new sense of co-operation and unity among journalists. Their efforts led to the formation of the Nigerian Press Association.

The leading spirit in this development was H. Antus Williams, editor of the *Nigerian Daily Telegraph*. H. Antus Williams was already an experienced journalist and nationalist by the late twenties. From a background of civil service employment from 1905 to 1917, he became sub-editor of the *Nigerian Spectator* in 1923–24, editor of the *Lagos Daily News* in 1927 and editor and proprietor of the *Nigerian Daily Telegraph* established in 1927. He was also the secretary of the Ebute Metta branch of the NCBWA. He was later to change his name to Akin Fagbenro Beyioku and to acquire a reputation for herbal medical skill.[100] On 17 August 1929, he invited his professional colleagues to a meeting to consider his proposals. The response was encouraging for with the exception of the *Pioneer* and the *Eleti Ofe*, all the existing newspapers were represented. The following resolution was unanimously carried.

> This meeting is of opinion that the time has arrived for the formation of a Nigerian Press Association and that the principal objects of such an Association should be to safeguard the interest of the local press, to raise its tone, to develop political thought and direct opinion on lines that would lead to the industrial, commercial and educational progress of the country.

Apart from the objects indicated in the resolution, the association wished to develop schemes for the attraction of local talents into journalism, to secure adequate wages for all engaged in newspaper work, to establish a library for the use of its members, to develop a co-operative scheme for the collection and distribution of news to the various newspapers and to settle disputes among members in their professional connection. Any editor dissociating himself from the association was to be denied official recognition. Members were to pay a monthly subscription of 2s and the Executive Committee was to comprise the Patron, Vice-Patron, President, Secretary, Treasurer and Librarian.

Tragically for the fate of the association, the election of officers apparently resulted in the exacerbation of differences. The details are not very clear but the view was later to be expressed by a leading foundation member that when it came to the election of an Executive Committee, 'the Association foundered, political bias being allowed to bias the deliberation of the meeting'.[101] Presumably, there was organised support for the more popular editors which aggravated mutual distrust. However, H. Antus Williams was elected secretary while Ernest Ikoli and S. H. Braithwaite were elected assistant secretaries. By November 1930, the association was virtually dead. To those who believed that the newspapermen ought to set an example of co-operation, the collapse of the association was a shameful event and for many years after, they campaigned, without success, for its revival.[102]

Notwithstanding the factionalism of the newspapermen, however, they readily sank their differences when occasion called for it. This was most effectively demonstrated when the Italo-Abyssinian War broke out in 1935. The Italian invasion of Ethiopia roused the quiescent Lagos public to new heights of nationalist fervour and the newspapers mirrored the militant mood in the passion with which they mounted an offensive against what was regarded as a war of African independence. Duse Mohammed Ali's *The Comet* most personified the embitterment of the educated Nigerians. It launched an Abyssinian Relief Fund to which the pan-Africanist editor and his wife contributed £5 and threw itself completely into the anti-Italian and anti-imperialism rallies. For a newspaper with a bias for international affairs, the Italian aggression became a consuming interest. For several weeks, in editorial articles as well as in Duse Mohammed Ali's popular columns 'Men and Matters' and 'About it and About', *The Comet* spearheaded the press and public demonstration of sympathy with Ethiopia.[103] Other newspapers like the *Nigerian Daily Telegraph* and the *Nigerian Daily Times*,[104] also played notable roles and the 'Ethiopian' unity of the journalists could not but provide an occasion for the renewal of the call for the resuscitation of the defunct Press Association. But as the popular enthusiasm cooled, the varius factions went their different ways and life continued along its impassive way.

In November 1937, a new sunrise emerged with the arrival of the *West African Pilot* established by Nnamdi Azikiwe. Before 1937, Azikiwe's academic and professional reputation was well known in West Africa on account of his critical articles on the West African Press in 1933 and his eventful role as editor of the *African Morning Post* in Accra, Ghana, from 1934 to 1937. With his popularity assured in a period of great opportunity provided by the absence of serious and respectable political newspapers, Azikiwe dramatically stirred the newspaper scene with a formula of striking techniques and rhetoric. The initial circulation of the *Pilot* was 9 000 as against the 6 000 of the *Daily Times* which, although it was distinctly conservative, had nevertheless dominated the newspaper field for eleven years. For large populations of people in and outside Lagos who for years had yearned for an effective purveyor of popular views and sentiments, for a symbol of increased political awareness and sophistication, the eloquent and sensational tone of the *Pilot* and its pugnacious political journalism, marked the beginning of a new era. And with the emergence of the new epoch of Nigerian politics and nationalism symbolised by the rise of the Nigerian Youth Movement in 1938, the Nigerian newspaper press stood on the threshold of a great institutional expansion and the attainment of the high tide of political influence.

Notes

1 14 March 1913, Also 3 October 1913.
2 14 July 1909. Also 2 January 1907. *Lagos Weekly Record*, 5 May 1906.
3 *Lagos Weekly Record*, 14 February, 13 June 1914.
4 *Lagos Daily Record*, 4 January 1930.
5 *Times of Nigeria*, 31 March 1914.
6 Perham, *Years of Authority*, pp. 138–73. Also P. C. Lloyd, 'Lugard and Indirect Rule', *Ibadan*, November, 1960, pp. 18–22.
7 *The Nigerian Gazette*, i, 4, 15 January 1914, pp. 130–71.
8 *Nigerian Chronicle*, 6 February, 1914; *Lagos Weekly Record*, 14 February 1914.
9 *Lagos Weekly Record*, 23 May 1914.
10 4 February 1914.
11 14 February 1914.
12 4 February 1914.
13 14 February 1914.
14 25 February 1914.
15 *Lagos Standard*, 25 February 1914; *Times of Nigeria*, 21 July 1914; *Nigerian Chronicle*, 30 January 1914: All the evidence indicates that flogging was not foreign to Yoruba people. In any case, sentences of flogging were imposed in the pre-Lugard period. Such sentences were regulated by the Corporal Punishments Limitation Ordinance, 1902, repealed by the Flogging Regulation Ordinance, 1903. See *Government Gazette*, 20 June 1903, p. 381.
16 See T. O. Elias, *The Nigerian Legal System*, London, 1954, p. 8.
17 30 January 1914. Zaria was the headquarters of Northern Nigeria at the time.
18 *Nigerian Daily Times*, 30 January 1932.
19 *Times of Nigeria*, 10 February 1914.
20 *Nigerian Chronicle*, 27 February 1914 and subsequent issues.
21 See for example, *African Messenger*, 30 March, 1 June 1922; Duse Mohammed Ali, 'The Provincial Courts Ordinance', in *Nigerian Daily Times*, 30 January 1932.

22 17 February 1914.
23 On 1 August 1919, he called attention to the haste with which Northern precedents were introduced into the South and observed '. . . the judicial reforms have fallen short of expectations and grave apprehensions continue to be manifested by many in this respect'. The previous year, on 17 September 1918, the Pioneer had remarked: 'Rightly or wrongly . . . and we do not propose to stop to consider the point . . . it was found necessary to pass the Provincial Courts Ordinance. . . .'
24 See *Times of Nigeria*, 1914.
25 4 January 1899.
26 *Lagos Weekly Record*, 19 July 1890; 12 September 1891. For details, see Fred I. A. Omu. 'The Nigerian Press and the Great War'.
27 *Nigeria Magazine*, No. 96, March/May, 1968, pp. 44–9.
28 15 and 22 April 1916.
29 8 January, 27 May and 3 June 1916.
30 *Lagos Standard*, 29 March, 5 April 1899; 12 April 1899; *Lagos Weekly Record*, 6 January 1900. C.O. 147/142, Denton to Chamberlain, 14 April 1899. Signatories included C. A. S. Williams, Dr Randle, John Jackson, R. B. Blaize, J. P. L. Davies, Leigh, Herbert Macaulay, Obasa of Ikeja and S. M. Harden.
31 15 and 22 April 1916.
32 *Report of the Proceedings at an Interview on the Water Rate Question* (Tika Tore Press, no date).
33 6 June, 23 May, 28 November 1914. See also *Lagos Standard*, 1 June, 17 June, 24 June, 1 July 1914.
34 *Report of the Proceedings*.
35 27 May and 3 June 1916. Also 16–30 September 1916.
36 2 and 9 September 1916; 3, 10 May 1930.
37 C.S.O. 1/33/60, Harcourt to Lugard, 20 September 1918.
38 *Lagos Weekly Record*, 20 and 27 January 1917.
39 See Chapter 6.
40 See *Times of Nigeria*, 6 August, 19 November 1918.
41 For details on the so-called Ijemo Massacre, see Perham, *Years of Authority*, p. 450.
42 23 February 1898. Also 25 January 1899.
43 22 March 1913.
44 22 March 1913; 2–16 March 1918.
45 *Nigerian Pioneer*, 7 December 1917; 1 February 1918.
46 *Lagos Standard*, 1 January 1919.
47 19 June 1918. Also 3, 10, 17 July 1918.
48 13 and 20 July 1918.
49 21 June, 5 July 1918. For attacks on the *Pioneer*, see *Standard*, 3, 10 July 1918.
50 Suggested were Griffin or Rev. A. W. Smith of the C.M.S. Oshogbo.
51 See for example, *Lagos Weekly Record*, 20 March, 27 March, 7 August 1920.
52 1–22 February 1919.

53 *Lagos Standard*, 7 May 1919.
54 *Lagos Weekly Record*, 9 August 1919.
55 *Lagos Standard*, 14 January 1920.
56 14 June 1919.
57 'Conspiracy against Eleko' by Herbert Macaulay. *African Messenger*, 27 October 1921.
58 *Lagos Weekly Record*, 15, 22, 29 November 1919; *Lagos Standard*, 14 November 1919; Also *Times of Nigeria* 6, 13, 20, 27 October; 3 November; 1–8 December 1919.
59 *Lagos Weekly Record*, 6 December 1919; *Lagos Standard*, 19 December 1919.
60 Begun in 1913 when the government, in keeping with its claim to possession of rights over land ceded in 1861, took over public land at Apapa. The Full (Supreme) Court in Lagos upheld the official view but the Privy Council rejected it.
61 *Lagos Weekly Record*, 6–20 May 1922; 20 January 1923. *Times of Nigeria*, 13 December 1920. Copy of letter, Henry Carr to the Eleko, 5 November, 24 November 1920; Eleko to the Private Secretary, Government House, Lagos, 29 November 1920; *Times of Nigeria*, 20 December 1920.
62 12 August 1925.
63 6 February–26 March 1921. *Times of Nigeria*. 13 December 1920. *Nigerian Pioneer*, 24 December 1920.
64 20 October 1921.
65 23 March 1922.
66 *Lagos Weekly Record*, 20 January 1923.
67 2 May 1925; See also *Nigerian Pioneer*, 29 May 1925; 1 January 1926.
68 See *Nigerian Daily Telegraph*, 26 March 1931; *Nigerian Pioneer* 10 July 1931.
69 See T. N. Tamuno, *Nigeria and Elective Representation, 1923–1947*, London, 1966, pp. 26ff.
70 1 March–31 May 1919.
71 See *Lagos Standard*, 13 July 1904.
72 31 August 1904.
73 *Gold Coast Leader*, 6 May 1905.
74 11 January 1905.
75 *Lagos Standard*, 22 March 1905.
76 'Veritas' to *Lagos Standard*, 5 April 1905.
77 *Lagos Weekly Record*, 27 February, 20 March 1915. *Nigerian Chronicle*, 26 February; 26 March 1915.
78 See *Lagos Weekly Record*, 10 July 1920.
79 *Lagos Weekly Record*, 7 and 14 July 1917; 7 February 1920.
80 *Lagos Weekly Record*, 7 February 1920.
81 According to Patriarch Campbell, people were reluctant to chair such meetings because 'Lagos politics were too full of intrigues ...' Among journalists who gave lectures were Thomas Jackson and R. Antus Williams, President of the Ebute Metta branch of the local committee.

82 The others were Prince Ephraim Bassey Duke of Calabar, Chief Essien Offiong Essien also of Calabar and Adeniyi Olugbile of Ebute Metta, Lagos.

83 See *Nigerian Pioneer*, 11 June 1920; Also 22 April 1921; 24 February, 3 March, 10 March 1922.

84 Minutes of the Nigerian Council, December 1920.

85 See also *African Messenger*, 10 March 1921; '. . . the opinion is that the Congress movement has only been used as a convenient excuse for insulting the whole of educated West Africa'.

86 *Lagos Weekly Record*, 7 June 1930.

87 *Constitution of the Nigerian National Democratic Party*, Lagos. n.d., p. 1. See *Lagos Weekly Record*, 9 June 1923.

88 See for example, 15 June, 22 June 1923.

89 See especially anonymous article possibly written by Ikoli headed 'The coming elections, a current of intrigues and falsehood'. *African Messenger*, 6 September 1923.

90 *Blue Books*, 1922, 1923. Also *Eko Akete*, 1 December 1923; 1 November 1924.

91 See issues of 30 June, 21 July, 29 July, 25 August 1923.

92 1–8 September 1923.

93 29 September 1923.

94 28 September 1923. Shyngle was Gambian; Adeniyi Jones, Sierra Leonian and Moore, Egba.

95 29 September 1923.

96 12–19 February 1927; 26 February–5 March 1927.

97 12, 13, 14, 15 June 1935. Compare the opinion of the *Lagos Daily News* on Cameron's accession to the governorship. 'What more do we want to recommend to us this great personality who had done more than sixteen years' work in the Nigerian Civil Service? Let us hope that the old ability has deepened with age and the power to inspire his colleague with a love of, and enthusiasm for work, the shrewdness and the sympathy evinced as the Chief Secretary to the Government would be keener to make Sir Donald's work in Nigeria a very big success to the progress of Nigeria.' (18 June 1931.) Herbert Macaulay, owner of the newspaper, was known to be on terms of friendship with Donald Cameron.

98 *Eko Akete*, 3 March 1923.

99 *Lagos Weekly Record*, 7 January 1930.

100 H. Antus Williams was born on 19 February 1890 to R. A. Williams one time President of the U.N.A. Church Organisation. He had his early education at the Jehovah Shalom School (U.N.A.) and the C.M.S. Grammar School in Lagos. Between 1905 and 1917, he worked in the Nigerian Railway and the Marine Department. In March 1938, he became personal secretary to Oba Falolu of Lagos. In the forties he became a church leader having founded the Universal African Model Church (22 December 1946). He was a member of the Ifa Cult in various Yoruba towns (Ife, Ilesha, etc.) and became the Awise of Lagos in 1944 and the Apesin of Isheri in 1948.

101 H. Antus Williams in *Nigerian Daily Telegraph*, 26 November 1937.
102 It appears that the Association was not revived until 1944. See *West African Pilot*, 14 February 1944.
103 For typical comments, see *The Comet*, 28 September 1935; 16 November 1935; 26 April 1936.
104 See *Nigerian Daily Telegraph*, 25 September 1935; 9, 10, 14 October 1935; 1 November 1935; *Nigerian Daily Times*, 6, 7 September 1935.

Epilogue

A remarkable feature of the history of the newspaper press since 1937 was the wider expansion and development of the industry. The enormous impact of the Second World War on society and politics encouraged the growth of newspapers, but the impetus was provided by the atmosphere of competition and enterprise generated by the leading newspapers. In their drive for leadership and greater recognition, the leading newspapers achieved significant improvements in the techniques of production and presentation as well as in conditions of service. In the process, they consolidated the new journalism and expanded the scope of its influence.

The great rivalry originated in the success of the *Pilot*. This became so outstanding in the 1940s that four provincial associates were established in various parts of the country.[1] And when at the end of the Second World War, nationalist thought and activity entered a new and decisive phase, the *Pilot* became the major engine of nationalist thought and propaganda, establishing itself as perhaps the leading newspaper in West Africa. The achievement of the *Pilot* drove the *Daily Times* to fierce competitive action, reflected in the decision in 1947 to sell controlling shares to the Daily Mirror Group of London. This was the beginning of an international relationship which was to last into the early seventies. The overall effect of the move was to transform the *Daily Times* into a modern newspaper with marked improvements in appearance, technical quality, distribution system and management. The *Pilot* responded with an ambitious reorganisation which stretched its resources. According to Nnamdi Azikiwe, the *Pilot* found itself engulfed not by a stream but by a roaring torrent.[2]

Another major newspaper, the *Daily Service*, also responded to the new challenge. Founded in 1933 and converted into a daily four years later, it had achieved only modest success and in the early 1950s, it merged with the *Nigerian Tribune* (based at Ibadan) and came under the control of the Amalgamated Press of Nigeria Ltd. In 1958, Roy Thomson of Canada and Britain went into partnership with a leading political party (the Action Group) to form the Allied Newspapers of Nigeria which absorbed the Amalgamated Press and launched the *Daily* and *Sunday Express* in 1960. The Allied Newspapers were out to dominate the provincial newspaper field and they established newspapers in such major towns as Benin, Jos, Kano, Onitsha and Uyo.

Lesser newspapers were by no means left out in the wind of change. To the limits of their financial capacities, they carried out improvements and helped to enhance the influence of the press and the prestige of the profesion of journalism. By 1960, the Nigerian press was probably the greatest and most developed press in Africa and the next fifteen years witnessed further improvements in the technical quality of newspapers as well as in the remuneration of staff. This was due largely to the entry of governments into the newspaper industry. From 1961 when the Federal Government established the *Morning Post* to provide better publicity for its activities, state governments have keenly entered the industry. By October 1974, all the states in the Federation, with the exception of Lagos State, had either established their own newspapers or were associated in a joint newspaper venture.[3]

Viewpoints differ as to whether governments should establish newspapers. Some believe that government-owned newspapers are a poor investment of public funds, that they are inherently dumb, unenterprising and ineffective. Others contend that given the financial constraints on newspaper publication, governments, particularly in a developing society, have an important role to play in the dissemination of information about official policies and programmes as well as in the general enlightenment and education of the people; that newspapers generally can play a constructive role without unrestricted liberty of criticism. Whatever the differences, it seems certain that the rise of government-owned newspapers has contributed significantly to the development of the newspaper industry particularly through modern equipment and high quality staff.

The growth and development of newspapers since 1937 has added a new dimension to the scope of their influence. The greater variety and sophistication of news and opinion presentation, for example, has helped to attract more readers, to facilitate the wider progress of ideas and to stimulate the growth of public opinion. Whether in pre-independence or post-independence era, Nigerian newspapers have played an active role in society, relaying news of politics and political strife and stimulating discussion and thinking on a variety of matters of public interest and importance. In the 1940s, the newspaper press played a crucial role in the reorientation of nationalism from an African or West African movement aimed at securing opportunities for effective African participation in administration into a national enterprise whose primary aim was the achievement of self-government and political independence. The prevailing temper was illustrated by the activities of the West African Press delegation which went to Britain in 1943. The delegation of eight West African journalists, which included Nnamdi Azikiwe, submitted to the British Government a memorandum which contained proposals for the achievement of independence within fifteen years. In the strategy of mass mobilisation, the press also provided the medium for the agitation of workers' grievances. The banning by the government in July 1945 of the *Pilot* and *Daily Comet* in the aftermath of the General Strike of June 1945 was a testimony to the new fraternity between labour and the press. However, although the newspapers kept the primary objective in sight, their mutual antagonism detracted from their effectiveness. The feud between the *Pilot* and the *Daily Service*, edited by Ernest Ikoli (1938–44) and S. L. Akintola, contributed to the regionalisation of nationalism and the crystallisation of inter-group tension and animosity which characterised political developments for a long time.

With the advent of responsible government in 1951 and the emergence of modern political parties as well as party-controlled administrations, old antagonisms were intensified and the atmosphere of politics and the press seethed with bitter rivalry and enmity. With few exceptions, the newspapers were owned or supported by the rival political parties (mainly the National Council of Nigerian Citizens (NCNC) and the Action Group (AG)) and it is one of the ironies of Nigerian history that in a crucial decade in the nation's development, a period which witnessed the taking of political and constitutional steps which led inexorably to independence, the newspapers were completely immersed in the vortex of partisan politics and were in no position to prepare the people for the challenges of independence and national unity. On the eve of independence, the leading political-party newspapers, which included the *West African Pilot*, the *Daily Service* and the *Nigerian Tribune*, and Dr K. O. Mbadiwe's *Daily Telegraph*, were locked in a vicious combat, and inter-personal communication between newspapermen of different political persuasion was at its lowest ebb. The ghost of the 1920s had assumed a more hideous form.

The first few years of independence saw little change in the political style of the newspapers. Indeed, the struggle for power among the politicians assumed a new fury and the competing party newspapers advertised their fanaticism. A few times, they acted together as in the successful agitation against the proposed Preventive Detention Act of 1963 but the pervasive mutual suspicion made for little regular co-operation and persistent mudslinging vitiated opportunities for constructive work. In the major events of the sixties – the Action Group crisis of 1962, the 1962–63 and 1963–64 Census, and the Federal Election of 1964 and its aftermath – the newspaper press provided a remarkable example of over-zealous and irresponsible partisanship and recklessness.

When the civilian government collapsed in January 1966, the newspaper press was foremost in self-criticism. Newspapers lamented their acquiescence in the corruption and mismanagement of the politicians and vowed to demonstrate greater courage and integrity. In the mood of relief and in the new atmosphere of promise signified by the expressed commitment of the military regime to correct the ills of society and to rebuild a framework for a more united and prosperous nation, the newspapers nostalgically affirmed a new loyalty to the legacies of the pioneer press.

How far were these hopes realised? It can be agreed that during the Gowon period of military rule, the newspapers worked earnestly for the enlightenment of the public and the wider appreciation of issues of importance by initiating debate on a variety of issues including the restoration of democratic rule, review of the Constitution, the creation of states, corruption, revenue allocation, Nigerianisation of the economy, free education and state control of schools. The civil war (1967–70) obliged the newspapers to embark upon propaganda in support of the Federal effort but this did not diminish interest in domestic political controversies. On the contrary, some of the hottest political debates took place during the national crisis. Government-owned newspapers were not totally left out. Although some indulged in toadyism or carried out only mealy-mouthed criticisms of the government, others, such as the *New Nigerian*, succeeded in establishing a reputation for integrity and leadership. The spirit of criticism and opposition in the press survived into the ninth year of military rule although signs of timidity and weakmindedness became increasingly evident. Whether this trend presaged a return to the twilight of civilian rule will ultimately depend upon the outcome of the long-standing conflict between liberty and authority in a dependent and an independent Nigeria.

In Chapter 6, we considered the nature of the conflict in the colonial period which issued in a curious dilemma. It was suggested that judged by the reluctance with which the press laws were administered, press freedom did not face a serious threat. Colonial governors and European officials were sensitive to criticism, but they seemed reluctant to restrict press freedom because, among other considerations, they had to seek prior authorisation by a Colonial Office often subjected to great pressure by influential liberal and humanitarian groups opposed to vindictive anti-African legislation. When Nigerians assumed power, a new situation rose. There was no excess of legislation, as might have been imagined, but prosecutions, especially of political opponents, were common and towards the end of the democratic period, the practice was introduced by which even local government councils banned unfriendly newspapers from circulating in their areas of jurisdiction. The view of the new leaders was that they could not afford opposition and criticism, that they were in a hurry to develop the country and that it was unpatriotic to distract public attention from the primary national objective by being hostile to the government. To this extent, any unfavourable criticism was seen to be destructive and worthy of repression, supposedly in the public interest. But this has always been the stock propaganda of authoritarian regimes and few persons of liberal persuasion would be impressed by it. The occasion for repressive action arrived in 1964 when some newspapers embarked upon certain revelations and speculations or what one newspaper described as 'periodic reckless attacks . . . against holders of public offices'.[4] The proposed newspaper law provided stiff penalties for the publication of false information which 'discloses or affects adversely any right, reputation or freedom of person which is entitled to protection'. A strong campaign of agitation led to important modifications. The fine of £500 for offending corporations was deleted and, in the case of individuals, imprisonment for between one year and three years was replaced with a fine of £200 or imprisonment for one year.[5] However, the Newspaper (Amendment) Act 1964 has remained extremely unpopular with journalists and liberal opinion generally. Persistent appeals continue to be made for its repeal.

The advent of military rule naturally aroused fears about the prospects of press freedom. Could the new rulers avoid the path of dictatorship? Would the newspapers resign themselves to an attitude of reserve and submission or would they, at the risk of trials and tribulations, seek to play a vocal role in the reform of society? Certain incidents of harassment, arrest and detention of journalists tended to justify the worst fears of the friends of press freedom in Nigeria but on balance, the situation was not a depressing one. Important Nigerian journalism leaders claimed in the early seventies that the Nigerian press was the freest in Africa.[6] Whether or not this was true, it did indicate a degree of satisfaction with the Nigerian situation.

Part of the explanation was related to the liberal disposition of the Federal military leadership. But the fear that a too liberal attitude could make nonsense of the implications of military rule, undermine the military government and erode public awareness of the military presence perhaps tended to result in sporadic demonstrations of military power. The future would be difficult to determine but any repressive enthusiasm would continue to be opposed by a strong tradition of free expression dating back to the nineteenth century.

Nigeria is passing through an epoch which is bound to be of critical importance in her history. The achievement of national development and nationhood depends not only on the quality of leadership but also upon the extent to which the mass of the people identify themselves with national objectives. Popular identification calls for a good measure of public enlightenment and general education. In other words, public opinion has to be mobilised in the overall interest of the nation through the agency of the mass media. The newspaper press, being the house in which all media men dwell, occupies a central position in the scheme of things. The role which it is allowed to play may determine whether the movement of growth and development will be in the right direction or not.

Notes

1 The *Eastern Nigeria Guardian* at Port Harcourt in 1940 (edited by A. K. Blankson); The *Nigerian Spokesman* at Onitsha in 1943 (editor, Olujide Somolu, who later became Chief Justice of the Western State); *Southern Nigerian Defender* at Warri in 1943 (editor, C. U. M. Gardner); *Daily Comet* at Kano in 1944 (editor, Anthony Enahoro).
2 Azikiwe, *My Odyssey*, pp. 311–12.
3 The six Northern states own the *New Nigerian* but Kwara also owns the *Nigerian Herald* and Benue-Plateau the *Nigerian Standard*. Other government-owned newspapers include the *Daily Sketch* (Western State); *Nigerian Tide* (Rivers); *Nigerian Chronicle* (South-East); *Nigerian Observer* (Mid-West); *Renaissance* (East Central). Lagos State considered the establishment of a newspaper in 1973 but eventually dropped the idea.
4 *Daily Times*, 10 September 1964.
5 See *Parliamentary Debates*, 1964. Also T. O. Elias (ed.), *Nigerian Press Law*, Edinburgh, 1969.
6 For example, J. K. Jakande, former President, Nigerian Guild of Newspaper Editors, in an address to the Guild. See *The People*, iii, 3 March 1971, pp. 12–17.

Appendix

LAGOS NEWSPAPERS

Name and frequency of publication	Dates	Editors	Owners
Lagos Times (f/w)	10 Nov. 1880–24 Oct. 1883; 6 Dec. 1890–Oct. 1891	Agbebi, 1880–83; W. E. Cole, 1890	R. B. Blaize
Lagos Observer (f)	4 Feb. 1882–12 July 1890	J. B. Benjamin	J. B. Benjamin
Mind (irregular)	1887	Ademuyiwa Haastrup	A. Haastrup
Eagle and Lagos Critic (m)	31 March, 1883–31 Oct. 1888	O. E. Macaulay	O. E. Macaulay
Mirror (w)	17 Dec. 1887–24 Nov. 1888	P. A. Marke	P. A. Marke
Iwe Irohin Eko (f)	3 Nov. 1888–16 July 1892	A. W. Thomas	A. W. Thomas
Lagos Weekly Times	3 May 1890–28 Nov. 1890	J. P. Jackson	R. B. Blaize
Lagos Weekly Record (w)	Jan. 1891–27 Dec. 1930	J. P. and T. H. Jackson	J. P. and T. H. Jackson, 1891–1913; 1914–30
Spectator (w) *Lagos Echo* (w)	1 July 1893–(?) Sept. 1894–97	? S. M. Harden(?)	? Lagos Printing and Publishing Company Limited
Lagos Standard (w)	16 Sept. 1894–28 Jan. 1920	G. A. Williams 1894–1919; J. A. White 1919–20	G. A. Williams 1894–1919; R. A. Williams 1919–20
Lagos Reporter (w)	23 Aug. 1898–18 July 1899	P. Mason	P. Mason

Name and frequency of publication	Dates	Editors	Owners
Wasp (w)	17 March–Aug. 1900	P. Mason	P. Mason
Nigerian Chronicle	20 Nov. 1908–26 Mar. 1915	Chris Johnson	Chris and E. T. Johnson
Astrological Mercury (irregular)	1909	Adeoye Deniga	Adeoye Deniga
New Age Herald (m)	1910	Adeoye Deniga	Adeoye Deniga
Nigerian Times (w)	5 April 1910–30 Oct. 1911	J. Bright Davies	J. Bright Davies
Herald Alore (m)	27 March 1913–(?)	Adeoye Deniga	Adeoye Deniga
Nigerian Pioneer (w)	18 Jan 1914–25 Dec. 1936	Irving 1914; Kitoyi Ajasa	K. Ajasa
Times of Nigeria (w)	13 Jan. 1914–29 June 1915; 6 June 1917–3 Nov. 1924	J. B. Davies, 1914–1920; Walter Edwin, 1920; Adamu I. Animashaun, 1920–24	J. B. Davies, 1914–1915. Limited Liability Company, 1917 Mohammedans, 1920–24
African Messenger (w)	10 Mar. 1921–4 Nov. 1928	E. S. Ikoli	E. S. Ikoli
Eko Akete (w)	7 July 1922–6 Apr. 1929; 4 March–14 Oct. 1937	Adeoye Deniga	Adeoye Deniga
Nigerian Spectator (w)	19 May 1923–27 Dec. 1930	R. A. Savage	R. A. Savage
Nigerian Advocate (w)	1 Aug. 1923–27 Dec. 1930	S. H. Braithwaite	S. H. Braithwaite
Eleti Ofe (w)	7 Feb. 1923–28 (?)	E. A. Akintan	E. A. Akintan
Advanced Opinion (w)	Aug. 1924–(?)	?	?
Nigerian Labour Bulletin (m d)	1924; 17 Mar.–23 June 1930	J. A. Olushola	J. A. Olushola
Lagos Daily News (d)	9 Nov. 1925–14 Jan. 1926; 1927–(1940)?	V. Babamuboni, 1925–26; J. A. Olushola, 1927; Herbert Macaulay & Frank Macaulay	Herbert Macaulay and J. A. Caulcrick
Iwe Irohia Osose (w)	1925–27	T. H. Jackson	T. H. Jackson
Nigerian Daily Times	1 June 1926–(Present day)	E. S. Ikoli 1926–29; A. A. C. Titcombe, 1930–38	Nigerian Printing & Publishing Co. Ltd, 1926–36; West African Newspapers Limited, 1936–48

Name and frequency of publication	Dates	Editors	Owners
Eko Igbehin (w)	1926–27	E. N. Awobiyi	E. M. Awobiyi
Nigerian Daily Telegraph (d)	12 Nov. 1927–10 Dec. 1937	H. A. Williams, 1927–31; Deniga, 1931; Duse Ali, 1932; Akaje-Mac-aulay 1932; Ikoli, 1934–35; Antus Williams, 1935–37	H. A. Williams, 1927–30; Nigerian Press Limited, 1930–1937; Aboyade Cole, 1937
Akede Eko (w)	Jan. 1928–(1953)	I. B. Thomas	I. B. Thomas
Nigerian Evening News (d)	1 June 1929–1 Nov. 1929	I. B. Thomas	I. B. Thomas
Nigerian Daily Mail (d)	14 Jan. 1930–2 June 1931	E. S. Ikoli	E. S. Ikoli
Lagos Daily Record (d)	1 Jan.–27 Aug. 1930	T. H. Jackson	T. H. Jackson
West African Nation-hood (d m)	18 Oct. 1930–31 Dec. 1934; Nov. 1932–Sept. 1933	G. E. Spencer	J. C. Zizer
Nigerian Daily Herald (d)	29 April 1931–32	E. Ronke Ajayi (Miss)	H. A. Williams
West African Sunday Digest (w)	5 April 1931–1934	J. C. Zizer	J. C. Zizer
Comet	21 July 1933–(1944)	Duse Mohammed Ali	Duse Mohammed Ali
Nigerian Evening Standard	5 July 1934–(?)	W. E. Akaje-Macaulay	W. E. Akaje-Macaulay
West African Pilot (d)	22 Nov. 1937–(present day)	Nnamdi Azikiwe	Zik Press Ltd
PROVINCIAL NEWSPAPERS			
Aurora [Calabar] (w)	Jan. 1914–17	W. Coulson Labor	W. Coulson Labor
Nigerian Herald [Onitsha] (w)	1921	?	?
Dawn [Aba, Calabar, Port Harcourt, Enugu] (w)	22 May 1923–18 Dec. 1937	W. Coulson Labor	W. Coulson Labor
Yoruba News [Ibadan] (w)	15 Jan. 1924–(1945)	D. A. Obasa	D. A. Obasa
Egba National Harper [Abeokuta] (m)	Sept. 1926–Sept. 1927	A. Folarin	A. Folarin

Name and frequency of publication	Dates	Editors	Owners
Nigerian Observer [Port Harcourt]	4 June 1930–32	L. R. Potts-Johnson	L. R. Potts-Johnson
Nigerian Protectorate Ram [Onitsha] (w)	22 Sept. 1930–(?)	S. Cole Edwards	S. Cole Edwards
Nigerian Echo [Aba] (w)	6 April 1933–15 Nov. 1934	A. Charles Howells	D.Joseph Emmanuel and A. C. Howells
Nigerian Weekly Dispatch [Onitsha] (w)	1933	S. Cole-Edwards	S. Cole-Edwards
Abeokuta Weekly News [Abeokuta] (w)	1934	D. O. Oke	D. O. Oke
Ijebu Weekly News [Ijebu-Ode] (w)	2 Sept. 1934–(25 Nov. 1940)	J. A. Olushola	J. A. Olushola
Nigerian Eastern Mail [Calabar] (w)	Aug. 1935–51	J. V. Clinton	C. W. Clinton
African Advertiser [Calabar] (w) *Nigerian Provincial Guardian* [Oshogbo] (w)	27 Dec. 1935– (1942) 21 Mar. 1936–(9 April 1938)	M. T. Oduntor Nottidge J. B. Layeni	M. T. Oduntor Nottidge J. B. Layeni
Osumare Egba [Abeokuta] (w)	7 Dec. 1935–5 Dec. 1936	S. K. Adenekan	D. A. S. Bamgboye
Nigerian Messenger [Onitsha] (w)	6 June 1936–(?)	?	?

d – daily.
w – weekly.
f – fortnightly.
m – monthly.

SPECIAL AUDIENCE NEWSPAPERS 1880–1937

DENOMINATIONAL NEWSPAPERS

The religious denominational publications are best considered under the various missions.

The Presbyterian mission

In 1885, in Old Calabar, the mission published an Efik-language monthly news-sheet, the *Unwana Efik*. Its duration is not known but it was supplanted by the *Obukpon Efik*. The *Old Calabar Observer* was founded in 1902 and abandoned two years later.

The Anglican mission

The C.M.S. in 1887 began to publish a local edition (in Lagos) of their London-based monthly *Gleaner*. Its place was taken four years later by the *Iwe Eko*. Described as 'a purely vernacular bi-weekly organ', it was inaugurated on 31 March 1891, by the Rev. J. Vernal. The Rev. Isaac Oluwole was Associate Editor and among the earliest contributors to the journal were Dr Mojola Agbebi (D. B. Vincent), E. H. Oke and J. A. Vaughan. The newspaper probably expired that year.

The most important Anglican, and indeed denominational, newspaper between 1880 and 1937, was the *In Leisure Hours*, established in 1910. It earned the attention of the people for its occasional sober incursions into Lagos politics. The monthly bilingual journal was started at Ibadan in May 1910 by two female missionaries in the C.M.S. Girls' Institute. Problems of printing and publishing (the journal was printed in England and this caused much postage expense and delay in publication) almost killed it in its first year. To save it from collapse, the C.M.S. Bookshop took over its management at the end of that year. Printing was carried out on the Egba Government Press until 10 June 1913, when the C.M.S. mission opened their new printing works. The *In Leisure Hours*, edited by successive Bookshop managers, survived into the forties.

The African Churches

African Churchmen occupy a significant place in the history of the early Nigerian newspapers. For not only were they some of the best contributors and columnists but also leaders of the African Church Movement founded and edited many important news-papers in our period. The *Standard, Chronicle, Times of Nigeria, Yoruba News, Eko Akete, Eko Igbehin, Kleti Ofe*, the *Daily Telegraph* and a few others were owned and edited by African Churchmen. The reason why African Churchmen were prominently engaged in newspaper press activity is not difficult to explain. In the first place, African Churchmen were among educated Africans who, for a variety of reasons (analysed in Chapter 2), took to the newspaper business to earn a living.

In the second place, they shared in the desire of educated Africans for media of nationalist expression. In the third place, they needed such media on religious grounds. The African Church Movement was a 'revolt against new policies and practices introduced by the missions to meet the situation created by the penetration, partition and subjugation of Africa by imperial European forces'. The African Churches were thus exposed to the ridicule and hostility of the missions whose propaganda media in Nigeria and overseas were highly organised and powerful. It was almost inevitable that the African Churches should take a lively interest in the press and not only answer their critics but also seek to propagate their values within the African community. It was noteworthy that eighty per cent of all the creative literature produced before 1920 were owed to the African Churchmen.

It might be imagined that the newspapers published by African Churchmen were necessarily propaganda sheets for the African Churches. This was not so. In fact, only the *Standard*, owned and edited by a foundation member of the U.N.A. (G. A. Williams), fully covered the activities of the African Church Movement. The role of this newspaper may probably explain why the African Churches were not disposed, until the second decade of the present century, to establish a religious denominational newspaper. A bilingual monthly magazine, the *African Hope* was founded in Lagos in 1918 by G. A. Oke, a young priest of the Jehovah Shallom branch of the U.N.A. but the governing body of the organisation refused to recognise it as the official publication. The *African Hope* was apparently short-lived but in 1934, the African Church Youngmen Improvement Society brought out the *African Church Chronicle*, a bilingual quarterly edited by Michael Lejuwon Epega. It was closed down in 1939 but resuscitated ten years later under a Board of Control with the Rev. S. O. Peters as secretary and editor.

The Methodist mission

The *Nigerian Methodist* was founded in 1925. While it served the immediate needs of the church organisation, the *Methodist* provided some coverage of world news and instructive biographies of great men in history. Financed in its first year and edited for a long time by the Rev. H. W. Stacey, principal of the Wesleyan Boys' High School, Lagos, it was apparently given up in 1927.

The Salvation Army

The *War Cry*, which continued from 1925 into the fifties, was completely given to devotional propaganda.

The Roman Catholic mission

The *Nigerian Catholic Herald* was founded in July 1924. Announced as the 'voice of the Catholic Church in Nigeria', it propagated the doctrines of Catholic teaching down to the fifties. Like *In Leisure Hours*, it cocasionally dabbled in local politics ventilating pro-Government views. Opponents of Herbert Macaulay employed the newspaper to harass him. Its chief contributor and one-time editor was A. B. Laotan.

OTHERS

The Lagos Customs and Trade Journal: A bi-monthly founded in 1911 and published under the authority of the Governor. The editor was the Comptroller of Customs. The journal was devoted to matters connected with the Imports, Exports and Shipping of Lagos. Contained from time to time judgments in important commercial cases and cause lists of civil actions for debt.

The Nigerian Journal, 1919: Official organ of the Association of European Civil Servants which was founded that year. From 1919 to 1929, it was printed in turn by the Government Printer, the Railway Press, the Akibomi Press and the Nigerian Printing and Publishing Company Limited.

Nigerian Law Journal, 1921–26: Inaugurated by A. Folarin, an Egba lawyer. Only five issues were published.

Circulation figures as in the
Blue Books, 1880-1937

(The list is incomplete, for a number of relevant *Blue Books* are not available).

1881	*Lagos Times*	60 fortnightly.
	Lagos Observer	480 every first and third Saturdays of each month.
1886	*Eagle and Lagos Critic*	200 monthly
1887	*Observer*	4 608 annually
	Eagle	1 320 ,,
1888	*Observer*	7 020 ,,
	Eagle	1 320 ,,
1889	*Observer*	7 200 ,,
	Mirror	—
	Iwe Irohin	6 650 ,,
1890	*Observer*	—
	Iwe Irohin	6 650
	Lagos Weekly Times	—
	Lagos Times	—
1891	*Observer*	—
	Iwe Irohin	5 00 annually
	Lagos Weekly Record	14 440 ,,
	Lagos Times	—
1892	*Weekly Record*	14 440 ,,
1893	*Weekly Record*	14 440 ,,
1894	*Weekly Record*	14 440 ,,
	Lagos Standard (Sept. – Dec.)	7 500 ,,
	Lagos Echo	27 040 ,,
1895	*Weekly Record*	25 800 annually
	Standard (Sept.–Dec.)	15 600 ,,
	Echo	24 960 ,,
1897	*Weekly Record*	31 200 ,,
	Standard	27 000 ,,
	Echo	20 800 ,,
1900	*Weekly Record*	30 000 ,,
	Standard	30 000 ,,
1903	*Weekly Record*	26 000 ,,
	Standard	26 000 ,,
1904	*Record*	26 000 ,,
	Standard	26 000 ,,

1905	*Record*	26 000 ,,
	Standard	26 000 ,,
1906	*Record*	500 weekly
	Standard	1 000 ,,
1907	*Record*	500 ,,
	Standard	1 050 ,,
1908	*Record*	500 ,,
	Standard	1 000 ,,
	Nigerian Chronicle	400 ,,
1909	*Record*	500 ,,
	Standard	500 ,,
	Chronicle	450 ,,
1910	*Record*	500 ,,
	Standard	500 ,,
	Chronicle	450 ,,
1911	*Record*	700 ,,
	Standard	580 ,,
	Chronicle	580 ,,
	Nigerian Times	400 ,,
	In Leisure Hours	1 500 monthly
	New Age Herald	200 quarterly
1912	*Record*	700 weekly
	Standard	700 ,,
	Chronicle	600 ,,
	In Leisure Hours	2 000 monthly
	Herald Alore	100 ,,
1913–19	No circulation returns	
1920	*African Hope*	600 monthly
	African Messenger	600 ,, (This paper was not founded in 1920 but in 1921).
	Record	–
	Nigerian Pioneer	500 weekly
	Times of Nigeria	230 ,,
1921	*African Hope*	600 ,,
	Messenger	1 200 ,,
	In Leisure Hours	1 650 monthly
	Record	–
	Pioneer	500 weekly
	Times of Nigeria	1 000 ,,
	Nigerian Law Journal	– ,,
1922	*African Hope*	600 monthly
	Messenger	1 200 weekly
	Eko Akete	500 ,,
	In Leisure Hours	1 500 monthly
	Nigerian Law Journal	–
	Pioneer	500 weekly
	Times of Nigeria	1 000 ,,
1923	*African Hope*	600 monthly

1923	Messenger	–	weekly
	Dawn	–	,,
	Eko Akete	1 000	,,
	Eleti Ofe	700	,,
	In Leisure Hours	1 400	,,
	Record	2 000	,,
	Nigerian Advocate	500	,,
	Nigerian Labour Bulletin	600	,,
	Nigerian Law Journal	–	monthly
	Pioneer	500	weekly
	Nigerian Spectator	–	
	Times of Nigeria	700	weekly
	Yoruba News	–	,, (This paper was not founded in 1923 but in 1924).
1924	Messenger	–	weekly
	Pioneer	500	,,
	Record	2 000	,,
	Advanced Opinion	200	,,
	Advocate	1 500	,,
	Labour Bulletin	500	monthly
	Times of Nigeria	700	weekly
	Yoruba News	500	,,
	Dawn	–	,,
	Eko Akete	1 200	,,
	Eleti Ofe	1 000	,,
	In Leisure Hours	1 400	monthly
	Nigerian Law Journal	–	,,
	Spectator	–	weekly
1925	Record	2 000	weekly
	Pioneer	500	,,
	Advocate	1 000	,,
	Spectator	–	,,
	Law Journal	–	monthly
	Messenger	–	weekly
	In Leisure Hours	1 400	monthly
	Eko Akete	880	weekly
	Eleti Ofe	700	,,
	Yoruba News	500	,,
	Lagos Daily News	500	daily
	Nigerian Methodist	800	monthly
1926	Nigerian Daily Times	1 500	daily
	Messenger	1 000	weekly
	Pioneer	500	,,
	Record	2 000	,,
	Eleti Ofe	700	,,
	In Leisure Hours	1 400	monthly
	Advocate	1 000	weekly
	Egba National Harper	–	monthly

1926	Nigerian Methodist	800	,,
	Yoruba News	300	weekly
1927	Pioneer	500	weekly
	Record	2 000	,,
	Advocate	1 000	,,
	In Leisure Hours	1 400	monthly
	Lagos Daily News	1 000	daily
	Nigerian Daily Telegraph	600	,,
	Nigerian Methodist	750	monthly
	Eleti Ofe	750	,,
	Yoruba News	300	weekly
	Daily Times	2 000	daily
1928	Daily Times	2 000	daily
	Pioneer	500	weekly
	Record	2 000	,,
	Advocate	1 000	,,
	Nigerian Daily Telegraph	1 000	,,
	In Leisure Hours	1 400	monthly
	Eleti Ofe	700	weekly
	Lagos Daily News	2 000	daily
	Akede Eko	800	weekly
1929	Nigerian Daily Times	3 500	daily
	Pioneer	500	weekly
	Record	2 000	,,
	Advocate	1 000	,,
	In Leisure Hours	1 400	monthly
	Dawn	1 000	weekly
	Eleti Ofe	700	,,
	Daily News	2 000	daily
	Akede Eko	800	weekly
	Daily Telegraph	1 000	daily
	Spectator	1 000	weekly
1930	Daily Times	3 000	daily
	Pioneer	500	weekly
	Record	2 000	,,
	Advocate	1 000	,,
	In Leisure Hours	1 400	monthly
	Dawn	850	weekly
	Eleti Ofe	700	,,
	Lagos Daily News	2 000	daily
	Akede Eko	1 000	weekly
	Daily Telegraph	3 000	daily
	Spectator	1 000	weekly
	Nigerian Observer	–	,,
	West African Nationhood	1 200	daily
1931	Daily Times	4 000	daily
	Pioneer	500	weekly
	Advocate	1 000	,,
	In Leisure Hours	1 400	monthly

1931	*Dawn*	850 weekly
	African Christian	8 000 monthly
	Yoruba News	400 weekly
	Daily News	2 000 daily
	Akede Eko	1 000 weekly
	Daily Telegraph	3 000 daily
	Nigerian Catholic Herald	2 000 monthly
	Nationhood	1 200 daily
	Nigerian Daily Herald	1 000 ,,
	Nigerian Weekly Despatch	1 700 weekly
1932	*Daily Times*	4 500 daily
	Pioneer	500 weekly
	In Leisure Hours	1 400 monthly
	Dawn	900 weekly
	Daily News	2 000 daily
	Akede Eko	1 000 weekly
	Daily Telegraph	1 000 daily
	Nigerian Catholic Herald	2 000 monthly
	Nationhood	1 200 daily
	Daily Herald	1 000 daily
	Weekly Despatch	1 700 weekly
	Yoruba News	400 ,,
1933	*Daily Times*	4 500 daily
	Pioneer	500 weekly
	Advocate	1 000 ,,
	In Leisure Hours	1 400 monthly
	Dawn	1 000 weekly
	Daily News	3 000 daily
	Akde Eko	1 000 weekly
	Daily Telegraph	3 000 daily
	Nigerian Catholic Herald	1 000 monthly
	West African Sunday Digest	1 200 daily
	Weekly Despatch	1 700 weekly
	Yoruba News	400 ,,
	Comet	4 000 ,,
1934	*Daily Times*	5 200 daily
	Daily News	2 600 ,,
	Pioneer	– weekly
	Advocate	– ,,
	Akede Eko	– ,,
	Daily Telegraph	– daily
	Catholic Herald	– monthly
	Nigerian Observer	1 200 weekly
	Sunday Digest	1 200 ,,
	Comet	4 000 ,,
	Nigerian Echo	750 ,,
1935	*Daily Times*	5 700 daily
	Pioneer	– weekly
	Advocate	– ,,

1935	In Leisure Hours	–	monthly
	Daily News	2 600	daily
	Akede Eko	1 000	weekly
	Daily Telegraph	3 000	daily
	Catholic Herald	1 000	monthly
	Nigerian Observer	2 000	weekly
	Comet	4 000	,,
	West African Star	500	,,
	Nigerian Eastern Mail	2 000	,,
1936	Daily Times	5 700	daily
	Pioneer	500	weekly
	Advocate	1 000	,,
	In Leisure Hours	1 400	monthly
	Daily News	2 600	daily
	Osumare Egba	3 000	weekly
	Ijebu Weekly News	700	,,
	Akede Eko	2 500	,,
	Nigerian Daily Telegraph	1 500	daily
	Nigerian Catholic Herald	1 000	monthly
	Nigerian Observer	2 000	weekly
	Comet	4 000	,,
	West African Star	500	,,
	Nigerian Eastern Mail	3 000	,,
	Service	1 500	quarterly
	African Advertiser	3 240	weekly
1937	Daily Times	5 900	daily
	In Leisure Hours	1 700	monthly
	Daily News	2 600	daily
	Akede Eko	2 500	weekly
	Nigerian Catholic Herald	1 000	monthly
	Nigerian Observer	2 000	weekly
	Comet	4 000	,,
	West African Star	340	,,
	Nigerian Eastern Mail	3 161	,,
	Osumare Egba	3 100	,,
	Ijebu Weekly News	1 000	
	Service	1 500	quarterly
	African Advertiser	3 800	weekly
	West African Pilot	9 200	daily
	African Church Chronicle	300	quarterly
	Catholic Life	1 300	monthly
	Nigerian Provincial Guardian	1 868	weekly

INTERVIEWS

Extensive private interviews were held with surviving pioneer journalists or their descendants chiefly in Lagos. I had access to only a few valuable papers but many people were very willing to offer information on various aspects of the early newspaper history. Below is a select list of people interviewed.

Date	Place	Name of Informant	Remarks
Various dates in May, 1964	Surulere	Senator Fagbenro-Beyioku	Son of Akin Fagbenro-Beyioku (H. Antus Williams) editor/ proprietor of the *Nigerian Daily Telegraph* and the proprietor of the *Nigerian Daily Herald*. The Senator, who was at the time a public servant, was something of a factotum in his father's enterprise.
Various dates in May, 1964	Ebute-Metta	Z. B. Laotan	Veteran journalist, died 15 March 1965 at 76. His connection with active journalism went back to the early twenties when he distinguished himself as a columnist. Appeared to be the most informed on the history of the early Nigerian press among the known surviving journalists.
Various dates in May, 1964.	Yaba	Alhaji Adamu I. Animashaun	Currently *seriki* of the Lagos muslims. Was for a time proprietor of *Times of Nigeria*.
Various dates in May, 1964	Lagos	Peter Jackson	Electrician and politician. Son and grandson respectively of Horatio Jackson and J. P. Jackson of the *Record*. Unlike Horatio, Peter did not follow his father's profession; nevertheless he knows much about his grandfather's enterprise and has filled in important gaps in his biography.
Various dates in May, 1964	Lagos	J. M. Odumosu	Production Manager, *Daily Times*. In the thirties, was head printer of Herbert Macaulay's *Daily News*.
,,	Lagos	Alhaji Babatunde Jose	Managing Director, *Daily Times* of Nigeria Limited.
,,	Lagos	Tunji A. Braithwaite	Managing Director, African Alliance Insurance Company, Lagos. Nephew of S. H. Braithwaite, editor *Nigerian Advocate*. He introduced me to the Braithwaite family.
,,	Surulere	Increase Coker	Business Manager, Nigerian National Press, Apapa. A well-known student of the Nigerian press, Coker knows quite intimately a number of pioneer journalists or their descendants.

Date	Place	Name of Informant	Remarks
16.4.65	Ikeja	Chief A. O. Adeshigbin	Son of Chief Adeshigbin of the Tika Tore Press. Retired Chief Magistrate. Although outside the country when his father was at the height of his printing business, he knows much about the Tika Tore Press that was useful.
18.4.65	Yaba	S. B. Agebi	Businessman. Formerly Circulation Manager, *Nigerian Daily Telegraph*.
19.4.65	Ikeja	J. V. Clinton	Writer and journalist. Formerly editor of the *Nigerian Eastern Mail*. Clinton is deaf but his son acted as interpreter. Clinton disclosed the names of a few of the early provincial journalists resident in Lagos. The information was followed up fruitfully.
28.8.64	Lagos	Isaac Thomas	News editor, *Daily Times*. Son of I. B. Thomas, editor/proprietor of the *Akede Eko* and the *Nigerian Evening News*.
21.9.64	Lagos	Kunle Akinsemoyin	Ministry of Information. Grandson of R. B. Blaize, proprietor of the *Lagos Times*.
21.9.64	Surulere	Chief Fred Anyiam	Author and journalist. Came to Lagos to settle in the thirties and well-informed on newspaper activity from then to the present day.

Bibliography

PRIMARY SOURCES

The major sources used in this study have been the newspapers themselves. Many have survived although generally incomplete. Two main collections are available.

I NIGERIAN NATIONAL ARCHIVES, IBADAN

African Advertiser, 27 December 1935–40.
African Messenger, 10 March 1921–4 November 1928.
African Sunday Digest, 5 April 1931–30 December 1934.
Akede Eko, 3 January 1929–53.
Comet, 21 July 1933–44.
Dawn, 22 May 1923–18 December 1937.
Egba National Harper, September 1926–September 1927.
Eko Akete, July 1922–December 1927; 4 March–14 October 1937.
Eko Igbehin, 1926–27.
Eleti Ofe, 7 February 1923–53.
Ijebu Weekly News, 15 August 1936–25 November 1940.
Lagos Daily News, 9 November 1925–14 January 1926; 2 July–31 August 1928; 2 November–31 December 1928; 1 March–29 October 1929; *1* April–31 December 1930.
Lagos Daily Record, 1 January–27 August 1930.
Lagos Observer, 1 February 1883–31 January 1884; 28 February 1884–22 January 1885; 21 January 1886–15 January 1887.
Lagos Standard, 7 January 1903–30 December 1903; 4 January 1911–27 December 1911; 15 August 1917–14 May 1919; 19 July 1919–28 January 1920.
Lagos Weekly Record, 1910; 18 August 1917–28 December 1918; 1919–1930.
Lagos Weekly Times, 3 May–29 November 1890.

Lagos Times, 10 November 1880–26 October 1881; 8 November 1882–24 October 1883.

Nigerian Advocate, 1 August 1923–27 December 1930.

Nigerian Daily Herald, 1 April–31 December 1931.

Nigerian Daily Mail, 14 January–2 June 1930.

Nigerian Daily Telegraph, 12 November–20 December 1927; 2 January 1930–10 December 1937.

Nigerian Daily Times, 1 June 1926–present day.

Nigerian Eastern Mail, 31 August 1935–50.

Nigerian Echo, 6 April 1933–15 November 1934.

Nigerian Evening News, 1 June 1929–28 November 1929.

Nigerian Labour Bulletin, 17 March–23 June 1930.

Nigerian Observer, 4 January 1930–31 December 1932.

Nigerian Pioneer, 10 August 1917–25 December 1936.

Nigerian Provincial Guardian, 21 March 1936–9 April 1938.

Nigerian Spectator, 19 May–29 December 1923; 31 January–28 November 1925; 8 and 15 January–24 and 31 December 1927; 7 January–29 December 1928; 4 and 11 January–20 and 27 December 1930.

Nigerian Times, 5 April 1910–present day.

Times of Nigeria, 6 June 1917–19 November 1918; 23 February 1919–27 December 1920, 3 January–26 December 1921; 2 January–25 December 1922; 1 January–10 December 1923; 9 June–3 November 1924.

West African Nationhood, 18 October–31 December 1930; 2 January–31 December 1931; November 1932–September 1933 (monthly).

West African Pilot, 22 November 1937–present day.

Yoruba News, 15 January 1924–45.

2 UNIVERSITY OF IBADAN LIBRARY

(a) *Macaulay Collection*

This includes a good number of some of the very early newspapers.

African Messenger, 10 March–29 December 1921; 12 January–21 December 1922; 3 January–6 March 1924; 13 March–2 October 1924; 26 February–31 December 1925.

Comet, 5 August 1933–11 July 1936.

Iwe Irohin, 1860–61; 1863–67.

Iwe Irohin Eko, 3 November 1888–18 October 1890; 1 November 1890–17 October 1891; 16 July 1892.

Lagos Daily News, 1925–26; 1927–36.

Lagos Observer, 4 February 1882–25 January 1890; 8 February–13 September 1890.

Lagos Reporter, 6 September; 17, 31 October; 7, 28 November–31 December 1898; 21 January–11 February; 16 May–19 June; 18 July 1899.

Lagos Standard, 18 September 1895; 2 October 1895–16 September 1896; 4 January–27 December 1905.

Lagos Times, 10 November 1880–24 October 1883; 6 December 1890–21 October 1891.

Lagos Weekly Record, August 1893–August 1893; 10 December 1919–4 September 1920; 1 October 1921–3 December 1921; 7 January–2 September 1922; 20 January–29 December 1923; 19 April–13 September 1924; 4 July–1 August 1925; 3 April 1926.

Lagos Weekly Times, 3 May–29 November 1890.

Nigerian Advocate, 1 August–16 December 1923.

Nigerian Daily Telegraph, 1 July–31 August 1929; 2–14 September –25 November 1929; 1 April–20 June 1931.

Nigerian Daily Times, 1 June 1926–present day

Nigerian Eastern Mail, 31 August 1936–30 June 1951.

Nigerian Pioneer, 31 January 1919–19 August 1921; 1922, 1925, 1926.

Times of Nigeria, 7 January 1914–29 June 1915; 5 July, 27 December 1920; 3 January–12 December 1921; 13 February, 6 March, 25 September 1922; 10 December 1923–30 June 1924.

Wasp, 17 March–30 June 1900 (Bound with Lagos *Standard* 1903–4).

West African Pilot, 22 November 1937–present day.

(b) *Ford Microfilms*

A microfilm collection of a number of the early newspapers which are at the British Museum Newspaper Library, Colindale Avenue, London.

(i) *Nigeria*

Anglo-African, 6 June–5 December 1863; 23 July 1864–30 December 1865.

Eagle and Lagos Critic, 31 March 1883–31 October 1888.

Lagos Observer, 2 March 1882–29 December 1888.

Lagos Standard, 6 February 1891–26 December 1896; 1900–21.

Mirror, 17 December 1887–24 November 1888.

Nigerian Chronicle, 20 November 1908–26 March 1915.
Nigerian Pioneer, 17 February 1914–13 July 1934.
Nigerian Times, 5 April 1910–31 October 1911.
Times of Nigeria, 6 January 1914–15 June 1915; 2 November
    1915–1 November 1920.
(ii) *West Africa*
Gold Coast Independent, 14 December 1895–30 September 1898.
Gold Coast Times, 28 March 1874–12 February 1885.
Independent (Freetown) 24 December 1874–23 May 1878.
West Africa, May 1900–December 1906.
West African Mail, April 1903–December 1907.
West African Reporter, 25 July 1876–December 1877: 1879–1884.
Western Echo, 18 November 1885–31 December 1887.

GOVERNMENT PAPERS

1 *Nigerian National Archives, Ibadan*
  (a) Despatches to Secretaries of State
      C.S.O. 1/1–C.S.O. 1/12, Colony of Lagos (1861–1906).
      C.S.O. 1/13–C.S.O. 1/18, Oil Rivers and Niger Coast
        Protectorate and Southern Nigeria. (1891–1906.)
      C.S.O. 1/19–C.S.O. 1/25, Colony and Protectorate of
        Southern Nigeria. 1906–14.
      C.S.O. 1/13 Nigeria (1914–15).
  (b) C.S.O. 7/1 Minute Books of the Executive and Legislative
      Councils, 1880–1923.
  (c) Official publications
      (i) *Blue Books*
          Colony of Lagos 1894–1905 (1895–6; 1898–9; 1901–2
            mission)
          Protectorate of Southern Nigeria 1904–05.
          Colony of Southern Nigeria, 1906–13 (1906–7 mission)
          Colony and Protectorate of Nigeria, 1914–38.
      (ii) *Gazettes*
          Colony of Lagos, 1886–1905
          Southern Nigeria, 1906–29.
          Nigeria, 1914–29
      (iii) *Handbooks*
          The Nigerian Handbook, 1916, 1919, 1922, 1925, 1926,
            1929, 1932, 1933, 1936.
          Southern Nigeria Handbook 1, 1912.

2 *Public Record Office, London*
C.O. 14/1. Copies of despatches ordered.

3 *High Court Records*
Held by the Ministry of Justice, Lagos. Records consulted included:
  (a) Record of Criminal Cases,
  (b) Record of Civil Cases,
  (c) Chief Registrar's Criminal Record Book.

4 *Register of Companies*
Open files of Companies in the former Ministry of Commerce and
Industry (now Ministries of Trade and Industry), Lagos.

PRIVATE PAPERS

1 *Macaulay Papers*
In the University of Ibadan Library.

2 *Animashaun Papers*
(Papers of Adamu I. Animashaun, currently Seriki of the Lagos
Muslims.) Relates mainly to the history of the *Times of Nigeria*.

INTERVIEWS
See Appendix V.

SECONDARY SOURCES

1 PRINTED SOURCES

(a) *On the Press*
Behrens, H. P. H., *Pretoria Press Story*, Pretoria, n.d.
Berger, M., *The Story of the New York Times 1851–1951*, New
    York, 1951.
Broughton, M., *Press and Politics in S. Africa*, Cape Town, 1961.
Clyde, W. M., *The struggle for freedom of the press (From Caxton
    to Cromwell)*, Oxford, 1934.
Coker, I., *70 years of the Nigerian Press*, Daily Times publication,
    Lagos, 1952.
Collins, I., *The Government and the Newspaper Press in France
    1814–1881*, Oxford, 1959.

Cook, Sir E., *Delane of the Times*, London, 1916.
Cranfield, G. A., *The development of the Provincial newspaper 1700–1760*, Oxford, 1962.
Detweiler, F. G., *The Negro press in the United States*, Chicago, 1922.
Emery, E., *The press of America*, New Jersey, 1962.
Frank, J., *The beginnings of the English Newspaper 1620–1660*, Cambridge, 1961.
Gollin, A. M., *The Observer and J. L. Garvin 1908–1914. A study in a Great Editorship*, London, 1960.
Grant, J., *The Newspaper Press: its origin, progress and present condition*, 3 vols, London, 1871.
Haig, R. L., *The Gazetter 1735–1797*, Illinios, 1960.
Jones, K., *Fleet Street and Downing Street*, London, 1919.
Jones-Quartey, K. A. B., *Problems of the Press*, London, n.d.
Janowitz, M., *The Community Press in an Urban Setting*, New York, 1952.
Kitchen, H. (ed.), *The press in Africa*, Washington, 1956.
Martin, K., *The Press the Public wants*, London, 1947.
Meyer, G. P., *Pioneers of the press*, New York, 1961.
Mott, F. L., *The news in America*, Havard, 1962.
Natarajan, S., *A history of the Press in India*, London, 1962.
Rea, R. R., *The English press in Politics 1760–1774*, Lincoln, 1963.
Read, D., *Press and People*, London, 1961.
Robinson, A. M. L., *None daring to make us afraid, a study of English periodical literature in the Cape Colony from its beginnings in 1824–1835*, Cape Town, 1962.
Schlesinger, A. M., *Prelude to Independence, The Newspaper war on Britain 1764–1776*, New York, 1958.
Steinberg, S. H., *Five hundred years of printing*, Edinburgh, 1955.
Steed, H. W., *The Press*, London, 1938.
Straumann, H., *Newspaper Headlines: a study in linguistic method*, London, 1935.
Times, The, History of the Times.
  Vol. I. *The Thunderer in the making 1785–1841*, London, 1935.
  Vol. II. *The Tradition established 1841–1884*, London, 1939.
  Vol. III. *The Twentieth Century Test 1884–1912*, London, 1947.
  Vol. IV. *The 150th Anniversary and beyond, Part I, 1912–1921*,
  Vol. V. *The 150th Anniversary and beyond, Part II, 1921–1948*, London, 1952.
Times, The., A Newspaper History, 1785–1935, London, 1935.

Weisberger, B. A., *The American Newspaper*, Chicago, 1961.
Wickwar, W. H., *The struggle for the freedom of the Press*, London, 1928.
Williams, F., *Dangerous Estate, The Anatomy of Newspapers*, New York, 1958.

(b) *General*

Ajayi, J. F. A., *Milestones in Nigerian History*, Ibadan, 1962.
Ajayi, J. F. A. and Smith, R. S., *Yoruba warfare in the 19th Century*, Cambridge, 1964.
Apter, D. E., *Ghana in Transition*, New York, 1963.
—, *The Political Kingdom in Uganda*, Princeton, New Jersey, 1961.
Awolowo, O., *Awo* (the autobiography of Chief O. Awolowo), Cambridge, 1960.
Azikiwe, N., *Zik, A selection from the speeches of Nnamdi Azikiwe*, Cambridge, 1961.
Barker, E. (ed.), *The Character of England*, Oxford, 1947.
Basden, G. T., *Niger Ibos*, London, n.d.
Biobaku, S. O., *The Egbas and their Neighbours, 1842–72*, Oxford, 1957.
Bovill, E. W., *The Golden Trade of the Moors*, London, 1958.
Burns, Sir A. C., *A History of Nigeria*, 3rd ed., London, 1942.
Campbell, R., *A Pilgrimage to my motherland, an account of a journey among the Egbas and Yorubas of Central Africa 1859–60*, London, 1861.
Coleman, J. S., *Nigeria, Background to Nationalism*, Berkeley and Los Angeles, 1960.
Crowder, M., *The Story of Nigeria*, London, 1962.
Curtin, P. D., *The Image of Africa – British Ideas and Action, 1780–1850*, Wisconsin, 1964.
Deniga, A., *Who's Who*, Lagos, 1934.
Dike, K. O., *Trade and Politics in the Niger Delta*, Oxford, 1956.
Elias, T. O., *British Colonial Law*, London, 1962.
—, *Government and Politics in Africa*, London, 1963.
—, *The Nigerian Legal System*, London, 1963.
Epelle, S., *The Promise of Nigeria*, London, 1960.
Evans, L. L., *The British in Tropical Africa*, Cambridge, 1929.
Ezera, K., *Constitutional Developments in Nigeria*, Cambridge, 1960.
Flint, J. E., *Sir George Goldie and the Making of Nigeria*, London, 1960.

Fyfe, C. H., *A History of Sierra Leone*, Oxford, 1962.
Hailey, Lord, *An African Survey*, revised 1956, London, 1957.
Hammond, J. L. and Hammond, B., *The Age of the Chartists 1832–1834*, London, 1930.
Hodgkin, T., *African Political Parties*, London, 1961.
—, *Nigerian Perspectives*, London, 1960.
Johnson, Rev. S., *History of the Yorubas*, London, 1921.
Jones, G. I., *The Trading states of the Oil Rivers*, London, 1963.
Jones-Quartey, K. A. B. and Passin, H. (eds.), *Africa: the Dynamics of Change*, Ibadan, 1963.
Kimble, D., *A Political History of Ghana, 1850–1928*, Oxford, 1963.
Lynch, Hollis, *Edward Wilmot Blyden, Pan-Negro Patriot, 1832–1912*, Oxford, 1964.
Lugard, F. D., *The Dual Mandate in British Tropical Africa*, Edinburgh and London, 1923.
Mackintosh, J. P., *The British Cabinet*, London, 1962.
Macmillan, A., *Red Book of West Africa*, London, 1920.
Nadel, S. F., *A Black Byzantium*, Oxford, 1942.
Newbury, C. W., *The Western Slave Coast and its rulers*, Oxford, 1961.
Payne, J. A. O., *Payne's Lagos and West African Almanack & Diary, 1879*, Lagos, 1879.
—, *Payne's Lagos and West African Almanack & Diary 1894*, Lagos, 1894.
—, *Table of Principal Events in Yoruba History*, Lagos, 1893.
Perham, M., *Lugard, the Years of Authority, 1898–1945*, London, 1960.
—, *Native Administration in Nigeria*, Oxford, 1937.
Plumb, J. H., *England in the eighteenth century, 1714–1815*, Aylesbury, 1959.
Sklar, R. L., *Nigerian Political Parties*, Princetown, 1963.
Smythe, H. H. and M. H., *The New Nigerian Elite*, Stanford, California, 1960.
Speed, E. A., *Lagos revised edition of Ordinances Orders*, London, 1902.
Tamuno, T. N., *The Evolution of the Nigerian State*, London, 1972.
Theal, G. M., *History of South Africa from 1795–1872*, vol. I, London, 1892.

Thomas, I. B., *Life of H. Macaulay*, Lagos, 1957.

Tilman, R. O., and Cole, T. (eds.), *The Nigerian Political Scene*, London, 1962.

Townsend, G., *Memoir of the Rev. Henry Townsend*, London, 1887.

Trevelyan, G. W., *British History in the nineteenth century and after 1782–1919*, 2nd ed., London, 1960.

—, *English Social History*, London, 1942.

Tucker (Miss), *Abeokuta or Sunrise within the Tropics*, London, 1853.

Wheare, J., *The Nigerian Legislative Council*, London, 1949.

Woodward, E. L., *The Age of Reform 1815–1870*, Oxford, 1938.

2 ARTICLES

Aderibigbe, A. B., 'The Ijebu Expedition 1892: An episode in the British Penetration of Nigeria reconsidered', Leverhulme History Conference September 1960, *Historians in Tropical Africa*, 1962, pp. 267–82.

Ajayi, J. F. A., 'Henry Venn and the Policy of Development', *Journal of the Historical Society of Nigeria*, i, 4, 1959.

—, 'British Occupation of Lagos 1851–61', *Nigeria Magazine*, 69, August 1961, pp. 96–105.

—, 'The Development of Secondary Grammar School education in Nigeria,' *Journal of the Historical Society of Nigeria*, ii, 4, 1936, pp. 571–36.

Aspinall, A., 'The Social status of Journalists at the beginning of the nineteenth century', *Review of English Studies*, xxi, January, 1945.

—, 'The circulation of newspapers in the early nineteenth century', *Review of English Studies*, xxi, January, 1945.

Ayandele, E. A., 'An Assessment of James Johnson and his place in Nigerian History, 1874–1917, Part I, 1874–1890', *Journal of the Historical Society of Nigeria*, ii, 4, December 1963, pp. 468–517.

—, 'An Assessment of James Johnson and his place in Nigerian History, 1874–1917, Part II, 1890–1817', *Journal of the Historical Society of Nigeria*, iii, 1, December 1964, pp. 73–101.

Fyfe, C. H., 'The Sierra Leone Press in the Nineteenth Century'. *Sierra Leone Studies*, 8, June 1957.

Gwam, L. C., 'Dr Edward Wilmot Blyden, M.A., DD., LL.D. (1832–1912)', *Ibadan*, March 1963.

Ikoli, E., 'The Nigerian Press 1900–1950', *West African Review*, xxi, 273, June 1950, pp. 625–7.

Jones-Quartey, K. A. B., 'Anglo-African Journals and Journalists in the Nineteenth and early Twentieth centuries', *Transactions of the Historical Society of Ghana*, iv, Part I, 1959.

—, 'Thought and Expression in the Gold Coast Press 1874–1930', *Universities*, iii, 3, June 1958, pp. 72–5; iii, 4, December 1958, pp. 113–16.

—, 'Sierra Leone's Role in the development of Ghana, 1820–1930,' *Sierra Leone Studies*, June 1958, pp. 73–84.

—, 'Sierra Leone and Ghana. Nineteenth century pioneers in West African Journalism', *Sierra Leone Studies*, December 1959, pp. 230–44.

—, 'A Note on J. M. Sarbah and J. E. Casely Hayford: Ghanaian Leaders, Politicians and Journalists, 1864–1930', *Sierra Leone Studies*, December 1960, New Series, 14, pp. 57–62.

Laotan, A. B., 'Brazilian Influence in Lagos', *Nigerian Magazine*, No. 69, August 1961.

Laoye I (Timi of Ede), 'Yoruba Drums', *Nigeria Magazine*, 45, 1954.

—, 'Yoruba Drums', *Odu*, 7, March 1969, pp. 5–14.

Nzekwu, O., 'Masquerade', *Nigeria Magazine*, 1960, pp. 134–44.

Okosa, A. N. G., 'Ibo Musical Instrument', *Nigeria Magazine*, December, 1962, 75, pp. 4–14.

Oton, E. U., 'Press of Liberia: A case study', reprint from *Journalism Quarterly*, xxxviii, 2, 1961.

—, 'Development of Journalism in Nigeria', *Journalism Quarterly*, (n.d.), pp. 72–9.

Sharp, G. F., Nigeria's First Daily Newspaper', *West Africa Review*, xxi, 274, August 1950, p. 920.

Webster, J. B., 'The Bible and the Plough', *Journal of the Historical Society of Nigeria*, ii, December 1963, pp. 418–35.

UNPUBLISHED THESES

Aderibigbe, A. A. B., 'The Expansion of the Lagos Protectorate 1861–1900', Ph.D., London, 1959.

Ajayi, J. F. A., 'Christian Missions and the Making of Nigeria 1841–1891', Ph.D., London, 1958.

Anene, J. C. O., 'The Establishment and Consolidation of Imperial Government in Southern Nigeria 1891–1904', M.A., London, 1952.

Ayandele, E. A. ,'The Political and Social Implications of Missionary Enterprise in the Evolution of Modern Nigeria, 1875–1914',
Ph.D., London, 1964.

Brown, S. H., 'A History of the people of Lagos, 1852–1886',
Ph.D., Illinois, 1964.

Herskovits, J., 'Liberated Africans and the History of Lagos
Colony to 1886', D.Phil., Oxford, 1960.

Ifemesia, C. C., 'British Enterprise on the River Niger 1830–1869',
Ph.D., London, 1959.

Lynch, H. R., 'Edward W. Blyden 1832–1912, and Pan Negro
Nationalism', Ph.D., London, 1964.

Mabogunje, A. L., 'Lagos: A study in Urban Geography', Ph.D.,
London, 1961.

Tamuno, S. M., 'The Development of British Administrative
control of Southern Nigeria 1900–1912; A Study in the Administrations of Sir Ralph Moor, Sir William MacGregor, and
Sir Walter Egerton', Ph.D., London, 1962.

Webster, J. B., 'The African Churches of Yorubaland 1888–1922',
Ph.D., London, 1963.

Index

279

Index

Index

Index

Macmillan, Allister, 53; *Red Book of West Africa*, 48
Manchester Chamber of Commerce, 139, 141, 142
Manchester Guardian, 128
Marina waterfront, in Lagos, 101, 103, 105; 'Samadu quarters', 125
Marke, P. Adolphus, 31
Mary, Queen of Scots, 224
Mason, Victor P., 38, 39
Mason, W. N., 90
'masquerade', 2
Maxwell, Dr (later Sir) John, 219; Commission, 219
May, Cornelius, 10
Mbadiwe, Dr K. O., 248
Memorial Hall, to Governor Glover, 106
Methodist Boys' High School, in Lagos, 22, 104
Methodist Episcopal Church, in New York, Committee of the Missionary Society, 6
Methodist Girls' High School, in Lagos, 22, 104
Methodist mission, 257
Miller Brothers (Liverpool), 92
Milton, John, 171
Mind, 153
Mirror, 31
Moloney, Governor, 31, 118, 120, 153
Monrovia, 230; Methodist Mission press in, 6; newspapers, 229
Moor, Ralph, 139, 175, 176, 192
Moore, Eric O., 50, 194, 219, 235
Moore, Miss Lucretia Cornelia Layinka, 47
Moorhouse, Acting Administrator Colonel H. C., 214, 223
Morel, E. D., 161, 162, 165
Morning Post, 246
Morrell, Phillip, 161
Mulford, F. B., 56, 234
Municipal Board of Health, 153, 154, 157
Muslims, 158, 223; *see also* Jamat Muslims

National Congress movement, 227, 228, 229, 231, 232
National Congress of British West Africa (NCBWA): scheme, 60, 66, 228, 231; Ebute Metta branch, 238
National Council of Nigerian Citizens (NCNC), 247

National Free Church Conference, at Hull, 157
Native Advisory Board, 141
Native Councils Bill, 140-1
Native Courts Ordinance (1906), 206
Native House Rule Ordinance and Colonial Church, 157
Native Pastorate Controversy, 9
Negro, The, 9, 10
New Age Herald, The, 58
New Era, 9, 13, 14
New Nigeria, The, 59
New Nigerian, 249
Newspaper (Amendment) Act, (1964), 250
Newspaper Ordinance (1903), 175, 177, 178, 179, 180, 181, 182, 191, 193
Newspaper Ordinance (1917), 192, 193, 194
Newspaper Registration Ordinance (1894), 18, 19
Nicholas II, Czar of Russia, 224
Niger Coast Protectorate, 192
Niger Company Limited, 94
Nigerian Advocate, 61, 224, 229, 234, 237
Nigerian Catholic Herald, 258
Nigerian Chronicle, 39-40, 80, 256; on Water Supply Scheme, 151, 152; on racial segregation, 161; on land tenure, 165; on Seditious Offences Ordinance, 187; on Provincial Courts Ordinance, 209, 210; and problem of Egbaland, 217, 218
Nigerian Daily Mail, 57, 66, 67, 224
Nigerian Daily Telegraph, 57, 66, 67, 78, 80, 86, 89, 93, 94, 182, 199, 237; Directory Scheme, 91; and H. Antus Williams, 238; on Italo-Abyssinian War, 239
Nigerian Daily Times, 57, 61-4, 67, 78; circulation supremacy, 86, 87; and advertising, 89, 93, 94; and freedom of press, 197; and Legislative Council elections, 236; and Italo-Abyssinian War, 239-40
Nigerian Educational Code, 228
Nigerian Evening News, 66
Nigerian Journal, The, 258
Nigerian Law Journal, 258
Nigerian Methodist, 257
Nigerian National Democratic Party (NNDP), xii, 51, 56, 65, 196, 232-3, 234, 236

286

Index